Money Matters

Money Matters

Consequences of Campaign Finance Reform in U.S. House Elections

Robert K. Goidel,
Donald A. Gross,
and
Todd G. Shields

ROWMAN & LITTLEFIELD PUBLISHERS, INC.
Lanham • Boulder • New York • Oxford

ROWMAN & LITTLEFIELD PUBLISHERS, INC.

Published in the United States of America
by Rowman & Littlefield Publishers, Inc.
4720 Boston Way, Lanham, Maryland 20706

12 Hid's Copse Road
Cumnor Hill, Oxford OX2 9JJ, England

British Library Cataloguing in Publication Information Available

Library of Congress Cataloging-in-Publication Data

Goidel, Robert K., 1967–
    Money matters : consequences of campaign finance reform in U.S.
House elections / Robert K. Goidel, Donald A. Gross, and Todd G.
Shields.
        p.   cm.
    Includes bibliographical references.
    ISBN 0-8476-8867-4 (cloth : alk. paper).—ISBN 0-8476-8868-2
(paper : alk. paper)
    1. Campaign funds—United States.   2. United States.   Congress.
House—Elections.   3. Elections—United States.   4. Voting—United
States.   I. Gross, Donald A. (Donald August), 1950–   .
II. Shields, Todd G., 1968–   .   III. Title.
JK1991.G65   1999
324.7′8′0973—dc21   98-52024
                                                                                        CIP

Printed in the United States of America

 ⊗ ™ The paper used in this publication meets the minimum requirements of
American National Standard for Information Sciences—Permanence of Paper for
Printed Library Materials, ANSI Z39.48–1992.

Contents

List of Tables and Figures   vii

1   Introducing Campaign Finance Reform   1

2   A Brief History of Campaign Finance and Finance Reform   15

3   Excessive Spending, Candidate Viability, and Free Speech   37

4   Electoral Competition and Campaign Finance Reform   57

5   The Question of Voter Turnout, Part I   85

6   The Question of Voter Turnout, Part II   107

7   Democracy and Citizen Involvement   123

8   Loopholes in the Federal Election Campaign Act   143

9   Improving the Electoral Process through Campaign Finance
    Reform   157

Appendix A: Statistical Basis for Chapter Four   175

Appendix B: Statistical Basis for Chapter Five   181

Appendix C: Statistical Basis for Chapter Six   185

Appendix D: Statistical Basis for Chapter Seven   189

References   199

Index   211

About the Authors   217

Tables and Figures

TABLES

3.1   Expenditures of Winners and Losers, 1994 and 1996 House
Elections   40

4.1   Estimated Effect of $100, in Candidate Spending on
Democratic Percentage of the Vote, 1994 and 1996   70

5.1   Estimated Effect of $100, in Candidate Spending on District-
level Voter Turnout   96

7.1   Effects of Incumbent and Challenger Spending on Measures
of Voters' Cognitive Engagement, 1994 and 1996   132

7.2   Effects of Party and Candidate Contact on Measures of
Voters' Cognitive Engagement, 1994 and 1996   132

9.1   Summary Evaluation of Three Campaign Finance Reform
Approaches   163

FIGURES

4.1   Spending Limits and Predicted Democratic Seat Loss, 1994   71

4.2   Spending Limits and Predicted Democratic Seat Gain, 1996   73

4.3   Matching Funds and Predicted Democratic Seat Loss, 1994   74

4.4   Matching Funds and Predicted Democratic Seat Gain, 1996   75

4.5   Full Public Financing and Predicted Democratic Seat Loss,
1994   76

4.6   Full Public Financing and Predicted Democratic Seat Gain,
1996   78

4.7   Partial Public Financing and Predicted Democratic Seat Loss,
1994   79

4.8   Partial Public Financing and Predicted Democratic Seat
Gain, 1996   80

5.1   Voter Turnout in Presidential Elections, 1960–1996   86

5.2   Voter Turnout in Midterm Elections, 1962–1994   87

5.3	Spending Limits and Aggregate Voter Turnout, 1994	97
5.4	Spending Limits and Aggregate Voter Turnout, 1996	98
5.5	Matching Funds and Aggregate Voter Turnout, 1994	99
5.6	Matching Funds and Aggregate Voter Turnout, 1996	100
5.7	Full Public Financing and Aggregate Voter Turnout, 1994	100
5.8	Full Public Financing and Aggregate Voter Turnout, 1996	101
5.9	Partial Public Financing and Aggregate Voter Turnout, 1994	102
5.10	Partial Public Financing and Aggregate Voter Turnout, 1996	102
6.1	Effect of Democratic Candidate Spending on Individual Voter Turnout, 1994	114
6.2	Effect of Republican Candidate Spending on Individual Voter Turnout, 1994	115
6.3	Effect of Democratic Candidate Spending on Other Voter Political Activity, 1994	116
6.4	Effect of Republican Candidate Spending on Other Voter Political Activity, 1994	117
6.5	Effect of Democratic Candidate Spending on Individual Voter Turnout, 1996	118
6.6	Effect of Republican Candidate Spending on Individual Voter Turnout, 1996	119
6.7	Effect of Democratic Candidate Spending on Other Voter Political Activity, 1996	120
6.8	Effect of Republican Candidate Spending on Other Voter Political Activity, 1996	121
7.1	Incumbent Spending and Respondent Familiarity with Incumbent, 1994	134
7.2	Challenger Spending and Respondent Familiarity with Incumbent, 1994	135
7.3	Incumbent Spending and Respondent Familiarity with Challenger, 1994	136
7.4	Challenger Spending and Respondent Familiarity with Challenger, 1994	137
7.5	Incumbent Spending and Respondent Certainty about Incumbent Ideology, 1994	138
7.6	Challenger Spending and Respondent Certainty about Incumbent Ideology, 1994	139
7.7	Incumbent Spending and Respondent Certainty about Challenger Ideology, 1994	140
7.8	Challenger Spending and Respondent Certainty about Challenger Ideology, 1994	140
7.9	Incumbent Spending and Respondent Concern about Election Outcome, 1994	141

7.10   Challenger Spending and Respondent Concern about
       Election Outcome, 1994   141
8.1   Political Party Soft Money Expenditures, 1992–1998   147
8.2   Independent Expenditures in House Races, 1978–1996   150

Chapter One

Introducing Campaign Finance Reform

In the 1992 presidential race, candidate Bill Clinton was openly critical of a campaign finance system that he said allowed large contributors to buy access and influence in Washington. Like many others before him, he called for fundamental reform. Four years later there were no reforms, and President Clinton became the single biggest fund-raising attraction in the history of American politics. After the 1996 presidential election, Republicans watched with pleasure as the Clinton administration and the Democratic National Committee had to respond to an ever-growing list of accusations involving campaign finance irregularities, including but not limited to illegal foreign campaign contributions. Alas, Republican happiness was short-lived, as their own party's campaign finance activities became subject to criticism for many of the very same behaviors undertaken by the Democrats, including illegal foreign campaign contributions. To many it seems that much of the current campaign finance system is best described by a comment made by a Clinton White House spokesman responding to charges of campaign irregularities: "It may be sleazy, but it is not illegal."

To look at current concerns about the influence of money on politics as something peculiar to the 1990s, however, misses a much deeper concern. The role of money in politics was present virtually from the beginning of the American Republic. For example, in the early decades of the American Republic, candidates were expected to provide the financial backing necessary to run for political office. As a result, "the system proved costly even for men of means, and only a few could afford to run" (Alexander 1992, 9). By the mid-1800s, self-financed candidates and political parties had turned to major business interests to help provide financial support for presidential campaigns. According to W. Lance Bennett (1996, 81), "the corruption of big money goes back at least to the Gilded Age of Robber Barons and the rise of industrial giants following the Civil War. . . . The Robber Barons purchased much of their political protection by financing electoral politics, an arrangement that culminated in the Republican party

1

funding system under the direction of Mark Hanna. The election of William McKinley in 1896, for example, was funded by something akin to a
tax on big business, whereby corporations and 'fat cat' entrepreneurs were
'assessed' contributions according to their wealth and prominence."

Large contributions from these wealthy "fat cats" dominated party and
candidate campaign financing at least up until the landmark reform efforts
of the early 1970s (Sorauf 1992). In 1971, Congress passed the Federal
Election Campaign Act, which requires fuller disclosure of candidate and
committee spending while also placing limits on advertising expenditures
in House and Senate campaigns. Equally important, while political actions
committees, PACs, had existed since the 1950s, the 1971 act provided a
legal basis for the creation and maintenance of these committees. More far-
reaching amendments to the act were passed in 1974 in reaction to the
Watergate scandal. At the time, the 1971 act and its subsequent amendments served as a major victory for political reformers. Larry J. Sabato and
Glenn R. Simpson (1996, 15) observe that "campaign finance reformers
were convinced in the mid-1970s that they had created a clean new world
for politics."

In a myriad of ways, however, the campaign reform efforts of the 1970s
have been undermined. Court cases, such as *Buckley v. Valeo* (1976) and
more recently *Colorado Republican Federal Campaign Committee v. Federal Election Commission* (1996), have undermined efforts at regulating campaign
activities. Party officials, interest group leaders, and political candidates
have continued to take aggressive actions to expand the legal boundaries
of campaign regulations. The Federal Election Commission, which has the
responsibility for policing campaign finance regulations, is generally described as weak and ineffective. The ineffectiveness of the FEC in regulating campaign activities has increased the willingness of candidates, parties,
and political action committees to engage in legally and ethically questionable campaign practices.

If the failures of the campaign reform efforts in the 1970s have made the
public even more concerned about the role of money in the electoral process, they have had just the opposite effect on those who study the role of
money in the electoral process. For many students of the electoral process,
the principal lesson of the reform efforts of the 1970s is that reform either
will fail or will create new, unintended consequences, many of which are
worse than the original impetus for reform (Sorauf 1988, 1992). For example, the growth of political action committees is often seen to be a direct
result of the 1971 Federal Election Campaign Act, which legitimized political action committee activity.

Beyond concerns about the negative effects of reform, many of the scholars writing on campaign reform also see positive effects from high-spending congressional races. Candidate spending, it is argued, is associated with

more competitive elections as well as a more involved and informed electorate. Reforming the electoral process, particularly reform that involves placing strict limits on spending, would only serve to diminish electoral competition while simultaneously depressing voter turnout and voter information (see, for example, Jacobson 1980; Sorauf 1992; Alexander 1992; Teixeira 1996). If these views appear to be widely accepted in the academic community, particularly among campaign finance specialists, they form something less than a consensus. First, multiple works by Jonathan S. Krasno and Donald P. Green (Krasno and Green 1993; Green and Krasno 1988, 1990) argue that spending limits would increase rather than decrease electoral competition. Second, once one moves beyond questions of spending limits and into questions of public funding, there is considerably less agreement within the academic literature as to the likely effects of campaign reform. Would communication vouchers worth $200,000 in advertising offset any negative effects of a $600,000 spending limit? The answer is not entirely clear, nor is it easily discernible from the academic literature.

POLITICAL PARTIES AND A CANDIDATE-CENTERED ELECTORAL PROCESS

Debates over the consequences of campaign finance reform are complicated by questions surrounding the changing nature of political parties in America. Understanding the nexus among candidates, political parties, and the electorate has always been critical to an understanding of elections in America. As such, the discontent with the role of money in contemporary elections can also be seen as linked to the shift from a party-centered electoral process to a candidate-centered process.

Walter Dean Burnham (1970) notes that with the rise of the Progressive movement in the 1890s, political parties began to lose influence over the electoral process. Voter participation and interest in elections have been on a consistent downward spiral ever since. For Burnham, this was a conscious attempt on the part of elites to weaken the only institutional mechanism (the political party) that was responsive to, and capable of organizing, the lower classes in a manner that might have challenged the economic status quo. While often differing with Burnham's interpretation of the role of elites, numerous other writers reach a similar conclusion about the "decline of party" (Broder 1971; Crotty 1984; Wattenberg 1990).

More than thirty years ago, V.O. Key Jr. (1964) emphasized the importance of analyzing American political parties in terms of three parts: the party in the electorate, the party in government, and the party as organization. This tripartite view of American political parties has dominated the academic literature ever since. Critics of the decline-of-party thesis argue that, while the thesis seems most persuasive when examining the party in the electorate, analyses of the party as organization and of the party in government paint a very different picture. Beginning with the analysis of Cornelius P. Cotter and colleagues (1984), most analyses indicate that party organizations at the national, state, and county levels are now stronger than ever. Moreover, analyses of partisan behavior in Washington, D.C., especially those examining party voting in Congress, indicate that party voting is now more common than it has been for more than twenty-five years (Aldrich 1995). This has led Joseph A. Schlesinger to conclude that "the decline-of-parties thesis is simply wrong" (1985, 1152).

John H. Aldrich, on the other hand, views these contrasting trends as creating "the central puzzle of understanding contemporary political parties" (1995, 244). For Aldrich, the resolution of the puzzle is simple: the old "modern mass political party," which had served the Republic since the days of Martin Van Buren, died in the 1960s. With the death of the modern mass party, the relevance of Key's tripartite view of political parties also died, for no longer would all three components of the party move together. In place of party-centered campaigns, we have the modern era of candidate-centered campaigns. The effective monopoly that parties held over nominations and elections for more than 150 years was broken in the 1960s. Money and new technologies now allowed candidates to win elections without depending on political parties.

Whether Burnham, Schlesinger, or Aldrich is correct in their entire interpretation need not concern us here. It is only important to recognize that contemporary candidate-centered campaigns are heavily dependent upon technological expertise and money. Political parties have changed in response to these developments. In a sense, political parties have become much more reactive to candidates and are much less proactive. They are very much service organizations, offering research and advice on such things as campaign managers, advertising agents and agencies, public opinion polls, and policy position papers. Political parties help "bundle" money and act as a general conduit for campaign funds. A cynic might even refer to this as money laundering. Finally, soft money that is officially used for party-building activities often provides a mechanism to offset a candidate's official campaign costs and a loophole to avoid federal campaign finance regulations.

The candidate-centered nature of contemporary campaigns and the emerging service role of political parties indicate why campaign finance reform is simultaneously a partisan and a nonpartisan issue. It is nonpartisan in that both parties have become accustomed to their new service role and are wary of proposals that might diminish that role. Further, candidates, particularly incumbents, are wary of losing the support mechanisms offered by political parties that simultaneously allow them a significant degree of independence from the parties. It is a partisan issue in that both parties remain wary of any proposal that might enhance the perceived advantage of the opposition party.

With the explosion of soft money, expenditures on behalf of candidates, and independent expenditures in 1996, it is argued that the description of election campaigns as candidate centered is no longer accurate. In this respect, much of the spending in contemporary congressional campaigns is, at least theoretically, beyond the control of individual candidates.[1] While this "new reality" may indicate a shift away from widely accepted notions of candidate-centered campaigns, it does not appear to have diminished the concerns of political parties and candidates regarding the potential consequences of campaign finance reform. Moreover, if campaigns have, in fact, spiraled out of control of individual candidates, they have not become "centered" on political parties but have, instead, become completely decentralized, lacking a center altogether.

PARTISAN CONSIDERATIONS AND CAMPAIGN FINANCE REFORM

Given the recent elections in which Republicans gained control of the House of Representatives and the Senate in 1994 and then maintained control of both chambers in 1996, questions regarding the likely effects of campaign reform have taken on even greater significance. For years, Republicans have argued that enacting public financing of congressional campaigns would limit their ability to gain control of the House of Representatives. Newt Gingrich (Republican, Georgia), for example, has argued that more, rather than less, money should be spent in congressional campaigns. Mitch McConnell (Republican, Kentucky), among others, has denounced campaign finance reform as a thinly disguised form of incumbent protection.

According to the logic conveyed in these public statements, it would be reasonable to conclude that the 1994 Republican Revolution would have been impossible had Democrats implemented campaign finance reform. Making this even more interesting is the fact that, in the two years immediately preceding the Republican Revolution, Democrats had their best opportunity in recent years to pass meaningful campaign finance reform. Intent on painting George Bush as antireform, and assured of a Bush veto, the Democrats passed campaign finance reform in 1992. After Bill Clinton's victory in the 1992 presidential election, Democrats were confronted with a president who promised to sign campaign finance reform. Yet the possibility that campaign reform would be enacted made congressional Democrats considerably more cautious. As described in the *Congressional Quarterly Almanac* (Campaign Finance Overhaul Dies 1995, 32), "the long history of the legislation was rich with evidence that many Democrats in both chambers shared GOP objections to establishing a system that would provide congressional candidates with federal subsidies. Other Democrats, particularly in the House, were deeply, if privately, opposed to an overhaul of the financing system that had protected their seats and majority status for years."

While the reform effort in the 103d Congress was eventually killed by a Republican-led filibuster, Democrats "set the stage for defeat by waiting until the eleventh hour to come up with a compromise version of a bill they had previously maintained would be a top priority in Clinton's first two years" (ibid.). In addition, a number of the key provisions of the legislation in the Senate version appeared to be unconstitutional.[2] Without going into undue detail at this point, it seems sufficient to note that if Democrats were serious about campaign finance reform, they had the opportunity to enact it. But did their failure to enact campaign finance reform contribute to their downfall in the 1994 elections? And did their failure to enact reform during the 103d Congress limit their ability to regain control of the House of Representatives during the 1996 elections?

A superficial glance at campaign fund-raising in 1994 would seem to suggest that money was at least partly responsible for Republican gains. While Theodore J. Eismeier and Philip H. Pollock (1996, 81) report that "money continued to roll into congressional campaigns in much the same way in 1994 that it had for the last several election cycles," they also observe that the number of Republican challengers with enough money to wage a credible campaign increased significantly in 1994. In a similar vein, James G. Gimpel (1996, 10) notes that funding for Republican challengers was "up some 42% over 1992." It is unlikely that money alone bought Republican victories in 1994, particularly given that many Republican challengers faced Democratic incumbents who outspent them and that spending in open-seat elections tended be fairly balanced. The increase in fund-raising did, however, place more Republican challengers in a position to be competitive than during any election in the recent past. Somewhat surprisingly, Eismeier and Pollock (1996) observe that had more money been devoted to those elections in which Democrats won by less than 55 percent of the vote, the 1994 Republican tidal wave might have been even more dramatic.

While money was not the sole cause of the Republican takeover, money was an important, if not primary, ingredient. So what would have happened had the source and amount of money spent in these elections been altered? Would spending limits have sentenced Republicans to an indefinite House imprisonment as the minority party?

If campaign finance reform might have altered the dramatic 1994 Republican takeover of the House of Representatives, reform might also have affected the ability of Republicans to maintain control of the House in

1996. Before the 1996 elections, numerous signals indicated a potential Democratic return to majority party status in the House. An ABC News Poll conducted on October 27, 1996, for example, indicates that 53 percent of respondents planned to vote for a Democratic congressional candidate.[3] Many of the seventy-three Republican freshmen elected in 1994 looked vulnerable to Democratic challengers bolstered by aggressive labor union support. Yet, on election day, the losses to the Republican Party were relatively minor. Not only did the Republican Party maintain control of the House of Representatives, it also successfully minimized the damage in a year that by all indications should have benefited Democratic candidates. At least one plausible explanation is that, through their newly acquired majority status, Republicans were able to use their fund-raising advantages to minimize losses during the 1996 House elections. But would Democrats have been able to win back control of the House of Representatives had campaign finance reform been enacted prior to the 1996 elections?

THE APPROACH OF THE BOOK

Our purpose in this book is to explore not only the likely effects of campaign finance reform on partisan control of the House of Representatives but also, more broadly, the likely effect of campaign finance reform on electoral competition, voter turnout, and voter information. In the debate over campaign finance reform, assumptions are frequently made regarding the likely impact of reform on the electoral process. The most frequently voiced assumption is that campaign finance reform would ultimately diminish electoral competition even beyond the general lack of competition present in congressional elections. This is not the only concern raised by critics of campaign finance reform. They also contend that reform would serve to depress voter turnout and decrease the quality of information that voters have about candidates (for a summary of these arguments, see Smith 1995). The problem with such assertions is that, while they have some basis in the academic literature on congressional elections, they have rarely been subjected to systematic analysis.

One goal of this book is to subject these criticisms to careful, systematic analysis. One of the keys in doing so involves carefully defining what is meant by the term *reform*. Often critics of reform assume that all reform proposals are created equal. Consequently, it is assumed that the same objections that can be made regarding spending limits can also be made regarding public financing schemes that involve any form of spending limits. As we show throughout the text, this is not necessarily true. Criticisms of spending limits are not always applicable to reform proposals involving public financing. Even more narrowly, criticisms of one form of public financing do not necessarily apply to all forms of public financing.

A second key to providing a more systematic examination of the criticisms of campaign finance reform involves the choice of methodology. Many critiques of campaign finance reform have been voiced without presenting much in terms of supporting evidence. Bradley A. Smith's (1995) well-written and strongly argued essay in the *Yale Law Journal* includes no original data analysis. Other works, such as Gary C. Jacobson's (1980) seminal *Money in Congressional Elections* and Alan I. Abramowitz's (1991a) more recent journal article are more systematic but examine a limited number of reform proposals. In addition, these works tend to focus solely on the impact that campaign finance reform has on electoral competitiveness without examining the likely impact on voter turnout and information.

A more systematic analysis of the likely effects of campaign finance reform requires that, along the lines of Jacobson (1980) and Abramowitz (1991a), our understanding of the effects of candidate spending be used to estimate the likely effect of campaign finance reform on the electoral phenomena of interest (that is, electoral competitiveness, voter turnout, and voter information). Recently, a few works have been written that include a more systematic analysis of the impact of campaign finance reform on electoral competition. Jonathan S. Krasno and Donald P. Green (1993) examine the impact of number of reform proposals based on their model of the congressional vote. They find that, in contrast to the conventional wisdom, spending limits would increase rather than decrease electoral competition. On a similar note, Robert K. Goidel and Donald A. Gross (1996) examine the predictions from a number of models across two election years. They find that conclusions regarding the likely effect of campaign finance reform on electoral competition are heavily contingent upon the model being employed. They also note that the conventional wisdom that campaign finance reform would ultimately serve to depress electoral competition appears to be true only in the case of spending limits, though even in the case of spending limits the effects are heavily contingent upon the model being employed. Once public subsidies enter the equation, the conventional wisdom breaks down. According to their analysis, there is little convincing evidence that spending limits combined with public subsidies would decrease electoral competition, unless spending limits are set at unrealistically low levels.

In its attempt to provide a more systematic examination of the effects of campaign finance reform, this book extends the work of Jacobson (1980), Abramowitz (1991a), Krasno and Green (1993), and Goidel and Gross (1996) by using simulations to estimate the likely effects of various versions of campaign finance reform. Simulations are not necessarily infallible. The results of the simulations are often tied to the assumptions made in estimating the model (Goidel and Gross 1996). In addition, simulations are often criticized for failing to adequately capture behavioral changes created by the reactions of strategic actors to changes in the economic or political environment. Should the rules of candidate spending be altered, strategic political actors would modify their behavior in an effort to maximize their political influence. Incumbents faced with spending limits, for example, might very well devote more time to shaking hands and less money to television. Similarly, while public subsidies might serve to attract higher quality challengers and open-seat contestants, they might also attract lower quality challengers more interested in the public subsidy than in actually winning the election.

A similar concern has been raised by Frank J. Sorauf's (1988) "Law of Unintended Consequences." The most recent wave of campaign finance reform, in the early 1970s, has had all sorts of political repercussions, many of which were unintended and ran counter to the overall goals of reform. For example, the legal recognition of PACs in the Federal Election Campaign Act, which was initially supported by labor organizations, has resulted in the explosion of business-oriented political action committees. While the reform was intended to quell some of the concerns about the role of special interests in the political process, many would argue that those concerns have been amplified in the postreform era.

Seen in this light, critics of reform may be correct in their suspicions that changes in the campaign finance system are likely to benefit incumbents. As political officeholders, incumbent representatives have already established an ability to manipulate the political system to their advantage. One could reasonably conclude that most incumbents would simply react to any changes in the political system, such as public financing of congressional campaigns, in ways that would ultimately benefit their efforts at reelection. In addition, any measure designed to alter existing campaign finance laws would have to first pass in both the House and the Senate. Would incumbent members of the House and the Senate pass campaign measures that would ultimately damage their chances at reelection?

Yet, if incumbents will be reacting to changes in campaign finance regulations, potential challengers and contributors will also be reacting in ways aimed at advancing their own strategic interests. One of the fundamental realities of congressional politics is that most challengers begin and end the election season as political unknowns. They begin with little, if any, financial support and name recognition, and they end with the same. Or as the L. Sandy Maisel (1982) title aptly describes it, they take the journey "from obscurity to oblivion." While public subsidies might help incumbents, most of the evidence suggests that public subsidies would do more to help challengers. In part, public subsidies might encourage more challengers with previous political experience to enter the electoral fray against a sitting incumbent. Public subsidies might also provide these challengers with the seed money necessary to solicit contributions from other sources, enabling even inexperienced candidates to raise additional money. In addition, if incumbents are limited in their spending, potential contributors might be more willing to invest their money in higher risk challengers. While readers may take exception to any or all of these examples, the key point for now is simply that, while critics of reform are correct in pointing out that reform may have a number of unintended consequences based on the strategic reactions of the political actors involved, it is unclear whether these unintended consequences would lead one to overestimate or underestimate the impact of campaign finance reform.

One appealing alternative to conducting simulations to gauge the likely effects of campaign finance reform involves looking at state-level campaign finance laws. Overall, analyses of individual states that have adopted some form of public financing yield inconsistent results. Herbert E. Alexander (1992, 146) observes that, "while excessively low spending limits can cause public financing to work to the advantage of incumbents, evidence exists that public funding programs have provided significant benefits to challengers." Looking more specifically at the system of public financing adopted by Wisconsin in 1977, Kenneth R. Mayer and John M. Wood (1995) find little evidence linking public financing to increased competition. Patrick D. Donnay and Graham P. Ramsden (1995), on the other hand, contend that, though a cursory glance at Minnesota's system of public financing might indicate that competition has declined over time, introducing a wider range of controls indicates that public financing has stimulated electoral competition. Research by Ruth S. Jones (1981, 358) investigating the partisan implications of public financing at the state level finds that, while systems of public financing tend to benefit the majority party, overall "any public funding may well be more beneficial to the minority than to the majority party." The recent work of Michael J. Malbin and Thomas L. Gais (1998) represents, perhaps, the most comprehensive effort at understanding the impact of campaign finance regulations on state-level elections. These authors conclude that, while public funding might increase electoral competition, it rarely achieves this effect because state public-financing schemes fail to provide adequate levels of funding.

One of the problems in these state-level analyses involves the question of what standard should be used to gauge the success (or failure) of campaign finance reform. If, for example, we find that competition is greater in states that have adopted some form of public financing than in states that have not, can we then conclude that public financing increases competition? Not if we have reason to believe that competition would have been greater in these states even without public financing. Similarly, a decline in electoral competition following the adoption of a system of public financing does not necessarily indicate that public funding is a failure, if it can be argued that the decline in competition would have resulted even if public financing had not been adopted.

This leads to an important question: How can legislative scholars best evaluate the likely effects of campaign finance reform on electoral competition? One potentially interesting, but impractical, response is that a pooled time-series analysis could be conducted that uses campaign finance data from a number of states and over a number of years. Unfortunately, while this approach is theoretically appealing, the availability of the state-level campaign finance reports and the logistical problems associated with collecting this data make such an approach impractical, at least in terms of evaluating the impact of reform in legislative elections.[4]

This leaves simulations as the most viable alternative to estimate the likely effects of various reform scenarios. This approach is appealing for a number of reasons. First, it is flexible enough to allow the testing of multiple reform scenarios. State-level analyses are limited to testing the efficacy of the reform proposal currently in place. Consequently, such analyses are limited in their ability to determine the likely effect of slightly different variations of the same general reform proposal. For example, though we might be able to determine that Wisconsin's system of public financing has resulted in decreased competition since its inception in 1977 (Mayer and Wood 1995), we are unable to determine how slight variations in their system of public financing would alter the level of competition. Second, while the results of the simulations are dependent on the assumption of the model employed (Goidel and Gross 1996), simulations provide a more stable foundation for making inferences than inferences based on the regression model alone.

In the following chapters, we use simulations to estimate the likely impact of various versions of campaign finance reform on electoral competitiveness (chapter 4), voter participation (chapters 5 and 6), and voter information (chapter 7). We do so in an attempt to provide reasonable, if still imprecise, estimates of the likely effects of campaign finance reform. We also attempt to gauge the impact of as wide a range of reform proposals as possible. In this respect, we attempt to estimate the effects of spending limits, matching funds, full public financing, and partial public funding through subsidies on electoral competition, voter turnout, and voter information. We hope that in estimating the likely effects of campaign finance reform to develop a sense not only of whether the assumptions of supporters and critics are accurate but also of how different types of reform affect each of the variables of interest (that is, competitiveness, turnout, and information).

Before we consider the simulations in more detail, we begin in chapter 2 with a brief review of the history of campaign finance reform in an attempt to highlight recurring problems that have plagued reform efforts. In chapter 3, we then consider some of the general arguments made against campaign finance reform that, for the most part, do not lend themselves to empirical examination. Chapter 4 examines the likely effects of various campaign finance proposals on electoral competitiveness. Chapters 5 and 6 then focus on questions of whether or not campaign finance reform would depress voter turnout, at both the aggregate and individual level. In chapter 7, we consider the implications of campaign finance reform on voter information; that is, would campaign finance reform lead to a less informed and less interested electorate? Chapter 8 then considers the issue of soft money and other loopholes in the Federal Election Campaign Act in terms of their impact on congressional campaigns. The use of soft money grew exponentially in the 1996 elections. Soft money is seen as especially important to understanding campaign finance reform because it has become linked to the political parties' growing service role and because it is often used to avoid current finance regulations. Soft money is also seen as especially problematic because its ambiguous nature (federal law does not make a legal distinction between hard and soft money) makes it difficult to analyze systematically as one would analyze hard money.

While we attempt to provide a balanced and objective analysis in each of the chapters, this is not, strictly speaking, an objective text. Part of our interest in writing a book on campaign finance reform stems from our belief that the opponents of campaign finance reform have been able to turn to political science for an ample supply of ammunition in arguing against campaign finance reform proposals. Not only do we see this as an inaccurate reading of the political science literature, but we also believe that the bulk of the evidence indicates that campaign finance reform with modest public subsidies and spending limits would enhance, rather than diminish, our system of democratic governance. In the concluding chapter (chapter 9), we summarize this evidence and present a convincing case that campaign finance reform would, on balance, improve the overall quality of American democracy.

NOTES

1. For a fuller discussion of these changes, see Citizens' Research Foundation 1997. The Task Force on Campaign Finance Reform was chaired by Herbert Alexander and included Janet M. Box-Steffensmeier, Anthony Corrado, Jonathan Krasno, Frank Sorauf, Michael Malbin, Ruth Jones, Gary Moncrief, John Wright, and Jeremy Wood as members.

2. The Senate version set limits on candidate spending without providing some form of public subsidy. In addition, it provided a tax on candidate contributions

should candidates spend above the designated limit. Both provisions seem to be in violation of the *Buckley v. Valeo* (1976) decision.

3. The results presented above reflect estimates for likely voters. The ABC News Poll was conducted October 26–27, with 717 likely voters. The margin of error was 4.5 points.

4. Recently, there has been a concerted effort at collecting data from a number of states making an analysis of a greater cross section of states possible. The results of this effort have been published in Joel Thompson and Gary Moncrief (1998). While the text represents a major contribution to the literature, it also reflects the problems inherent in comparative state campaign finance research, including difficulties in obtaining data from various state agencies. As the concluding chapter notes, "There is not evidence [from the states] . . . to conclude that public finance would succeed or fail in meeting the goals of reformers" (Jewell and Cassie 1998).

Chapter Two

A Brief History of Campaign Finance and Finance Reform

The interrelationships among money, elections, politics, and social power have remained problematic since the very first elections in the United States. At its root, the pervasiveness of money in the electoral process threatens the principle of one person, one vote. As Herbert Alexander (1992, 162) observes, "Reconciliation is needed between a theory of democratic government and a set of economic conditions—how to hold to the egalitarian assumption of 'one person, one vote' (and 'one dollar'?) in the face of unequal distribution of economic resources." This concern pervades American politics regardless of whether the money enters the political system legally, through political action committees, or illegally, through vote buying. While scholars may debate the reality, the fact that money has the potential to distort democratic process, both in its legal and illegal manifestations, is beyond question.

Throughout American history, political corruption has been common and widespread. While reforms have eliminated some of the more outrageous forms of political corruption, reform efforts have typically been followed by creative new efforts and techniques to circumvent the intent of reforms as well as by official apathy toward the enforcement of reform provisions. The recurring nature of corruption in American politics is perhaps best expressed by Larry J. Sabato and Glenn R. Simpson (1996, 10) who observe that "even when scandals have been followed by reforms, inevitably corruption finds a way to thrive in the new environment. The result is that wave upon wave of corruption washes over American democracy, despite all attempts to erect a seawall sufficiently strong to prevent it. Corruption is truly a staple of our Republic's existence."

In fact, much of the problem with reform efforts is that they tend to develop in response to specific activities or scandals, with the resulting reforms focusing on specific activities such as vote buying, bribery, or the

15

elimination of certain types of campaign contributions. As a result, efforts at comprehensive reform of the campaign finance system have been rare. Only in the 1970s has there been any effort to try to control all types of monetary contributions.

The evolution of campaign finance and reform efforts in the United States is an evolution that is not clearly defined in terms of specific time points, locations, or specific events. It is an evolution that is intertwined with political, social, and economic developments in the country as a whole, developments that often differed significantly in particular states or regions of the country. Regulation of campaign finance developed over time as a patchwork of regulations issued by local, state, and federal governments responding to particular developments in local, state, and national affairs. With these caveats in mind, it is possible to think of the evolution of campaign finance in terms of five time periods. As we shall see, each period is best thought of in terms of practices widely utilized to finance elections in the context of the political, economic, and social developments of the times.

THE FORMATIVE YEARS, 1789–1824

To appreciate the nature of elections and campaign finance in the earliest years of the Republic, it is best to begin by considering the meaning of the phrase, "standing for office," which reflects the British tradition of the former colonies.[1] The social and political aristocracy of the time would select candidates from among themselves. The candidate for office would neither openly promote his candidacy nor promulgate his political views among the electorate. As he stood for office, voters were to recognize the "obvious qualities" of the candidate. While candidates today "run for office" and plead with voters to vote for them, a direct appeal to masses of voters would have simply been seen as socially unacceptable in the earliest years of the Republic.

George Washington stood for office when he became president. He had no real competition, and he did not openly promote his candidacy. Further, only four of the eleven states casting electoral votes in the first presidential election even allowed individual citizens to vote directly for electors. The norm against campaigning for office was so strong that some states had laws against campaigning for office. Even Thomas Jefferson, champion of the common man, could not initially buck the norms against openly campaigning for office. When he first sought the presidency, he used a botanical tour of the country as his official explanation for his campaign tour. The nature of the electorate was also fundamentally different from what we see today. To be able to vote, one had to be a property owner.

Women could not vote. And, of course, slaves could not vote. Only about one out of every five people in the country met all of the qualifications for voting, and these were widely scattered throughout the states. The small, widely dispersed electorate and the prejudicial norms against openly campaigning for office necessarily meant that campaign costs remained minimal.

Even in this primitive electoral atmosphere, however, there were attempts to influence the electorate; and there were campaign costs to be paid. Liquor was often used to attract voters. George Washington bought an average of one and a half quarts of liquor per voter when he first ran for office in 1757. According to George Thayer (1973, 25), "The success of this system and its entrenchment in the public heart could be gauged two decades later when James Madison was defeated for reelection to the Virginia legislature because he refused to distribute whiskey to the voters. A committee reviewing his case refused to interpret gifts of liquor to the voters as bribery or corruption." Newspapers were another campaign expense during the early years of the Republic. At the time, newspapers were partisan undertakings with no attempt to exhibit balance and objectivity. Both the Federalists and the Democratic-Republicans, the infant party organizations of the time, used money to purchase newspapers and other printed materials to publish their partisan writings. As was the custom of the day, Thomas Jefferson used his own money to publish partisan materials.

As we can see, elections in the late eighteenth century were primitive affairs with minimal costs, which were generally absorbed by the candidates themselves. This is not without significance, because candidacy was focused within an indigenous aristocracy that could afford to pay campaign expenses. Furthermore, early campaign techniques themselves would eventually become the focus of reform efforts. As early as 1811, Maryland passed a law to prohibit the sale of liquor on election day in an attempt to minimize the use of alcohol as an enticement for voters.

As the Republic began to move into the first quarter of the nineteenth century, two highly related developments occurred that would forever change the nature of elections and campaign finance in America. The first of these was the growing importance of the so-called common man. This change initially developed momentum in the Southern states and eventually swept the nation. While electioneering and openly running for office was continuing to be snubbed in much of the North during the early 1800s, it started to become widespread throughout much of the South. Property requirements for voting began to be eliminated. Universal manhood suffrage swept through much of the South and the Western frontiers of Kentucky and Tennessee. By 1828, twenty of the twenty-four states casting electoral votes for the president had their electors linked to popular vote outcomes. The second development was the establishment of organized political parties.[2] In the very first Congress, legislative factions developed in response to the policies of the Washington administration, especially the financial proposals suggested by Washington's secretary of the treasury, Alexander Hamilton. The Federalists backed the Washington administration, while the Anti-Federalists generally opposed the administration. While these factions were often very cohesive when voting in Congress, they lacked many of the characteristics traditionally associated with political parties. They had little or no organization outside of the government, and they lacked linkages to the electorate. Eventually, these factions did, however, form the basis for the first American political parties.

Particularly important in this regard was the development of the Democratic-Republican Party under the leadership of Thomas Jefferson. Beginning in Anti-Federalist opposition to the Federalist policies of the Washington administration and with its base of support in the more open political culture of the South, the Democratic-Republican Party would become the first mass-based political party in the United States. Soon, political machines began to develop in the nation's cities as an effective mechanism for voter mobilization, and campaigning for office became the norm throughout the nation.

Throughout the first quarter of the nineteenth century, campaign costs remained minimal. The candidates and small groups of donors paid for the costs that were incurred. However, the stage was set for significant increases in campaign costs. One now had to campaign for office; the nation had grown, and universal manhood suffrage now required large numbers of voters to be contacted; and political party units were now in place to help facilitate voter mobilization.

THE GROWTH YEARS, 1828–1876

The election of 1824 brought an abrupt end to the era of one-party Democratic-Republican rule, as America's first mass-based party broke into two factions, an Adams/Clay faction and a Jackson faction. The former would eventually become the Whig Party, while the later became known as the Democratic Party. The election of 1828 would be the first in which popular vote returns would be a dominant factor in determining the electoral vote outcome. Campaign costs began to rise as advisors and political parties undertook organizational efforts to get out the vote for their chosen candidate.

The need for mass voter appeals and political party organizational efforts made it clear that it was no longer possible for most candidates to run self-financed campaigns or campaigns financed by a few individuals. A source of funds was needed, and patronage provided a natural reservoir. By 1828, patronage systems were already well developed in many municipal and state governments. The Tammany Hall campaign fund, for example, received 6 percent of all New York City employees' weekly paychecks. Patronage on the federal level took on renewed vigor after Jackson's victory in 1828 and the outright nurturing of the spoils system. By 1876, almost all federal officeholders, including congressmen and senators, were expected to make annual contributions to the party.

Patronage and the spoils systems became a source of revenue and a source of increased expense as corruption began to expand. Paying individuals to vote in the proper manner became a common practice in many parts of the country. While government employees' required donations to the party continued to be a prime source of revenue, additional funds were needed; so the search for campaign contributors expanded. As Thayer states (1973, 29), "Contributions often came in the form of cash packed in satchels or carpetbags, no questions asked. In 1839, Whig lobbyist Thurlow Weed raised $8,000 from New York merchants, and the money was delivered in a bandana handkerchief. No one appeared to think it unusual."

As the nation moved toward midcentury, the ever-growing need for campaign funds resulted in the search for men of wealth who could help the parties and their candidates. Individuals such as Du Pont, Belmont, Astor, Cooke, Vanderbilt, Tilden, and McCormick are some of the people who began to help bankroll candidates. The link between the rich and economically powerful campaign contributor and the needy candidate and political party had been forged. Not only had the leaders of the industrial revolution realized that government policies and regulations could affect their industries, there was also much to be made from government spending itself. The Du Ponts made millions by supplying the government with black powder. Government payoffs, kickbacks, and other forms of graft and corruption soon became a way of life. The Credit Mobilier became the first major scandal to exemplify what would become a way of life in Washington and other seats of government for years to come. The Credit Mobilier was the name of a corporation established to construct the country's first transcontinental railroad. Important congressmen were given shares of stock in the company in order to avoid any embarrassing questions being asked on Capitol Hill. The company had been making massive profits by overcharging the government, as well as through other forms of graft and corruption. As the facts of the case eventually became known, political careers were destroyed and the Grant administration became tainted with the image of corruption. Perhaps most important, calls for political reform never materialized.

By 1876, the stage was set for perhaps the most corrupt era in American political history. There were millions of voters to be contacted. The mass political party had become a way of life. As the industrial revolution continued to pick up steam, there were millions of dollars to be earned and a nation to be conquered. Patronage and numerous forms of political corruption had become institutionalized. Initial calls for reform were generally ignored at the federal level and only minimally successful at the state and local levels. The only successful attempt to limit the common practices of the day was an 1867 naval appropriations bill that prohibited any government employee, or any naval officer, from levying political assessments on naval yard workers.

THE GOLDEN DAYS OF GRAFT AND CORRUPTION, 1876 to 1932

As the nation moved through the last quarter of the nineteenth century and the beginning of the twentieth century, the country experienced perhaps its most openly corrupt era in its history. It was a brash rough-and-tumble era, in which government corruption was widespread and openly tolerated. To use the phrase of Thayer, it was "the golden age of boodle." As he states (1973, 37), "never has the American political process been so corrupt. No office was too high to purchase, no man too pure to bribe, no principle too sacred to destroy, no law too fundamental to break." In the midst of such corruption, movements for reform took root. From 1876 to 1932, four reform measures were passed by Congress aimed directly at campaign financing. Numerous other measures to "clean up" the political process at the local, state, and federal levels became part of the Progressive agenda.[3] Many of these reforms, such as the Australian ballot, primaries, and the civil service system, remain today. In the context of campaign financing, however, most of the reform efforts merely ended up being exercises in futility.

As the era began, assessment for government employees was a common practice at the local, state, and federal levels. Some states had varying fee schedules for different types of officials, while others, such as Louisiana, had a flat rate as high as 10 percent of the salary. Other forms of official corruption such as kickbacks, preferments, and outright bribery were used to finance candidates and political party affairs. And although Rutherford B. Hayes became president in 1876 on a platform calling for civil service reform, Congress remained uninterested in reform. Hayes's four-year presidency became an ongoing battlefield over the civil service reform issue.

It is perhaps most ironic that the Civil Service Reform Act of 1883 was signed into law by President Chester Arthur. Arthur had been removed from his position in the New York customhouse by President Hayes because of widespread incompetence and corruption. Moreover, Arthur had long opposed civil service reform. The assassination of President Garfield by an individual who felt that he had been denied an expected presidential appointment, however, inflamed public opinion against the entrenched spoils system. Dramatic gains by the Democrats in the congressional elections of 1882 helped ensure passage in Congress. To the surprise of many, Arthur signed the legislation. For the first time in American history, federal jobs in Washington were to be filled on the basis of competitive examinations, and assessments on civil servants were banned.

After the passage of the Civil Service Reform Act and similar laws in a number of states, businesses became an even more important source for campaign funds. The laissez-faire attitude dominant at the time, typified in the behavior of the "robber barons," helped solidify the connections between business and politics. At times, entire legislative chambers were controlled by monied interests. According to W. Lance Bennett (1996, 81), "the Robber Barons purchased much of their political protection by financing electoral politics. . . . The election of William McKinley in 1896, for example, was funded by something akin to a tax on big business, whereby corporations and 'fat cat' entrepreneurs were 'assessed' contributions according to their wealth and prominence."

The election of 1896 was of critical importance to much of the business community, which feared the populist agenda of William Jennings Bryan and other economic reformers. Coinage of silver, protective tariffs, antitrust proposals, and the overall antibusiness tone of the Bryan campaign made it quite easy for Mark Hanna to collect funds for McKinley and the Republican Party. Estimates suggest that the McKinley campaign outspent the Bryan campaign by a ratio of ten to one. The overwhelming might of corporate money had proved its point. The presidential election four years later had many of the same dynamics and the same outcome. Money had truly become the mother's milk of politics.[4] Campaign monies were used to advertise in the printed press, organize rallies, and travel. Money was also used to purchase votes. Election officials were paid off to report the desired outcome. Money was even used to purchase office. Until the passage of the Seventeenth Amendment in 1913, U.S. senators were still being selected by state legislatures. In many cases, the cost of purchasing the vote of a state legislator could go as high as $20,000 in order to ensure that he voted to elect the correct U.S. senator.

In the context of such overt corruption, scandals were merely waiting to become the subject of public debate. As written accounts of political abuses at the state and local levels became ever-more commonplace, the public mood took an ever-more cynical attitude toward business and government. Scandals eventually provided the impetus for new federal legislation aimed at minimizing corruption. Corporate contributions to political parties and candidates had become a way of life during the last part of the nineteenth century. In the first decade of the twentieth century, a legislative investigative committee obtained evidence that some of the nation's largest insurance companies, Aetna, New York Life, and Prudential among others, had been using policyholders' money for a variety of political purposes. The Republican National Committee, for example, had received $75,000. These revelations, and the growing anticorporate mood of the time, resulted in congressional passage of the Tillman Act of 1907. Once the Tillman Act went into effect, corporations and national banks were prohibited from contributing funds to candidates for national political office.

As part of his overall Progressive agenda, in 1907 Teddy Roosevelt called for fundamental changes in campaign finance regulations. He called for the full disclosure of campaign funds, limits on campaign contributions, and government subsidies of campaign expenses. Attempts to implement Roosevelt's agenda were merely a matter of time. Before the presidential election of 1908, candidates Bryan and Taft promised to limit certain types of campaign contributions. After questions were raised over whether or not each man had actually kept his promise, Congress passed a campaign disclosure bill. The Publicity Bill of 1910 required that the receipts and expenditures of all political committees be filed with the clerk of the House of Representatives within thirty days after the election. A year later, Congress passed amendments to the Tillman Act to require representatives and senators to file financial disclosure statements with the clerk. Total contributions and expenditures for House and Senate races were also limited to $5,000 and $10,000, respectively.

Soon, another well-publicized scandal, Teapot Dome, hit the American scene. In 1921 two oil tycoons were given oil-drilling rights on federal lands that had been previously set aside as U.S. Navy petroleum reserves. Edward Doheny and Harry Sinclair obtained these rights, without competitive bidding, from Interior Secretary Albert Fall. Disgruntled competitors complained, and a congressional investigation was soon under way. It was found that Fall had illegally received approximately $400,000 for granting the drilling rights to the oilmen. Fall was forced to resign and eventually was sent to prison. More important, the scandal help set the stage for further legislation as Congress passed the Corrupt Practices Act of 1925. The act stands as Congress's single attempt at extensive campaign finance reform prior to the 1970s. The law continued the ban on bank and corporate contributions. Reporting requirements were strengthened and extended to include nonparty political committees. And campaign expenditure limits were raised to between $10,000 and $25,000 for U.S. Senate races and between $2,500 and $5,000 for U.S. House races.

As the era came to a dramatic close with the stock market crash of 1929 and the election of Franklin Roosevelt in 1932, it might appear as though the Progressive agenda of reform had won the day. Much of the reform movement had become law. The merit system was firmly in place in the federal government, the Australian ballot had become a way of life, primaries were being used in more than ten states, antitrust legislation had been passed, and the federal government had passed extensive campaign finance reform. Much of the political system had been fundamentally changed by the reforms of the late nineteenth and early twentieth centuries. However, in the context of campaign finance, the reforms proved to be more illusion than reality.

Even though reform efforts were also being undertaken at the state and local levels, many state and local governments did not institute reforms. As late as 1966, only nineteen states had some form of prohibition against the solicitation of funds from state employees. Often, such laws were difficult to enforce because of their ambiguity over what was meant by a solicitation. Many states continued to allow corporate contributions. Vote buying continued unabated in many locales. And, as prohibition helped lead to the growth of organized crime, links between organized crime and political officials often became widespread. It soon became clear that the federal reform efforts instituted during the first quarter of the twentieth century were simply unworkable. Corporate contributions were sometimes simply ignored and creative techniques were developed to circumvent the ban on corporate contributions. Executive salaries were sometimes increased with the understanding that the increase was to be contributed to the appropriate candidate or political party. The campaign reporting requirements were essentially useless because the legislation lacked any real enforcement provisions. The reports were submitted to the clerk of the House and were therefore generally unavailable for public scrutiny. The campaign reports were kept for only two years. Often, candidates simply did not file reports. Evasion of the expenditure limits was quite simple. Certain types of expenditure were excluded from the limits, and candidates could simply claim that they simply did not know about a given expenditure. In the case of *Newberry v. U.S.* (1921), the Supreme Court stated that congressional regulation could not extend to primaries and nominating activities; any spending for activities before nomination were therefore not covered by federal law.

As Frank J. Sorauf (1992, 6) observes, "All of this regulation scarcely impeded the flow of campaign money. Much of the reform legislation, both of Congress and the states, seems to have been passed with the loopholes tailored in. . . . Not surprisingly, there were no prosecutions under the 1925 law, from its origin to its repeal in 1971."

THE NEW DEAL ERA, 1932–1968

After the Great Depression began in 1929, public intolerance of the most blatant forms of corruption continued to grow. As a result, corruption was forced underground, making it even more difficult to control. Money, however, remained a main ingredient of a successful campaign, and the Democratic Party remained in serious financial trouble throughout the 1930s. Much of the initial money to help fund the party came from wealthy individuals who had personal contacts with Franklin Roosevelt. Many of these same individuals eventually found themselves employed in government jobs. By 1936, labor union funds had become an additional source of revenue for the Democratic Party and its candidates. As the business community became increasingly uneasy with the direction of the Democratic Party, corporate-related money expanded its role in the Republican Party.

Reform efforts followed a familiar pattern: concern over specific activities; the passage of legislation despite the reluctant support of politicos; efforts to circumvent the intent of the legislation; and finally, little or no enthusiasm for enforcement. In 1939, the Hatch Act was passed after it gained momentum from reports, never proven, that Senator Barkley of Kentucky had used Works Progress Administration workers in his reelection campaign. The law extended the prohibition against political activities by civil servants to include almost all federal employees. A year later, legislation extended coverage to include all employees of state agencies financed in whole or in part by federal dollars. The 1940 legislation also installed a new $3 million campaign-spending limit and set a maximum contribution limit of $5,000 per person. In 1943, Congress passed the Smith-Connally Act, which temporarily prohibited labor unions from contributing to national political organizations. Four years later, the Taft-Hartley Act made the ban permanent and extended the ban to include expenditures on behalf of a candidate.

These and earlier efforts to reform the campaign finance system helped spawn numerous creative mechanisms to circumvent the law, which often formed the basis for many of the creative financial activities that we see today. The $3 million limit on campaign expenditures was quickly overcome by the creation of multiple campaign committees. The original political action committees, PACs, were the creation of labor unions as a means to get around the provisions of Taft-Hartley. The $5,000 limit on contributions was avoided by giving to multiple committees or contributing funds before the start of the official reporting period.

By the late 1950s, America had a campaign finance system that, according to Frank Sorauf (1988), had six salient characteristics, five of which are particularly relevant in the present context. First, campaigns were financed primarily by large contributors. Sorauf provides evidence that in 1952 about two-thirds of all the money spent on federal elections came from contributions of $500 or more. Second, vestiges of patronage and preferments, while relatively unimportant at the national level, remained a significant source of funds in numerous states and locales. Third, political parties remained the primary financial intermediaries between candidates and contributors. Fourth, solicitors remained central to the campaign finance system. Personal contacts with the affluent contributor continued to remain critical to the financial stability of the party. And fifth, regulation of campaign finance had been an exercise in futility. Numerous openly corrupt behaviors had been marginalized; however, most reform efforts fell victim to the problems of evasion, avoidance, and nonenforcement.

Two significant developments during the 1950s and 1960s were the foundations upon which changes in campaigns and campaign finance would be built. The first of these was the development of new campaign technologies in which the nonprint media would play a major role. While public opinion polls had been used in the 1940s and 1950s, it was the Kennedy campaign of 1960 that first used them to help guide campaign strategies. Radio had been used for much of the twentieth century, but the new medium of television took off in the 1950s. The media age was born, and campaign costs began to skyrocket. The continued growth in new campaign technologies would continue unabated.

The second, and highly related, development was a change in the fundamental nature of political parties and their relationships to candidates and campaigns. As stated in chapter 1, some see this change as the decline of political parties while others see it as an evolution of political parties. In either case, political parties began to loose their grip on the American public and their own candidates for office. The new technologies themselves helped exacerbate the declining importance of parties. Whereas candidates once relied upon thousands of party workers to help them gauge public opinion, public opinion polls soon would become the standard for gathering information. The candidate would no longer need thousands of party workers to hand out information. Television would present the message to millions. Although Alexander Heard (1960) could correctly claim that political parties were the primary intermediaries between candidates and contributors in the 1950s, by the late 1960s political parties were beginning to lose much of their financial intermediary role.

THE MODERN ERA, 1968 TO THE PRESENT

For many Americans today, "the sixties" conjures up memories of upheaval, disillusionment, and change. In many ways the events of the late 1960s and early 1970s helped create a climate of political reform not seen since the days of the Progressives. As early as 1961, President Kennedy appointed a commission to analyze costs in presidential elections. Campaign finance reform was once again part of the national agenda. Campaign costs continued to spiral upward, and by the late 1960s, Democrats began to feel that they were losing the campaign funding race to Republicans. Many traditional large contributors to the Democratic Party were lost as a result of upheavals associated with the Vietnam War. The upheavals at the 1968 Democratic convention resulted in calls for reform to "open up" the party. The stage was set for the most significant attempts to reform the overall campaign finance system in our nation's history.

In 1971, Congress passed two major pieces of legislation that deal directly with campaign finance: the Revenue Act of 1971 and the Federal Election Campaign Act. The Revenue Act created a special campaign fund for presidential and vice presidential elections into which taxpayers could divert a dollar of their tax liability. As for the Federal Election Campaign Act (FECA), many of the objectives were not fundamentally different from earlier reform efforts. It continued the prohibition against contributions by corporations and labor unions. However, the law did provide a clear legal basis for the creation and maintenance of business and labor political committees. Campaign reporting and disclosure requirements were tightened and extended the provisions to include primaries. And, for the first time, federal law took direct aim at the growing cost of media advertising, as strict limits were placed on the amount of money candidates could spend on media advertising. Congressional and senatorial candidates were limited in their spending on media advertising to an amount equal to $50,000, or ten cents per voting-age resident of the district or state, whichever total was larger. Primaries and the general election were treated separately, so in any single election year a candidate could actually spend twice the amount specified above.

On June 17, 1972, burglars were caught breaking into the Democratic Party headquarters in the Watergate complex in Washington, D.C. Thus began a two-year saga that became the most widely documented and most publicized political scandal in American history. It would ultimately bring down a presidency. For almost two years, millions of Americans saw testimony that documented burglary, illegal campaign contributions, enemies lists, coercion to induce campaign contributions, money laundering, conspiracy to cover up illegal activities, and other scandalous actions too numerous to list. The public outcry demanded action, and in 1974 Congress passed a series of amendments to the FECA that represent the most comprehensive effort to reform and regulate campaign finance in our nation's history. The 1974 FECA amendments had five major categories of provisions:

1. Limits on Contributions. Individual contributions to candidates for federal office were limited to $1,000 per candidate per election. In any given election year, this meant that one could give a candidate a total of $2,000 ($1,000 for the primary season and $1,000 for the general election). PAC and party committee contributions were limited to no more than

$5,000 per candidate per election. An overall, or total, contribution limit of $25,000 was placed upon individual contributors. These contribution limits were not indexed for inflation and, with the exceptions to be noted later, remain in force to this day.

2. Limits on Expenditures. Limits were placed on what candidates for the House, the Senate, and the presidency could spend seeking election or re-election. Individuals were limited on what they could spend on behalf of their own campaign. Finally, limits were imposed on what individuals or organizations could spend advocating the election or defeat of a candidate.

3. The Creation of the Federal Election Commission. The Federal Election Commission was created to help implement and enforce federal law. It was to receive the financial reports of all candidates for federal office and other political organizations and would be responsible for the public disclosure of this information. It had power to issue certain types of regulation and could act as the initial arbiter when disputes arose over the interpretation of federal law. And, it had the power to undertake initial investigations into accusations of illegal activities.

4. Disclosure Requirements. Candidates for federal office were required to submit quarterly reports to the Federal Election Commission, which made these records public. Record keeping and disclosure requirements covered both campaign contributions and expenditures.

5. Public Funding of Presidential Elections. The 1971 Revenue Act had created a tax checkoff system to provide funds for a presidential election campaign fund. The 1974 FECA amendments created a two-tier funding system—one for the primary season and one for the general election—that candidates could accept or reject. During the primary season a candidate would receive matching funds up to a specified spending limit. Additional provisions created criteria that had to be met in order to receive matching funds and criteria for the cutoff, and potential reinstatement, of federal dollars. In the general election cycle, candidates received a flat sum of money. Most of the funding provisions were indexed to inflation. For example, while each major party candidate received $21,800,000 for the general election in 1976, the amount grew to $61,800,000 in 1996. Finally, there were provisions that specified the criteria that had to be met for minor party candidates to receive federal dollars.

The 1974 FECA amendments stand as our nation's greatest effort to gain control of the campaign finance system. Soon after the passage of the law, however, it was challenged in court, and many of its main provisions were declared unconstitutional. If the 1974 FECA amendments represent our nation's greatest attempt to regulate campaign finance, the case of *Buckley v. Valeo* represents the greatest impediment to comprehensive campaign regulation. It, and subsequent Court decisions, gutted much of the letter and intent of the 1970s reform efforts.

The *Buckley* decision did uphold the constitutionality of the reporting and disclosure requirements, the funding of the presidential election campaigns, and most of the limits on campaign contributions. Most important, however, the Supreme Court ruled that spending is a form of free speech. Attempts to limit spending, at least without some accompanying form of public financing, violate First Amendment protections of freedom of expression. One consequence of this ruling is that, to pass constitutional muster, spending limits must be voluntary, though acceptance of spending limits can be encouraged by providing public subsidies to those candidates abiding by the limits. A second consequence is that spending limits, even in combination with public subsidies, cannot preclude the possibility of wealthy candidates spending as much of their own money as they desire in an attempt to "buy" the election. Finally, one cannot limit expenditures by individuals or groups that spend independently of the candidate.

After the *Buckley* decision, Congress, in 1976, acted quickly to reestablish the constitutionally acceptable aspects of FECA in order to have the provisions ready for the 1976 election. Additional amendments were passed in 1979 that merely reflected attempts to fine-tune the law and, in 1993, the tax checkoff for the Presidential Election Campaign Fund was raised to three dollars. Of more significance were additional Court decisions and an increasingly indifferent Congress that helped to further limit and restrict campaign finance regulation. In *Colorado Republican Federal Campaign Committee v. Federal Election Commission*, for example, the Court extended the *Buckley v. Valeo* decision by allowing political parties to engage in unlimited independent spending. Moreover, investigations of campaign irregularities by the Federal Election Commission often have long delays because Congress has not been willing to adequately fund the commission. In Washington, most now see the Federal Election Commission as a paper tiger. Given these developments, current federal law can now be described as follows:

1. Limits on Contributions.   For a single calendar year, individual contributions are limited to $1,000 per candidate per election, $20,000 to a national party committee, $5,000 to any other single political committee, and an aggregate total of $25,000. Multicandidate political committees are limited to $5,000 per candidate per election, $15,000 for a national party committee, and $5,000 for any other political committee. Other political committees are limited to $1,000 per candidate per election, $20,000 for a national committee, and $5,000 for any other political committee. Political party committees are limited to $1,000 per candidate per election unless it is a multicandidate committee, in which case the limit is increased to $5,000 per candidate per election. In addition, political party committees can contribute only $5,000 to any other political committee. A national party committee, its national senatorial campaign committee, or some combination of the two can contribute $17,500 to any Senate candidate in the year in which he or she seeks election. Finally, any of the follow types of contributions are prohibited: anonymous contributions, cash contributions of more than $100, and contributions from banks, corporations, labor unions, and foreign nationals.

2. Reporting and Disclosure Requirements. All candidates for federal office and all political committees that operate in federal elections must file reports that are then made available for public inspection by the Federal Election Commission. The names of any contributor who gives more than $200 per year must be identified. Other information that must be reported include cash on hand, loans, spending figures, receipts, money transfers, dividends, and interest.

3. Expenditure Limits. Only presidential candidates who agree to accept public funding have limits on what they can spend during the primary election period and the general election period. These limits were set in 1976 at $10 million for the primary season and $20 million for the general election.[5] Cost-of-living allowances are used to adjust these figures for every presidential election year. Thus, the figures were $27,600,000 for the primary season and $55,200,000 for the general election in 1992 and $31 million and $61,800,000 for the two cycles in 1996. Certain fund-raising costs, up to a maximum of an additional 20 percent, are exempt from the spending limits. Political parties that accept public funds for their conventions are limited to a 1974 amount of $4 million, with a cost-of-living adjustment bringing the totals to $11 million in 1992 and $12,360,000 in 1996. The national committees of each political party may spend money, in addition to direct contributions, on behalf of their House, Senate, and presidential candidates. The limits, in 1974 dollars that are annually adjusted for cost of living, are as follows: $10,000 for House candidates in states that have more than one congressional district; $20,000 or two cents per voter, whichever is greater, for each Senate candidate or House candidate in single-district states; and, two cents per voter for the presidential candidate. By 1994 these figures had increased to $29,300 for multidistrict House races and between $58,600 and $1,325,415 for Senate races. The same spending limits apply to state political party spending on behalf of House and Senate candidates.

4. The Federal Election Commission. The Federal Election Commission is a six-member independent regulatory agency. Its members are appointed by the president subject to the advice and consent of the Senate. It administers the public funding provisions for presidential elections and is responsible for public disclosure of all federal campaign finance reports. It has investigation authority, has the authority to issue regulations and advisory opinions, and can conduct hearings.

5. The Public Funding of Presidential Elections. Candidates for the presidency can elect to receive public funding. To qualify for public funding during the primary season, a candidate must raise $5,000 in each of twenty states, counting only the first $250 of each contribution. After a candidate qualifies, the federal government will match the first $250 of each contribution up to a total not to exceed one half of the total spending limit. There are also provisions for cutting off federal matching dollars if a candidate does poorly during part of the primary season; there are also reinstatement provisions. Each major party's convention nominee gets a flat sum of money to spend during the general election period equal to the respecified spending limit. Minor party candidates can receive money if their party received at least 5 percent of the vote in the last election. The actual amount depends upon the vote percentage that the party received in the last presidential election. New party candidates can receive retroactive funding if they receive at least 5 percent of the vote. Finally, each major party can receive funds, up to the full amount of the spending limit, for their convention, while minor parties can receive a lesser amount depending upon how their candidate fared during the previous presidential election.

The current federal campaign finance laws are clearly the most extensive that we have ever seen in American history. At the same time, the contemporary campaign finance system remains highly controversial partly because of the ingenious steps undertaken to circumvent the intent, if not the letter, of current law. We conclude our historical discussion of the modern era, therefore, by briefly discussing nine characteristics of the contemporary campaign finance system that help define its character and potential for controversy.

First, there is no question that campaign expenditures for all federal elections have increased greatly over the last twenty-five years. All indications are that, in the absence of new campaign reform laws, costs will continue to increase far in excess of the inflation rate. In 1976, the aggregate cost of all U.S. Senate and House campaigns was $115,500,000. By 1994 the aggregate cost had risen to $725 million. While the average cost of winning a House election was $87,200 in 1976, by 1994 the average cost was $529,020. The average cost of winning a Senate seat rose from $609,100 in 1976 to $4,300,000 in 1994. Campaign costs are likely to continue to escalate because of the perceived need to continue to run high-technology, candidate-centered campaigns, which place a major emphasis on the importance of media.

Second, PACs play an ever-increasing role in modern campaigns. PACs are important as a source of direct funds for candidates and a source of funds for independent expenditures, an issue that is discussed below. The total number of PACs grew dramatically from the early 1970s to the late 1980s, at which point their numbers began to level off. There were 608 federally registered PACs in 1974; there were 4,268 in 1988. PAC contributions have also grown significantly. House and Senate candidates received

$12,500,000 from PACs in 1974 and a record $189 million in 1994. In 1994, about a quarter of all money raised by Senate candidates came from PACs, while winning House candidates received about 40 percent of all their money from PACs.

The proliferation of PACs is very much the result of federal campaign finance regulations. PACs were originally an innovation of the labor movement and used as a mechanism to circumvent federal prohibitions against direct contributions by labor unions. Corporations and banks now use PACs to circumvent federal prohibitions against direct contributions by banks and corporations. In addition, one often sees a proliferation of PACs within a given industrial sector as a means to circumvent limits on campaign contributions. Since it would be illegal for a PAC representing the American Petroleum Institute to contribute $100,000 to a single candidate, one merely creates ten different PACs representing ten different oil companies, and each contributes $10,000 to the same candidate. The role of PACs in contemporary campaigns is perhaps one of the most contentious issues in the campaign finance debate. Critics view PACs as a direct threat to representative democracy, claiming that the average citizen is overshadowed by the organized power of special interest groups that are able to buy policies favorable to their own agenda. PACs are defended by those who view them as reflecting the pluralist idea of American democracy, wherein the average citizen has influence in government by his or her affiliation with organized interests.

A third characteristic of the contemporary campaign finance system is that candidates are beginning to receive more and more of their campaign money from out-of-district sources. It is often difficult to specify the geographical source of PAC contributions, and data collected by the Federal Election Commission do not allow one to identify the location of individual contributions of less than $200. Nevertheless, all indications are that, today, candidates for federal office, especially for the Senate, are receiving more money from out-of-district sources than they have in the past. Critics suggest that this nationalization of the system of campaign contributions poses a direct threat to the traditional linkage between an elected representative and his or her constituency.

Fourth, there is a great imbalance in the availabilty of resources between incumbents and challengers. In most recent elections, incumbent House candidates outspent challengers by a ratio of 3.5 to 1. Incumbent Senate candidates outspent challengers by a ratio of 2 to 1. More than 70 percent of PAC contributions go to incumbents. These financial advantages of incumbency are in addition to other advantages that accrue to incumbents: name recognition, the franking privilege, the ability to undertake casework, and other taxpayer subsidies. In fact, the majority of congressional elections every two years are elections in name only. The reality in most

congressional elections is that one has a well-known, well-financed, entrenched incumbent facing a little-known challenger who begins with little
campaign money and is simply incapable of raising significant funds. Given
the imbalance in resources between most incumbents and most challengers, it is not surprising that incumbents consistently win more than 90
percent of the elections in which they choose to compete. Critics suggest
that the lack of competition in congressional elections is only exacerbated
by the imbalance inherent in the current campaign finance system.

Fifth, soft money has continued to take on increasing importance and
has therefore become increasingly controversial. Soft money is simply a way
to avoid the contribution limits, expenditure limits, and disclosure requirements of current federal law. Soft money is money that would be illegal if
spent directly in connection with federal elections. The money is solicited
from banks, corporations, labor unions, individuals, and other organizations and funneled through designated nonfederal accounts of the national political parties. The money is laundered to state political parties,
which spend the money on activities that affect national elections. Because
there are minimal record-keeping requirements in connection with soft
money, and some debate over exactly what is considered to be soft money,
exact figures on the amount of soft money in any campaign are difficult to
specify. However, estimates are that in 1992 more than $87 million in soft
money was collected by the two major parties. Soft money totaled $85 mil-
lion in 1994 and more than $200 million in 1996.

Soft money seems to have first become a significant financial procedure
to circumvent federal law in the presidential election of 1980. Since 1980
it has taken on increasing importance as the dollar amounts have continued to grow and the prohibition against using the money in direct connection with federal election has become increasingly ambiguous. Attempts at
regulatory enforcement are minimal. Efforts to eliminate the big contributor from the campaign finance system, as seen in the 1974 FECA amendments, have effectively been neutralized by the soft money loophole. Individuals are once again able to contribute large sums of money.

Sixth, independent expenditures are another characteristic of the contemporary campaign finance system that is often seen as a loophole in current law. Because of the *Buckley* decision, individuals or groups may spend
as much money as they wish to support or oppose candidates for federal
office. There may be no coordination or cooperation with any candidate
when such money is spent. Independent expenditures first gained significant public awareness in 1980, when the National Conservative Political Action Committee (NCPAC) targeted a number of liberal Democratic senators for defeat. Four eventually lost their reelection bids. As has been the
case in other types of spending, independent expenditures have continued

to increase. Estimates of independent expenditures that totaled $300,000 in 1978 had risen to $11,100,000 in 1992 and to $5,200,000 in 1994.

The seventh characteristic of the contemporary campaign finance system is that many questionable campaign practices continue and that there are ongoing efforts to find new ways to circumvent federal law. In their book, *Dirty Little Secrets,* Larry Sabato and Glenn Simpson (1996) discuss a number of corrupt campaign practices that can be readily documented, among them dirty campaign tricks, street money, legislative perks being used to help reelection bids, telephone sleaze campaigns, and vote fraud. In addition to such corrupt activities, there are ongoing efforts to develop new ways to raise money that can be used to circumvent federal and state laws. For example, a practice known as bundling is used to undermine campaign reporting requirements and avoid certain contribution limits. Bundling simply involves having a person collect checks for a candidate. The person collecting the checks often represents a particular interest group or PAC. The PAC can receive credit from the candidate for raising the money, but the official source of the money becomes registered as being from the specific individuals who wrote the checks.

The eighth characteristic of the contemporary campaign finance system is that it is a candidate-centered system in which political parties primarily play a service role.[6] As stated in chapter 1, the effective monopoly that political parties held over nominations and elections for more than 150 years was broken in the 1960s. Money and new technologies now allow candidates to win elections without depending on political parties. Political parties have changed in response to these developments. They are very much service organizations, offering research and advice on such things as campaign managers, advertising agents and agencies, public opinion polls, policy position papers, and raising campaign funds. Political parties often bundle money, act as a conduit for campaign funds, and launder soft money to help its candidates win office.

The ninth characteristic of the contemporary campaign finance system is that reform continues to be part of the national agenda but that there is little consensus on the particulars of reform. Given the public rhetoric of our public officials, it would seem that few individuals are satisfied with our current campaign finance system. However, reform of our current system is problematic because of basic philosophical and partisan differences over the need for specific reforms. It is difficult to even obtain consensus on the nature of the problems. Numerous individuals, Newt Gingrich for example, do not even accept the premise that elections have become too expensive. In this context, Congress has struggled to pass meaningful campaign finance reform. A Republican-led filibuster in the Senate stopped campaign finance legislation in the 100th Congress. Although reform legislation did pass the House and the Senate in the 101st and 103d Congresses on party-line votes, differences could not be resolved in the conference committee. President Bush vetoed legislation that was passed by the 102nd Congress. More than ninety bills to reform the campaign finance system were introduced in the 104th Congress. None passed.

In the 105th Congress we again saw a large number of bills introduced to change the contemporary campaign finance system. These bills differ a great deal in terms of the problems they address. Some are narrow in focus and are aimed at specific items such as the elimination of soft money, PAC contributions, or the elimination of contribution limits altogether. Others are more inclusive and would attempt to limit spending by providing funding or other benefits to induce candidates to adhere to voluntary spending limits. Some propose a constitutional amendment to overcome the limits on federal action imposed by the *Buckley* decision. The diversity seen in the large number of bills being introduced suggests that the Congress, and the nation, still lacks a consensus on how to reform the campaign finance system. Given this lack of consensus, and the partisan makeup on Capital Hill, it would seem unlikely, in the absence of a major scandal, and even in the presence of numerous minor scandals, that comprehensive reform will be passed during the next few sessions of Congress.

CONCLUSION

Throughout the history of the American Republic candidates for elected office have always needed votes, and money has always been a necessary ingredient in obtaining votes. The interrelationships among money, elections, politics, and social power have remained problematic from the first elections in America to the election of Bill Clinton in 1996. Attempts at regulation of campaign finance developed over time as a patchwork of regulations issued by local, state, and federal governments responding to particular developments in local, state, and national affairs.

The nature of the campaign finance system at a particular time in our nation's history can be best understood in terms of the dominant political, social, economic, and cultural norms of the time. In the earliest years of the Republic, campaign costs were minimal because of the small and widely dispersed electorate and the prejudicial norms against openly campaigning for office. As the electorate expanded and mass political parties became the primary intermediaries between the electorate and the candidate, campaign costs increased and parties became dominant actors in the campaign financing system. As campaign costs continued to escalate and the nation continued to industrialize, the link between the rich and economically powerful contributor and the needy candidate and political party became solidified. As new campaign technologies continued to develop and the mass media campaign came of age in the 1960s, political parties began to lose much of their traditional financial intermediary role as campaigns became candidate centered.

Reform efforts throughout American history have followed a familiar pattern: concern over specific activities, a specific event or set of events that helped the passage of legislation despite the reluctant support of politicos, efforts to circumvent the intent of reform, and finally little or no enthusiasm for enforcement. Candidates for office almost always feel the need for additional revenue, and special interests have almost always tried to use money to obtain an advantage in the political process. Failure to recognize these two facts has doomed most reform efforts. Future reform efforts are also likely to fail if they do not recognize these two simple facts. As can be seen when the Civil Service Reform Act banned assessments on federal civil servants, reform works only when the public demands immediate action, will not accept the development of loopholes, and is ever vigilant to guarantee that the law is enforced.

NOTES

1. Works that provide much of our understanding about the early years of campaign finance are George Thayer (1973), Louise Overacker (1932), and Alexander Heard (1960).

2. Perhaps the best historical account of the early development of political parties in America can be found in Wilfred E. Binkley (1964).

3. Further discussion about the Progressive movement can be found in Richard Hofstadter (1956).

4. The phrase "money is the mother's milk of politics" originated with Jesse "Big Daddy" Unruh, who served as speaker of the California state assembly. Quoted in Herbert E. Alexander (1992).

5. Although the law was reconstituted after the *Buckley* decision in 1976, the expenditure limits are actually specified using 1974 as a base year. Thus, the actual limits for the presidential election in 1976 were $10,900,000 and $21,800,000 for the primary and general election, respectively.

6. With the growth of soft money and independent expenditures during the 1996 elections, it has been argued that campaigns are now beyond the control of individual candidates. See Citizens' Research Foundation (1997). Still, political parties primarily play a service role in modern American politics.

Chapter Three

Excessive Spending, Candidate Viability, and Free Speech

The purpose of this chapter is to outline some of the general arguments regarding campaign finance reform that are difficult to empirically verify. How, for example, might one determine whether too much or too little money is being spent in congressional elections? Too much compared to what? Compared to the advertising budgets of major corporations? Compared to spending in past elections? While we make no pretensions that we are able to "solve" the issues raised in this chapter, we hope to at least address many of the concerns that have been raised about campaign finance reform.

ARGUMENT #1: THE AMOUNT OF MONEY SPENT IN CONGRESSIONAL CAMPAIGNS IS REALY NOT THAT MUCH

Frequently, opponents of campaign finance reform argue that the money being spent in congressional elections is really not exorbitant. Expenditures in electoral campaigns, these critics point out, pale in comparison to the amount of money spent by major corporations in their yearly advertising campaigns. For example, "Americans spent two to three times as much money in 1994 alone on the purchase of potato chips. Procter & Gamble and Philip Morris Company, the nation's two largest advertisers, spend roughly the same amount each year on advertising as is spent by all political candidates and parties" (Smith 1996, 1059).

This analogy between corporate advertising and campaign spending, however, is objectionable on a number of grounds. First, implicit in the analogy is an assumption that when voters choose between candidates they are making a choice similar to the decision between Pringles and Ruffles Brand potato chips. Yet, voting decisions should, at least theoretically, be different from a choice between consumer products. Ideally, we would prefer that voters have more information about political candidates than they have about potato chips, even if public opinion surveys indicate that voters frequently fall short of this mark. In addition, when consumers err in the decision between competing products, in most instances, they can easily return to the store to purchase the other brand. Returning political candidates who prove to be less than promised is not quite as easy. Not only is the choice between candidates offered only every two years in House elections, but the decision to try a different brand is based on the decision of more than a single consumer. If the economic market worked in a similar fashion, consumers who voted for Pepsi would be forced to drink Coca-Cola if 50 percent + 1 percent of the voting population opted for the "real thing."

Whether this ultimately means that less rather than more money should be spent in congressional campaigns is not entirely clear, but it should be apparent that comparing campaign spending to spending on product advertising is not entirely appropriate. It is often argued that the nature of democratic choice justifies more rather than less candidate spending presumably because such spending results in a more informed citizenry. A more detailed examination of the thesis is considered in chapter 7; for now, we simply raise a question: Do consumers really learn more about Pepsi and Coca-Cola as a result of their advertising campaigns? And if so, what exactly is it that they learn? That Michael Jordan drinks Pepsi? In this respect, if candidate expenditures are, by and large, devoted to television and radio advertisements in which candidates are packaged as consumer goods, why would we expect the average voter to have any greater understanding of candidate issue positions than the average consumer has of the ingredients of Coca-Cola?

Fortunately, other bases of comparison exist that provide greater insight into whether or not too much money is being spent in congressional elections. First, one can compare campaign spending in U.S. elections to campaign spending in other Western democracies. On this count, elections in the United States are clearly longer and more expensive than elections in comparable Western European democracies. However, because of differences in political systems, particularly in terms of the party-centered nature of parliamentary elections and provisions for public subsidies in many of these nations, such comparisons offer little guidance in judging the relative expense of U.S. elections.[1]

Second, if one compares current spending to spending in past elections, one finds that even after controlling for inflation, campaign spending has increased dramatically over the last two decades (Magleby and Nelson 1990). Though Frank J. Sorauf (1992) notes that campaign spending may have leveled off in the late 1980s, in light of the 1996 elections such a conclusion appears to have been a bit premature. Campaign spending may have leveled off during the late 1980s and early 1990s, and may do so again in the future if competition wanes or if partisan control of Congress stabilizes within the next few election cycles. Still, it is unclear exactly what this means in terms of whether too much or too little money is spent in congressional elections. Unfortunately, it is difficult to escape Herbert E. Alexander's conclusion that "there are no universally accepted criteria by which to determine when political campaign spending becomes excessive" (Brookings n.d.).

In part, perceptions of too much or too little campaign spending may be affected by public perceptions regarding the outputs of the political process. Perhaps the amount of money spent on election campaigns would seem more acceptable if citizens truly believed that the result is "the best Congress money can buy" (see Stern 1988) or, for that matter, if the electoral process appeared to produce exceptional candidates in terms of their competence and integrity. Yet, this is clearly not the case. While causality is difficult (if not impossible) to prove, increased spending is associated with an increasingly alienated, apathetic, and uninvolved citizenry, which sees little reason to trust political institutions or politicians. As Senator Fred Thompson (Republican, Tenn.) has noted, "The American people look at a system where we spend so much time with our hand out for so much money from so many people who do so much business with the federal government who we're basically regulating and legislating on. They look at that system and the amounts of money that are involved nowadays. They don't have much confidence in it" (Schmitt 1997).

Yet, while many reformers lament the high levels of spending in election campaigns, the more glaring shortcoming of congressional campaign finance is not with the level of spending but with the source and the distribution of campaign money. Frequently, public interest groups, such as Common Cause and the Center for Responsive Politics lament the high costs of congressional campaigns as though the spending in these campaigns were the central problem. On this point, critics of campaign reform are at least partially correct. The problem with congressional campaigns is not the exorbitant expense but the inequities in the process of campaign fund-raising. If all candidates could raise $2–3 million in "disinterested" money to spend in House campaigns, there might be some residual concern about the costs of campaigns, but much of the public concern about money in elections would be alleviated.[2] But, to paraphrase V. O. Key Jr. (1964), citizens are not fools. They are well aware that, even if money does not buy elections outright, a candidate with money has a clear advantage over a candidate without money. In this respect, concerns over campaign fund-raising are not simply rooted in the recognition that certain candidates have almost unlimited resources at their disposal, they are also rooted in the recognition that too many candidates lack resources.

In 1994 and 1996, as in all recent election years, those candidates who raised more money had clear electoral advantage. As can be seen in table 3.1, the candidate who spent the most money won in 84 percent of contested elections in 1994 and in 92 percent of contested elections in 1996. In 1994, money appears to have been less decisive in those elections involving Republican open-seat winners and successful Republican challenges to Democratic incumbents. For Republican open-seat winners, only 58 percent of winners outspent their opponent, while only 31 percent of successful Republican challengers outspent the Democratic incumbent. In 1996, successful Democratic challengers were, on average, outspent by their Republican opposition, but they still won. In every other type of race in 1996, the candidate spending the most money was, on average, more likely to win. To some scholars, the fact that some candidates outspend their opponents and still lose is a sure sign that money cannot buy elections. This is

Table 3.1   Expenditures of Winners and Losers, 1994 and 1996

	1994	1996
All races		
Winners ($)	534,833	689,859
Losers ($)	320,070	290,056
Winners outspending losers (%)	84.2	91.8
Open-seat races		
Republican winners ($)	539,756	724,422
Democratic losers ($)	523,800	544,538
Winners outspending losers (%)	58.1	68.0
Democratic winners ($)	668,713	780,333
Republican losers ($)	831,615 [a]	544,538
Winners outspending losers (%)	88.9	81.8
Incumbent races		
Republican incumbent winners ($)	506,246	718,052
Democratic challenger losers ($)	179,880	233,995
Winners outspending losers (%)	96.2	96.7
Democratic incumbent winners ($)	520,253	592,568
Republican challenger losers ($)	151,756	190,253
Winners outspending losers (%)	97.1	96.7
Democratic incumbent losers ($)	944,573	710,406
Republican challenger winners ($)	675,828	123,615
Winners outspending losers (%)	30.6	100.0
Republican incumbent losers ($)	---- [b]	1,085,439
Democratic challenger winners ($)	----	993,97
Winners outspending losers (%)	----	47.4

[a]This figure is inflated by one candidate that spent over $4,000,000.
[b]No Republican incumbents were defeated in 1994.

certainly true to the extent that money provides no guarantee of electoral success. Yet it is also true that having more money than your opponent is a distinct electoral advantage in congressional elections, second perhaps only to the incumbency advantage in terms of electoral impact. Most of the candidates who won but were outspent were not exactly impoverished. On average, those candidates that either defeated a sitting incumbent or that won in an open-seat election spent in excess of $500,000.

Taken as a whole, the data reflect Gary C. Jacobson's (1980) observation that money is a necessary but not sufficient condition for electoral success. Or put more simply, money does not buy elections, but without money a candidate is almost certain to lose. The data also reflect the overall concern with money in American politics: too few candidates are able to raise the money necessary to be competitive. Despite the high level of partisan turnover during 1994, the number of competitive seats in 1994 actually declined compared to 1992 (Duncan and Lawrence 1995).[3] Part of the reason, beyond the 52 uncontested seats, was that in just over 100 seats at least one candidate who spent less than $50,000 was facing an opponent who spent, on average, just under $400,000.[4]

As a general rule, incumbents are able to raise (and spend) about as much money as they deem necessary. Incumbent representatives begin the campaign with a base of individual donors they can readily turn to for financial support. Well positioned within the Washington community, incumbents can also solicit political action committee contributions without much investment of time or energy. While some political action committees have clear ideological and partisan biases, most pursue legislative rather than electoral strategies. As a general rule, PACs that follow such a strategy care less about who is in office than about their access to and influence over the representative, regardless of the official's partisan or ideological leanings. For incumbents, a great deal of money is there simply for the asking. Frank J. Sorauf (1992), for example, notes that popular accounts of PACs trying to buy votes from incumbent representatives are often inaccurate. At least as often, it is the incumbent representative pressuring political action committees for contributions. Whatever the exact nature of the relationship, as a source of campaign financing in congressional elections, PAC money tends to be more available to incumbents than to challengers.

Unlike incumbents, challengers must first prove that they are viable before they can begin to raise the money necessary to mount a credible campaign. Most challengers fail this test and, consequently, fail to raise much money. Even viable nonincumbent candidates, however, have to build a fund-raising organization, often from scratch. The more expensive the campaign, the earlier these fund-raising efforts have to begin. Often, potential candidates have to begin raising money more than a year in advance of the election. Many potentially qualified candidates decide how much money it would take to run a competitive campaign, and how much time and effort they would have to devote to raising this money, and then simply decide not to seek elected office.

Although these inequities in fund-raising have been well documented in the existing literature, they have not generally resulted in increased calls for campaign finance reform. Oddly enough, while challengers may be disadvantaged in raising campaign money, they have a distinct advantage in terms of spending it. With few exceptions, most studies examining the impact of candidate spending on election outcomes have found that, on a dollar-for-dollar basis, challenger spending yields a much larger percentage of the vote than incumbent spending (Jacobson 1978, 1980, 1985, 1990a; Green and Krasno 1988; Goidel and Gross 1994). For critics of campaign reform, one implication of this finding is that, if challengers are to defeat incumbents, they need to be unrestricted in the amount of money they are allowed to spend. More to the point, critics argue that placing limits on challenger spending (even if some form of public subsidy were provided) would have the unintended consequence of reelecting more incumbents.

Though that is possible, given that over 90 percent of incumbents are routinely reelected, it is hard to imagine that reform could make incumbents any safer. Consider, for example, that 1992 was remarkable, at least in part, because the percentage of incumbents seeking reelection who were defeated in either the primary or the general election dropped below 90 percent for the first time since 1974. In 1994 and 1996, both election years in which the partisan balance in the House of Representative was in question, more than 90 percent of incumbents were reelected. It is unclear how giving candidates money, or limiting their spending, could result in elections any less competitive.

In addition, while critics of reform may have the spending side of the equation correct (though this too is debatable), the failure to enact reform means that, at least in most elections, challengers will languish because they are unable to raise enough money to mount a serious electoral challenge. An analogy could be made to certain third world countries in which, although the cost of living is extremely low, only tourists and the few residents who have money can enjoy this low cost of living. So it is for congressional challengers: a small group of challengers may benefit from an advantage in terms of the dollar-for-dollar return on spending enjoyed by challengers, but to the overwhelming mass of challengers such an advantage means very little. In this context, reformers should acknowledge that campaign finance reform might limit the effectiveness of those challengers who, under existing rules, can raise and spend large sums of money. Yet it should also be acknowledged that this is a relatively small subset of all congressional challengers. In the 1994 and 1996 elections, spending limits set at $600,000 would have affected about 15 percent of congressional challengers, while spending limits of $800,000 would have affected less than 10 percent of all challengers.

Overall, two simple realities define U.S. House elections. First, challengers need money to mount competitive campaign efforts. Without money, any advantage in spending on a dollar-for-dollar basis compared to incumbents means very little. Second, in general, the market of political campaign contributions fails to provide challengers with an amount of funding sufficient to mount a competitive campaign. Most political scientists, even those who generally are opposed to campaign finance reform, recognize that, if the goal of reform is to make the electoral process more competitive, the key to doing so involves funneling money to challengers. In 1994, one of the keys to Republican success involved ensuring that Republican challengers received adequate funding to mount a serious campaign. According to James G. Gimpel (1996), Republican challengers in 1994 were able to increase their spending by 42 percent, compared to 1992. Similarly, as Theodore J. Eismeier and Philip H. Pollock (1996) observe, the key difference between 1994 and previous election years was that in 1994 more Republican challengers were able to raise enough money to mount a credible campaign. These authors also note, however, that the overall flow of PAC money during the 1994 elections was remarkably similar to the flow of PAC money in past election cycles. PACs continued to show a bias in favor of incumbents, while challengers found it difficult to convince political action committees that they were viable candidates despite relatively clear signs of a major electoral upheaval. In fact, Eismeier and Pollock contend that had business- and trade-oriented political action committees not been so conservative in their contribution strategies, the "earthquake" of 1994 might have been even more dramatic. As these authors note, "If more Republican money had flowed into these marginal races instead of the coffers of safe incumbents, the damage to Democrats could have been worse" (41).

One notable difference in fund-raising practices in 1994 compared to previous years was an increase in the number of candidates investing, and in many cases investing heavily, in their own campaigns. According to the Eismeier and Pollock (1996, 86) study, "In primaries and general elections for the House in 1994 some 163 candidates contributed $50,000 or more to their own campaigns. Thirty-nine supported their own campaigns with more than $200,000, including 6 who contributed or loaned more than $1 million." While 43 of the top 50 self-contributing candidates eventually lost (ibid.), the level of self-investment in political campaigns raises a number of normative concerns.

First, the trend may indicate that there is a certain level of self-investment that is required before outside investors will take a campaign effort seriously. Gary C. Jacobson observes that "even (nonincumbent) candidates without personal wealth normally must be prepared to invest some of their own money to pay start-up costs—about $20,000 is typical of a serious contender—and to demonstrate commitment, with little hope of recouping any of it if they lose" (1992, 78).[5] What does this required self-investment mean for congressional elections? Does it mean that only candidates who can afford to lose $20,000 (or more) of their own money need apply?

The perception that political office is available only to wealthy Americans is hardly new to American politics. As early as the Washington administration, candidates for public office were limited to individuals who could afford to provide financial backing for their own campaign (Alexander 1992). Still, the perception that elected office is limited to the wealthy contradicts the democratic ethos characteristic of the American political culture. If $500,000 is required to run a competitive election campaign, and $20,000 or more is required as an entrance fee into the political arena, many reasonable citizens may conclude that politics is best left to those who can afford it.

Ultimately, the question of whether too much money is being spent on election campaigns has to be placed within a context that includes the average American voter. If $500,000 seems a trifling sum compared to the advertising campaigns of major corporations in the United States, it seems an enormous sum to working-class and middle-class Americans. The level of spending in congressional election campaigns creates tensions within American democracy not because spending in campaigns is inherently evil but because it sends a clear signal to average Americans that only the wealthy, or individuals with close ties to the wealthy, can successfully compete for elective office. These tensions are heightened further when political campaign contributions are valued more by political parties and candidates than voting or grassroots mobilization (Verba, Schlozman, and Brady 1995).

ARGUMENT #2: CAMPAIGN CONTRIBUTIONS REFLECT THE CANDIDATE'S ELECTABILITY

If there is an inequity in the way contributions are dispersed in congressional elections, many critics of reform would say, so what? Contributions are simply a sign of a candidate's appeal to voters: popular candidates raise more money than unpopular candidates, likely winners raise more money than likely losers. While there may be some truth here, this line of reasoning is inherently elitist. Implicit in the logic is an assumption that all citizens could contribute if they only decided to do so. Yet, all citizens are not able to participate in politics with the same level of resources (see, for example, Verba, Schlozman, and Brady 1995). Existing research shows that contributors are not reflective of either the general public, defined as all eligible voters, or the voting public, defined as those voters that actually voted (Sorauf 1992; Verba, Schlozman, and Brady 1995). Contributors tend to be better educated and to have higher incomes and higher-status occupations than noncontributors. If contributions reflect democratic appeal, it is only if one so narrowly defines what is meant by the term *democracy* that it includes only those citizens with the resources and the motivation to contribute to political candidates.

Taking this logic to its extreme, if contributions reflect a candidate's popular appeal, why hold elections at all? Why not just have contests to see which candidates can raise the most money from political contributors—excluding, of course, self-contributions? The argument that fund-raising ability reflects a candidate's popular appeal also ignores the geographic base of candidate fund-raising. Increasingly, candidates are turning to sources outside their districts to raise campaign money, potentially pitting their geographic constituency against their funding constituency (Sorauf 1992). One can reasonably question whether fund-raising success reflects a candidate's popular appeal within the district or a more practical appeal to campaign contributors who may have little, if any, connection to the geographic constituency (but see Wright 1996 for an opposing view).

Finally, the assumption that the marketplace of political contributions reflects a candidate's electoral prospects is difficult to establish empirically. Do candidates who successfully raise money perform strongly in elections because they are politically popular? Or does the money actually buy votes, such that candidates become politically popular by spending money? For first-time candidates who have little political experience, it is often difficult to accurately gauge their electoral prospects. Many first-time candidates defy political oddsmakers and do much better than expected, particularly when one accounts for the limited amount of money that they are able to devote to their campaign. Indictment or no indictment, most observers were surprised when Republican Michael Patrick Flannigan defeated Dan Rostenkowski in an overwhelmingly Democratic district. Similarly, political observers were also surprised when Democratic incumbent Dan Glickman was defeated in Kansas's Fourth Congressional District in 1994 by Todd Tiahrt's grassroots conservative campaign.

Most untested candidates are not so fortunate, but every election cycle a number of underrated challengers come surprisingly close to knocking off a sitting incumbent. In the next election cycle, with the experience of the previous campaign under their belt, many of these previously untested candidates try again. More often than not, they are better funded but lose again anyway. One might be tempted to conclude from this failure the second time around that money didn't matter, that it was some other factor that contributed to the candidate's unexpected success during the first election. When the candidate was underfunded and wasn't given much of chance, she ran about as well as when she was better funded and had name recognition to build on from the previous campaign. We prefer a different interpretation: money did matter, but it mattered the first time around when the challenger didn't have it. In the two years before the next election, most incumbents adjust their behavior in preparation for an even more competitive election the next time around. Whatever vulnerability these amateur politicians exposed in their first election attempt is less likely to be a vulnerability during the second campaign. Even if one assumes that incumbents would have taken the initial challenge more seriously had the opposing candidate been better funded, it is difficult to escape the conclusion that more money the first time around would have increased the odds that one (or more) of these "close but no cigar" first-time candidates would have won.

The broader point here is that estimating a candidate's electoral chances is more art than science, but it is particularly problematic when the candidate is relatively untested. Without political experience, the campaign money market generally assumes that the candidate is not electable—unless, of course, the candidate is willing and able to invest a substantial sum of her own money into the race. Most often, this is the correct assumption, but at least occasionally it is incorrect. And in those cases where the market errs, it generally errs in favor of incumbents and in a manner that leads to less competitive elections.

ARGUMENT #3: REGULATING CAMPAIGN FINANCE ALWAYS FAILS

Because politics is about the allocation of values in society, politicians, consultants, and their legal advisors have an incentive to push the boundaries of any legal reform as far as possible. The laws governing campaign finance have in the past routinely succumbed to these types of pressure, so much so that it is hard to imagine any reform legislation that would not at least in part be undermined by such efforts. A prime example of this is Newt Gingrich's work through GOPAC on behalf of Republican congressional candidates. GOPAC was designed to create a farm team of Republican state legislators. Because state campaign finance laws are often less restrictive than national laws, GOPAC was able to attract large individual contributions—contributions that far exceeded the federal contribution limits established by the Federal Election Campaign Act—and to avoid federal disclosure requirements. Despite clear evidence that GOPAC was indeed attempting to influence federal elections, Gingrich maintained that the organization was subject to state rather than federal campaign finance laws (see Sabato and Simpson 1996 for more thorough discussion).

Attempts to pervert the spirit, and the letter, of campaign finance regulations have not been limited to the Republican Party. Democrats benefited tremendously during the 1970s and 1980s from in-kind contributions from labor unions, that is, contributions of goods and services that were not subject to federal limits. In fact, the very techniques developed by labor unions to circumvent federal contribution limits were later used by conservative groups. As Larry Sabato and Glenn Simpson (1996, 27) observe, "The Right's adoption and successful execution of many of the Left's tactics enabled Republicans and their allies to develop extraordinary organizational and financial strength by circumventing some of the principle post-Watergate reform laws." Because there is often an electoral advantage to be gained in violating the spirit and letter of campaign finance regulations, both parties have done so. But does this mean that limits on either campaign contributions or on campaign spending are doomed to failure? Perhaps. But we are not ready to concede that such regulations are always doomed to failure.

First, electoral reforms have not always failed. The adoption of the Australian, or secret, ballot is a perfect example of a reform effort that reduced, though did not eliminate, political corruption in the form of vote buying. Civil service reform is another example of successful electoral reform, in which clear, unambiguous limits were placed on political activity (see chapter 2). As these examples illustrate, reform efforts can be successful but only when the rules are clearly written, when there is adequate enforcement, and when there is significant public demand for reform and public attentiveness to its enforcement. Attempts to regulate campaign finance have been notable for their ambiguity and for an almost complete absence of enforcement. In addition, while reform efforts have frequently been generated by public pressure, particularly following major political scandals, public attentiveness to campaign finance issues has generally been lax.

Second, from a legal standpoint, we as a society attempt to regulate a variety of behaviors that we cannot possibly control. Drugs are a prime example. No one truly believes that we can ever eliminate drug use in our society through strong law enforcement, tough sentencing, and programs devoted to education and rehabilitation. Yet, while there have been calls to legalize drugs in the United States, it is unlikely that Congress will ever pass legislation legalizing the recreational use of marijuana or cocaine. Why? Because as a society we place a value on attempting to control drug use even if we cannot possibly eliminate it.

Although one might argue that the influence of money in the political process is not nearly as harmful to our society as drug use, a compelling argument can be made that because money potentially subverts democratic processes, the role of money in politics is of graver concern. Drug use may adversely affect society, it may disrupt the social order by increasing violent crime, but it does not undermine the legitimacy of democratic governance. The point here, of course, is not that drugs should be legalized, or for that matter, that they are less harmful than the influence of monied interests in electoral and legislative politics, but that society attempts to regulate certain behaviors even when regulation is more than likely doomed to failure.

Third, as every text on campaign finance acknowledges, enforcing campaign finance legislation has never been given high priority (Jackson 1990). Critics of the Federal Election Commission frequently refer to it as a toothless dog, meaning that it lacks much of an enforcement mechanism. If public officials have frequently violated the spirit of campaign finance regulations, it is at least in part because they realize that violations will not be aggressively pursued by the FEC. Returning to the example of drug use, imagine if legislation regulating the use of controlled substances was simply never enforced. It is hard to imagine how such legislation could ever have much of an impact on drug use. Similarly, it is hard to imagine how campaign finance regulations can have much of an impact if they are only weakly enforced. As Brooks Jackson (1990, 2) notes, "The FEC's weak enforcement has made the campaign finance laws a fraud on the public. Such a sham reform not only breeds contempt for those laws among lawmakers themselves, but also produces in turn contempt among the voters for politicians and the political process. This should not be surprising, since even the most honest candidates, seeing violations by their opponents go unpunished, feel tremendous pressure to cheat. This leads to a competitive cycle in which a loophole opened by one side is widened by the other, so that eventually there is little left of the original intent of the law."

Imagine being in a college class in which cheating was not only tolerated but in which honest students were penalized with lower grades. Such a class is analogous to the campaign finance system that currently reigns over American politics. Cheating not only is allowed, it is rewarded. It is no coincidence that former Speaker of the House Newt Gingrich and President Bill Clinton in many ways led the way in stretching the boundaries of campaign finance regulations. Both achieved status as leaders of their respective political parties at least in part because they proved to be skilled fund-raisers. If, on occasion, they pushed the limits too far, it is because the political incentives for doing so outweighed any potential costs. In defense of the FEC, even when violations of federal campaign finance laws have been pursued, violators have found an ally in the courts. In reviewing campaign finance violations, the courts have generally preferred to interpret campaign legislation very narrowly, encouraging politicians to violate the spirit and, in many cases, the letter of the law.

ARGUMENT #4: CAMPAIGN SPENDING IS FREE SPEECH

By now the Supreme Court decision in *Buckley v. Valeo* equating campaign spending with free speech has become an accepted part of the regulatory environment governing campaign finance. Rather than argue with the principles set forth in the decision, most texts simply accept its ruling as a political reality (but see Rosenkranz 1998). Still, the decision in *Buckley v. Valeo* is worth reconsidering in this context because the decision continues to hamper efforts at political reform.

The basic thrust of the Court decision is that campaign spending is equivalent to free expression. As a result, individuals are allowed to engage in unlimited spending as part of their First Amendment freedoms. Any limits placed on candidate expenditures must be voluntary rather than coercive, meaning that individuals should be able to choose not to abide by legal spending limits. The more recent Court decision in *Colorado Republican Federal Campaign Committee v. Federal Election Commission* (1996) extended the *Buckley v. Valeo* decision by allowing parties the constitutionally protected right to engage in unlimited independent spending.

Despite the *Buckley v. Valeo* decision, however, the courts have never recognized an absolute right to freedom of expression. The courts have recognized that limits can be placed on the time and location of expression and that freedom of expression must be weighed against other societal values, such as national security and the right to a fair trial. More narrowly, the courts have upheld or let stand limits on product advertising, including truth in advertising laws, and limits on the advertising of such products as tobacco, alcohol, and pharmaceuticals. Unlike political speech, the courts have generally limited so-called commercial speech to an intermediate level of First Amendment protection.

Even within the political arena, the courts have been willing to limit political expression. Consider for example the case of Ralph Forbes (*Arkansas Educational Television Commission v. Forbes 1998*). Forbes, an independent candidate in Arkansas' Third Congressional District, was denied participation in a public debate sponsored by the Arkansas Educational Television Network. The publicly owned television station airing the debate made the editorial decision that the Forbes' candidacy was not viable, a position borne out by the 3 percent of the vote Forbes received in the general election and ultimately endorsed by the Supreme Court. Placed within the context of rulings on free speech, the collective implications of the *Buckley* and *Forbes* decisions are clear: the ability to disseminate one's views in the mass media is constitutionally protected if one can afford it; otherwise, it is granted at the editorial discretion of the news media. As the juxtaposition of these two cases illustrates, the question raised by the *Buckley* decision is not just whether free speech is protected but also whose free speech and at what costs to other equally compelling democratic values.

Among other academics criticizing the *Buckley* decision, Sorauf (1994, 1349) laments that the Court's "greatest error was to dismiss without discussion the assertion of Congress' substantial interest in protecting the integrity of the electoral process. It had long conceded that interest in approving state limitations on fundamental issues such as the right to vote and the right to become a candidate. More than any other articulated interest, this interest in protecting the integrity of the electoral process for decades served to justify legislative action to protect fairness and confidence in democracy's popular choices." As a result of the decision, not only have certain "monied" voices been able to speak more loudly and more frequently but also popular confidence in elections and political candidates has continued to erode. Perhaps this would have been the case anyway. Certain voices are always advantaged regardless of the type of political system, and public confidence in the electoral process cannot be casually attributed to a single Supreme Court decision. Yet in equating money with free speech, the Court in *Buckley v. Valeo* not only recognized that some voices speak louder than others, it also legitimized this reality.

Oddly, however, in striking down spending limits as unconstitutional, the Court left standing limits on political contributions under the argument that such limits serve a compelling government interest. The compelling government interest in the case is that large, unlimited contributions might create and foster public perceptions of political corruption. According to the decision, the perception—not the reality—of corruption is adequate to demonstrate a government interest compelling enough to limit individual, political action committee, and political party contributions. As Kenneth Levit (1993, 473) observes, "In limiting its conception of corruption to the quid pro quo variety, the Court ignored the role excessive campaign spending plays in compromising the electorate's confidence in the democratic process."

A recent Twentieth Century Fund report concurs, arguing that the government's compelling interest in maintaining the integrity of the electoral process outweighs its First Amendment protections. The Supreme Court, the report argues, could overturn *Buckley v. Valeo* on relatively narrow constitutional grounds requiring a balance between free speech protections and a compelling government interest to protect the sanctity of the democratic process without threatening the protection of First Amendment freedoms (Rosenkranz 1998). On this point, the number of legal scholars who believe that *Buckley v. Valeo* needs to be overturned is striking. In an exchange in the *American Prospect,* Joshua Rosenkranz and Andrew Shapiro argue that there are "more than 100 prominent constitutional scholars who believe the Supreme Court should overrule Buckley. . . . The overwhelming majority of these scholars believe that Buckley can be overturned on narrow grounds without . . . eviscerating free speech law" (Rosenkranz, Shapiro, and Morrison 1998).

Given the makeup of the current Supreme Court, it is unlikely that the legal conception of corruption will be broadened any time in the near future. As a result, reformers are left with two options, each of which suffers from serious limitations. First, they can devise reform in such a way that it does not intentionally violate the *Buckley v. Valeo* precedent. Even with the best of intentions, however, newly adopted reforms will likely be challenged in the courts and may be overturned. In this respect, one need look no further than the debate over recent reform efforts to gauge the diversity of opinion on what is allowed under the provisions of *Buckley v. Valeo*. Senator Mitch McConnell (Republican, Kentucky) has argued that spending limits amount to "punishment if you choose to express yourself beyond the government-prescribed amount" (Clymer 1997). Yet, referring to the same legislation, fellow Senator Fred Thompson (Republican, Tennessee) notes that "this idea that we are going to cut off somebody from saying something or that we are going to shut people up is simply not true. It makes interesting rhetoric, but it is not in this bill" (Schmitt 1997).

If the constitutionality of various reform efforts is frequently in question, the fact that any significant reform effort will be challenged in the courts is not. As a result, good intentions can result in legislation that, even if passed, may be overturned either in whole or in part by the Supreme Court. Passing legislation and subjecting it to Supreme Court interpretation may, however, present the best, and perhaps the only, opportunity for devising reform that gets around—or results in a decision that overturns—*Buckley v. Valeo*.

The second option for reformers is a constitutional amendment, several of which have been offered during recent sessions of Congress. None of these proposed amendments have had much chance of passing, much less of being ratified. While most (though not all) reformers cringe at the idea of a constitutional amendment, the severe limitations imposed on reform by the *Buckley v. Valeo* decision, plus the potential that future reform efforts will be undermined by Court decisions, leave reformers with little choice. Because Congress is itself unwilling, or unable, to pass either reform legislation or successfully propose a constitutional amendment, reformers should consider pushing for a national convention through state governments. Even if unsuccessful, support garnered in a few states for a national convention would apply direct pressure both on Congress to pass reform and on the Supreme Court to reconsider its *Buckley v. Valeo* decision. While the *Buckley* decision continues to impede reform efforts, there is little reason to believe that the decision has attained the status of eternal law.

ARGUMENT #4: POLITICAL CONTRIBUTIONS DO NOT
INFLUENCE LEGISLATIVE ROLL CALL VOTES

Establishing a clear causal relationship between political contributions and political influence has proven a more difficult task than one might initially assume. At a very basic level, it is easy to establish a strong correlation between the money a legislator receives and the way he or she votes on legislative issues. The problem, however, is in establishing causality. Are political action committee contributions actually influencing legislative decision making? Or are political action committee contributions simply rewarding those legislators who supported them in the past?

Once a legislator's ideology and partisanship are entered into the analysis, the effect of contributions on voting decisions appears to be considerably less significant (both statistically and substantively) as a determinant of legislative decision making. As a result, academic studies tend to conclude that, while PAC contributions may not be unimportant in legislative decision making, they are considerably less important than other more pertinent influences: partisanship, ideology, and constituency (Chappell 1982; Welch 1982; Wright 1985, 1990; Grenzke 1989).

Yet, if academic studies have failed to produce the cliché-ridden "smoking gun" for the connection between money and influence, they have also not cleared the suspect of all charges. First, academic studies yield evidence that PAC contributions may influence less visible, less partisan issues (Evans 1986; Jones and Keiser 1987; Schroedel 1987). Second, if PAC money fails to buy much influence over legislative decisions, it does buy access to key decision makers (Wright 1996). Put simply, contributors are more likely to be in position to present their case before individual congresspersons and before congressional committees and subcommittees than are noncontributors. Additional research has found that contributions are related to interest group lobbying efforts, which in turn are believed to exert a significant impact on congressional voting decisions (Rothenberg 1992; Langbein and Lotwis 1990; Wright 1990). Third, in most academic studies it is assumed that contributions explain only the variance in roll call voting not already explained by partisanship and ideology. Yet findings that PAC contributions exert a small, often insignificant, impact on roll call voting after controlling for ideology and partisanship means only that PAC contributions do not exert a substantial independent effect on voting decisions. Such findings do not account for the possibility that PAC contributions influence roll call decisions through, rather than independent of, partisanship and ideology.

Even if there were absolutely no evidence of outright vote buying, however, it is still possible that money buys legislative influence. Waiting until voting decisions on the floor of the chamber may be too late, if the real influence of political contributions occurs earlier in the legislative process. In this respect, PAC money may have its most profound influence by affecting what is in the legislation in the first place. Because interest group representatives are recognized experts within their specialization, they are often consulted regarding the content of legislation (Wright 1996). Similarly, more subtle interest group influence, for example dampening the enthusiasm (or opposition) a legislator has for a particular bill, may also occur. As a result, representatives may still vote against the interest group's position, but they may not attempt to persuade other legislators to do likewise. They may also refrain from offering floor amendments or using procedural maneuvers to delay or kill the legislation. Such subtle forms of legislative influence, to the extent that they exist, defy empirical, quantitative investigations. As UCLA law professor Daniel Lowenstein (1990, 333–34) comments, "There is no 'smoking gun' in this, or in most cases, but neither is there reason for anyone other than a criminal investigator to search for one. The campaign contribution is pervasive. It is present in legislators' talks among themselves, in their meetings with lobbyists and in lobbyists' evaluations of their own tactics and strategies. . . . Are contributions the only consideration in the legislative deliberations? Of course not. Are they the dominant consideration? Probably not in most cases. But they are always there, and their effect can never be isolated or identified with precision."

An additional critique of these works involves the burden of proof. In criminal trials, the burden of proof is placed on the prosecutor who must demonstrate guilt "beyond a reasonable doubt." Yet being acquitted of a crime is not quite the same as being proven innocent. Acquittal simply means there is insufficient evidence to convict. O. J. Simpson was acquitted of murdering his ex-wife, but most Americans, particularly white Americans believe he was guilty as charged. In the social sciences, the burden of proof is placed on the researcher attempting to establish a relationship. Like the judicial system, failure to find a statistically significant relationship does not mean that the "suspect" is innocent, only that there is insufficient evidence to conclude that the observed relationship did not occur by chance.

The burden of proof issue is perhaps best illustrated in terms of Type I and Type II error. As graduate students (and sometimes as undergraduates), social scientists are taught the difference between Type I and Type II errors. Type I errors occur when one incorrectly assumes that there is a relationship between two variables when in fact there is no relationship. In the present case, this would involve reaching the incorrect conclusion that there is a relationship between political contributions and voting decisions when, in reality, there is no relationship. Type II errors occur when one incorrectly assumes that there is no relationship between two variables when there is a relationship. In our example, this would involve concluding that there is no relationship between money and votes when, in fact, there is a relationship.

As a student, one is taught that one must weigh the potential risks that each type of error implies for the analysis, but as researchers we focus almost entirely on Type I errors. Analyses that focus on the relationship between money and voting decisions assume that the risk of a Type I error is greater than the risk of Type II error. But what is the greater risk? Incorrectly concluding that there is not a relationship between contributions and voting decisions? Or incorrectly concluding that there is a relationship when in fact there is none? If one considers the implications for democratic governance, clearly the former is more worrisome than the latter. In the first instance, if our conclusion is incorrect, special interests continue to buy influence over legislative decisions—ultimately, undermining democratic processes and public faith in democratic procedures.

In addition, because such analyses attempt to discover the systematic effects of money on legislative behavior, they may miss individual corruption. In other words, how many legislators must be "bought" by special interest money before we find significant effects? Would influencing the vote of one or two legislators on a key piece of legislation turn up significant at the .05 level? Would influencing the outcome of just one legislative roll call vote per session turn up as statistically significant? Considering a 1982 vote to overturn a ruling by the Federal Trade Commission requiring that used cars have stickers on their windows indicating known defects, John R. Wright (1996) argues that, at most, contributions from used car dealers could have influenced fourteen votes. While Wright contends that even this figure likely overestimates the influence of contributions from the Automobile Dealer's Election Action Committee, the analysis raises important normative questions. If political contributions influence just a single vote per congressional session, is public concern over the influence of money in the legislative process justified? Should we be concerned only if the number of legislators influenced alter the outcome? And at what point does public concern over the role of money in the legislative process become justified?

Finally, in a democratic system of governance, perception is important, even if it conflicts with reality. In 1992, the economy may have been better off than voters realized, yet George Bush was still defeated in his bid to be reelected president. In the area of campaign finance reform, the influence of PAC contributions and, more generally, of special interests over the legislative process may be greatly exaggerated; yet perceptions of corruption persist. Because these perceptions undermine support for democratic institutions and processes, they should not be dismissed as yet another indication of public ignorance.

CONCLUSION

Overall, what can we conclude from this chapter? First, there are no acceptable criteria for judging whether or not spending in congressional elections is excessive. However, the inequities in campaign fund-raising provide ample cause for public concern about the fairness of the electoral process. The costs of campaigning are high enough that citizens are more than aware that people of similar means and backgrounds cannot successfully compete for public office. If spending is deemed "too high," it is not because some absolute standard exists but because of public concerns that political office and political influence is beyond the reach of average citizens. Second, the ability to raise and spend money at least in part reflects a candidate's political viability. However, a lack of money does not always mean that voters are rejecting a candidate's message (or image). A message that is never heard cannot be rejected. Moreover, to the extent that money buys votes, it is difficult to separate electability from fund-raising success. As such, it is unclear whether money follows or creates candidate success. Finally, the burdens of campaign fund-raising may lead many politically viable candidates to decide not to seek elected office.

Third, attempts to place limits on contributions and spending have generally failed. The 1996 presidential election serves as a case in point, in that both political parties aggressively circumvented federal spending limits. Yet, it is overly simplistic to assume that all future attempts at limits will also fail. Reform efforts have been unsuccessful for a variety of reasons, but perhaps no reason looms larger than the concerted lack of effort put into enforcing reform. Regulation without enforcement simply will not work, but when there is a commitment to reform and adequate enforcement, as was the case with civil service reform and the adoption of the Australian ballot, the potential for successful electoral reform is considerably higher.

Court decisions provide a more difficult obstacle to reform advocates. Based on *Buckley v. Valeo* and on the more recent case of *Colorado Republican Federal Campaign Committee v. Federal Election Commission* allowing the Colorado Republican Party to engage in unlimited independent expenditures, any reform will, at a minimum, be subjected to Court challenges. As Levit (1993, 470) comments, "today's reformers would do well to remember that the effort to alter election law ends not in the legislative arena but in the courts, where judges have zealously guarded the First Amendment values threatened by regulation of the political process." Yet it is possible that at some point the Court might decide that First Amendment protections have to be weighed against the government's interest in maintaining the integrity of the electoral process.

Finally, while the research investigating the connection between political action committee contributions and roll call votes has failed to deliver convincing evidence of vote buying, it does provide suggestive evidence that contributions may buy political influence on at least some votes. It also provides convincing evidence that contributions buy political access. Regardless of the effects, it is clear that many contributors are engaged in a rational, instrumental attempt at influencing legislative outcomes. While political action committee contributions are only one part of this strategy, and are insufficient to guaranteeing preferred outcomes, political action committee contributions do provide groups with a valued commodity—political access. By and large, it is a commodity that would not be available without contributions.

NOTES

1. The best and most recent account of comparative campaign finance is Herbert E Alexander and Rei Shiratori (1994).

2. By disinterested money, we mean money that is not raised from groups seeking access in or influence over the political process.

3. In 1994, 97 elections were decided by 55 percent of the vote or less. In 1992, 112 elections were decided by 55 percent of the vote or less.

4. The average for Democrats facing Republican challengers who spent less than $50,000 was $423,901. For Republicans facing underfunded Democratic opponents, the average was $364,803.

5. The $20,000 figure is from Clyde Wilcox 1988.

Chapter Four

Electoral Competition and Campaign Finance Reform

At a minimum, it is the ability of the citizens to "throw the bums out" at the ballot box that defines democratic governance. Yet, by this standard, elections to the United States House of Representatives are not very democratic. Since the 1950s, 90 percent of House incumbents have, on average, won reelection. Even in the historic 1994 midterm elections, 90 percent of all incumbents seeking reelection, and 84 percent of Democratic incumbents, were returned to office. Drawing on the resources of office, and the unique nature of House districts, incumbency proves to be a nearly insurmountable obstacle to real (and potential) challengers in House elections.

What has been perhaps more troubling than incumbent success rates, however, has been the trend, first noted by David Mayhew (1974), in which incumbents not only won but also won with an increasing margin of victory. Other indicators of incumbent electoral strength suggest as well that, at least up until 1992, House elections became less competitive over time and that congressional incumbents were the prime beneficiaries of declining competition.

Uncompetitive elections present a dilemma to democratic governance: How can public officials be held accountable if the threat of electoral defeat is minimal or diminishing? Within the United States constitutional framework, this dilemma is particularly compelling as it applies to the House of Representatives. Unlike the more aristocratic Senate, the House was intended to "have an immediate dependence on, and an intimate sympathy with, the people" (Federalist No. 52, 1787). Ultimately, it was through the electoral process, particularly through frequent elections, that this sympathy was to be created and maintained. Frequent elections, it was believed, would ensure frequent turnover (primarily through electoral defeat), which in turn would ensure that the House of Representatives closely reflected popular will. Yet, as recently as 1992, Alan I. Abramowitz and Jeffrey A. Segal observed that the United States Constitution had been turned on its head. The Senate, designed to be insulated from popular opinion, has in fact become more responsive to changing political winds. The House, in contrast, has inoculated itself from shifts in national political and partisan trends.

While this thesis may require some revision in light of the 1994 Republican Revolution, the question of whether the United States House of Representatives is adequately responsive to national trends remains within the scope of academic debate. Despite the dramatic turnover during the 1994 elections, incumbent representatives maintain a formidable arsenal of weapons, which if wielded correctly allow them to focus constituent attention away from national politics and toward more local concerns. Gary C. Jacobson (1996, 10), for example, observes that, despite the high partisan turnover, "the electoral value of incumbency remained at a high level in 1994. . . . The 1994 elections were, on this dimension, entirely normal." In fact, "without the incumbency advantage, the Democratic minority in the 104th Congress would [have been] considerably smaller."

The 1994 midterm elections have been depicted as an earthquake; but the 1996 elections have been described as status quo elections, in which incumbency reasserted itself. Writing just before the 1996 elections, *Congressional Quarterly* reporter Ronald Elving (1996) observed that "with the elections of 1996 little more than a fortnight away, incumbency appears suddenly to be back in style. . . . The outlook for the great majority of Senate and House incumbents is also remarkably roseate." Belying the value of incumbency, however, was an election year that, despite its minimal partisan turnover, was actually quite competitive by historical standards. Before the election, *Congressional Quarterly* classified 174 of the 435 House races in 1996 as competitive. By comparison, in 1994, only 147 seats, a relatively high number by historical standards, were classified as competitive. National opinion polls also indicated the potential for major turnover in the House of Representatives. Consistently, results based on a generic congressional ballot indicated that a majority of citizens preferred Democratic to Republican congressional candidates. Yet, when the smoke cleared, relatively little had changed as a result of the 1996 congressional elections. Republicans entered the 105th Congress controlling only three seats fewer than they controlled in the 104th Congress. So what happened? The answer to this question has much to do with the value of incumbency and with the role of money in House elections.

SOURCES OF THE INCUMBENCY ADVANTAGE

One of the more widely cited and agreed upon facts about congressional elections is that incumbents are at a tremendous advantage over challengers in running for reelection. As Morris P. Fiorina, David W. Rohde, and Pater Wissel (1975, 24) characterize it, "According to popular stereotypes, few congressmen are defeated; few resign or retire; moreover, their longevity is legendary. . . . Representatives come to Washington, settle in, establish themselves within the congressional context, and eventually develop a vested interest in the status quo." Perhaps the only addendum that needs to be offered to their characterization is that, increasingly, members of Congress voluntarily leave office. While many of these departures reflect changing partisan control of the House, others appear to be strategic, reflecting a realization on the part of the member that a tough reelection campaign and, possibly, an electoral defeat are looming in the next election cycle (Hall and Van Houweling 1995; Groseclose and Krehbiel 1994; Kiewiet and Zeng 1993; Jacobson and Kernell 1983).[1]

Although there is a general consensus that an incumbency advantage exists, there is less agreement as to its source and as to why the advantage appears to have grown over time, if in fact it has grown over time. In general, there have been two schools of thought regarding the source of the incumbency advantage, one focusing on institutional resources, the other emphasizing changes within the electorate that have ultimately benefited incumbent candidates (see, for example, Cox and Katz 1996).

From an institutional perspective, research has consistently singled out casework and constituency service activities as a prime contributor to the incumbency advantage. Casework may include helping constituents receive their social security checks or tracking down their family members serving in the military overseas. By helping constituents in their day-to-day dealings with the bureaucracy, incumbents can reap electoral profits that cross party lines (Fiorina 1990). The increase in resources devoted to constituency service has coincided with an increase in incumbent vote margins (Mayhew 1974). Furthermore, larger state operating budgets are associated with greater incumbent electoral success (Holbrook and Tidmarch 1991, 1993; King 1991; Cox and Morganstein 1993, 1995). Despite these findings, however, an empirical connection between constituent service and district-level voting returns has proven elusive (Fiorina 1989; Johannes and McAdams 1981; Ragsdale and Cook 1987; but see also Serra and Moon 1994; Serra and Cover 1992; Romero 1996; Yiannakis 1981).

A similar story can be told regarding the electoral effects of pork barrel legislation (more neutrally referred to as distributive politics). Anecdotes about pork barrel politics are widespread, including stories about the renovation of Lawrence Welk's home and studies of salmon reproduction, so much so that pork anecdotes may dominate public perceptions of government spending. Yet, if projects like the National Wetlands Research Center located in Louisiana's Seventh Congressional District seem like pork to those outside the district, they are viewed as essential government spending to those within the district. While it seems likely that an incumbent's ability to attract federal dollars to the district has a significant impact on incumbent electoral success, a direct connection between federal dollars and electoral votes is difficult to establish empirically (Feldman and Jondrow 1984; Rundquist and Griffith 1976; Ray 1980). Still, distributive politics (and by extension, activities such as casework and constituency service) may have important indirect effects on campaign contributions and candidate quality (Stein and Bickers 1994, 1996). In addition, the positive effects of "bringing home the bacon" may also be contingent on the representative's ideology. More fiscally conservative representatives may not receive the same electoral yield for federal projects as their more liberal colleagues (Sellers 1997).

While institutional resources undoubtedly contribute to the incumbency advantage, the difficulty in establishing a clear empirical link between these types of activity and the incumbent's percentage of the vote at the district level has led political scientists to look to changes in the electorate for sources of the incumbency advantage. The most noted (and most noteworthy) change within the electorate over the last few decades has been the weakening of individual attachments to political parties. While some question the significance of this change, the evidence for the weakening of the political party in the electorate is overwhelming. In national surveys, citizens have become less inclined to identify themselves as either Republicans or Democrats. When actually casting a ballot, individual citizens have been more willing to "split the ticket," voting for Democrat candidates for some offices and Republican candidates in others (see, for example, Wattenberg 1990). Though recent elections have witnessed an increasingly polarized party in government and an increasing congruence in voting in congressional and presidential elections, the historical trend is toward weakened partisan attachments within the electorate.

For incumbent House members, the decline of the party in the electorate is generally good news. While there is no reason that incumbents should necessarily benefit from this trend, incumbent politicians, particularly incumbent representatives, have proven adept at appealing to an increasingly independent electorate (Jacobson 1997b). In part, this reflects the unique nature of House districts. House districts rarely merge with existing geographic boundaries or media markets, making campaigning difficult and, depending on the district, quite expensive. Because of this, candidates who are known throughout the district have a tremendous advantage over candidates who are not known. To the extent that incumbents have successfully served the district through casework activities, "brought home the bacon" in federal government dollars, and avoided the appearance of ethical improprieties while in office, they will not only be recognized by constituents but will also generally be evaluated positively.

As a result, incumbents who occasionally diverge from constituent opinion may, in effect, buy electoral security through diligent constituent service.

If the deck appears to be stacked in favor of incumbents, challengers do at least occasionally run and win against an incumbent. For one, while a more independent electorate may translate into larger victory margins for incumbents, it also translates into a more volatile electorate (Jacobson 1997b). Incumbents who have faced lackluster competition in past election cycles may find themselves suddenly vulnerable to an experienced, well-financed challenger. Though much of the academic literature focuses on incumbency and the advantages it confers, the structure of competition in congressional elections is determined largely by the decision of potential challengers to enter (or to refrain from entering) the race (Cox and Katz 1996). The greater competitiveness witnessed in Senate elections is often attributed to the more visible, more politically experienced, and better-funded challengers whom Senate elections tend to attract (Abramowitz and Segal 1992).

Generally speaking, successful challenges include at least one or more of the following ingredients: (1) a challenger with previous elected experience, (2) a well-funded campaign, (3) national party tides that favor the challenger's party, and (4) ethical improprieties involving the incumbent. These ingredients are not independent of one another. Strategic challengers consider national party tides, their ability to raise money, and any potential ethical problems facing the incumbent before deciding to run. Other than avoiding political scandals, incumbent behavior is also relevant to the decision making of strategic challengers. In years that look bad for their political party, incumbents can focus on the tangible benefits they have provided to the district or on the service they have provided to constituents, in an attempt to insulate themselves from national partisan tides. In 1996, Republican incumbents minimized the potential electoral damage of a "bad" year by moving away from their national party leadership, a move encouraged by party leaders concerned about losing majority control of the chamber. As Jacobson (1997a, 156) observes, "the Republican's brief flirtation with responsible party government succumbed to the desire of individual members to win reelection and of the party as a whole to keep its majority."

While we have already mentioned some of the factors that affect the decision making of potential challengers, clearly one of the most important involves the burden of raising enough money to run a competitive race. L. Sandy Maisal (1994, 37), in a study of potential candidates identified by state caucus participants in the 1992 national conventions of the Democratic and Republican Parties, notes that "the key factor [discouraging potential candidates from running] seems to revolve around leveling the financial field." On a similar note, Janet Box-Steffensmeier (1996) presents convincing evidence that incumbent campaign "war chests" help to deter quality candidates from running against incumbents (see also Goidel and Gross 1994). As these works illustrate, the herculean task of raising money, combined with an opponent who is often well financed and well versed in the art of campaign fund-raising, deters potential candidates from entering the election.

MONEY AND CONGRESSIONAL ELECTIONS

The literature on the impact of money on House election outcomes can all, in some form or fashion, be traced to the seminal work of Gary Jacobson (1978, 1980, 1985, 1990a). According to Jacobson, incumbents receive very little electoral benefit from their campaign spending. In fact, looking at multiple election years, Jacobson consistently found that the more an incumbent spent, the lower the percentage of vote the incumbent received on election day. Jacobson surmised that incumbent spending yielded little benefit because incumbents were already known commodities with established reputations. Other than countering claims made by the challenger or reinforcing prior attitudes regarding the incumbent, incumbent campaign spending appeared to buy very little.

Jacobson's conclusions regarding the impact of incumbent campaign spending have been subjected to frequent criticism within the literature (Green and Krasno 1988, 1990; Goidel and Gross 1994; Thomas 1989; Erikson and Palfrey 1998; Gerber 1998). Generally speaking, these criticisms focus on two related questions: How does one control for the strength of the challenge facing an incumbent? and How does one account for the myriad of ways that expectations affect electoral outcomes? Studies of the role of money in congressional campaigns have been hindered by the fact that the amount of money raised and spent in an election campaign is largely a function of electoral expectations. An incumbent who appears vulnerable is more likely to attract an experienced challenger, who in turn is more likely to raise enough money to run a competitive campaign. Vulnerable incumbents, realizing that they are vulnerable, will also generally spend more money than safe incumbents (though this is not always the case). As a result, it is often difficult to decipher when campaign spending is the cause of more competitive elections and when spending simply reflects elite expectations that an election will be competitive.

While the effectiveness of incumbent spending is the subject of frequent debate in the literature, there is greater consensus regarding the effect of challenger spending. Spending by challengers is extremely effective in terms of its marginal return on the percentage of the vote. First and foremost, challengers largely unknown in the district are able to use campaign spending to buy name recognition. Without gaining some unspecified threshold of name recognition, challengers are almost certain to be defeated by better-known incumbents. Second, even if challengers become a known quantity in the district, they still have to make a convincing case that they would be a better representative of the district's interests than the incumbent, and making that case requires money.

The problems for challengers arise not in spending money but in raising it. In order to raise money, challengers first have to prove that they are electorally viable, an obstacle that most challengers never overcome. In this sense, challengers "are classic victims of a downward spiral of electoral expectations" (Sorauf 1992, 79–80). Given little chance of defeating incumbents, challengers struggle to raise enough money to run competitive campaigns. Without money, challengers often fail to solidify support among their own partisans, much less make inroads into incumbents' electoral base.

Of the major sources of campaign funding—individuals, parties, and political action committees—only parties consistently provide much support for challengers in House campaigns. Challengers, it has been noted, "get party money for reasons having to do with the goals of the party; it is important for a party not to forfeit an office by default, if only to maximize voter appeal for the whole ticket of party candidates" (Sorauf 1992, 78). Of the potential contributors to congressional campaigns, political parties have the greatest incentive to give to potentially competitive challengers. Frequently, these contributions are made with the expectation that party contributions will spawn contributions from other sources, by signaling other potential contributors that the race is likely to be competitive.

In contrast with political parties, political action committee contributions generally reflect a strategy of risk aversion, preferring the safe bet (that is, the incumbent) even when the challenger may be more ideologically appealing. The primary exception to this general rule is the willingness of organized labor to contribute to Democratic challengers, though even labor contributions go overwhelmingly to incumbents. As the majority party in the 1970s and 1980s, Democratic Party leaders were extremely successful in adapting to the proliferation of business- oriented political action committees, despite the fact that business interests are often ideologically more closely aligned with the Republican Party. Democratic Party leaders, particularly former majority leader and whip Tony Coelho, convinced these business-oriented PACs to contribute to Democratic incumbents to maintain access and influence in the Democratically controlled House of Representatives. Because of the preference of business-oriented PACs for incumbents rather than partisans, their proliferation worked to the short-term advantage of the Democratic Party—at least as long as they controlled the chamber.

The loss of majority status in 1994 limited the fund-raising of Democratic incumbents and challengers alike. As Jacobson (1997a, 152) observes, "The Republican takeover of Congress transformed the campaign money market. Democrats no longer had the majority status and committee control to attract campaign contributions from business-oriented political action committees (PACs), which after 1994 were free to follow their Republican hearts as well as their pocketbooks in allocating donations. Not only did such PACs have less reason to contribute to incumbent Democrats, they also had less reason to worry about contributing against incumbent Democrats, whose ability to retaliate against interests that funded their opponents had diminished sharply." Others have made similar observations. Marjorie Randon Hershey (1997, 211), for example, writes that after the 1994 elections "Republicans began to get the majority of PAC money. . . . By June 1996 the Center for Responsive Politics found that Republican candidates were pulling in $3 in PAC money for every $1 received by Democrats." The fact that 1996 turned out to be a strong Democratic year, however, probably saved Democrats from the full financial brunt of the change in majority control by encouraging PACs to "hedge their bets" (Jacobson 1997a, 153).

If incumbents are advantaged in raising PAC money, they are equally advantaged in raising money from individual contributors. Though an incumbent's attraction to individual contributors may reflect the incumbent's overall campaign skill and service to the district, it also reflects the fact that the incumbent began the election with a campaign organization and a list of potential donors already in place.

Journalist Dwight Morris has spent a considerable amount of time during the past few election cycles tracking how candidates actually spend their money (Fritz and Morris 1992; Morris and Gamache 1994). One of the principal findings of his work is that much of the money spent in congressional campaigns is spent on items that have little to do with communicating with voters. Dispelling the myth that rising campaign costs are created by television and radio advertising costs, much of the money spent in congressional campaigns is directed toward maintaining permanent campaign organizations: "The $543,248,774 price tag attached to the 1992 campaigns was attributable in large part to the fact that most members of Congress have created their own state-of-the-art, permanent political machines that operate 365 days each year, during off-years as well as election years" (Morris and Gamache 1994, 10). With permanent campaign organizations in place, incumbents have an institutional campaign fund-raising mechanisms in gear before challengers might even consider entering the race. As a result, the real source of rising campaign costs comes not in communicating with voters but in maintaining a campaign organization even in years without an election.

The picture confronting congressional challengers in raising money can only be described as dire. Challengers are overmatched in every avenue of potential campaign support. Lacking anything equivalent to the permanent campaign organizations of the incumbent, challengers generally have to build campaign organizations from scratch. The one potentially viable source of campaign risk capital, the political party, lacks the resources to compensate for the overwhelming disparity in PAC and individual contributions favoring incumbents. Overall, two conclusions regarding the effect of money in congressional campaigns appear to be incontestable: (1) money is no guarantee of electoral success, and (2) candidates without money lose.

MONEY AND ELECTORAL SUCCESS

In 1994, in Texas's Twenty-fifth Congressional District, Ken Bentsen, nephew of Lloyd Bentsen (former Texas senator, vice presidential candidate, and Clinton secretary of the treasury), won election to the House of Representatives despite being outspent by more than $3.5 million. While Bentsen spent more than $900,000, his opponent, Gene Fontenot, spent a grand total of $4,658,585—more than any other House candidate during the 1994 election cycle. Ken Bentsen wasn't the only candidate in 1994 to be greatly outspent and yet still win election to the House. Michael Patrick Flanigan won a seat despite being outspent by just under $2.5 million. His opponent in the race, Dan Rostenkowski, however, was handed a multi-count federal indictment just days before the election. The indictment proved enough to overcome a multimillion dollar spending deficit in a heavily Democratic district that Rostenkowski had controlled for decades.

Winning an election while being outspent is not confined to the 1994 election cycle. In 1996, incumbent Republican Fran Cremeans (Republican, Ohio) outspent his opponent, former Representative Ted Strickland, by more than a million dollars; yet Cremeans was still defeated. On a similar note, in Washington's Ninth Congressional District, incumbent Randall Tate outspent his opponent by more than $800,000 but came up short on election day, losing to challenger and state senator Adam Smith.

If money can't buy love, these examples illustrate that money can't buy elections either. In 1994, in races when Republican challengers defeated Democratic incumbents, they were, on average, outspent by approximately $300,000. Republican candidates were even outspent in 40 percent of the open-seat races won by a Republican candidate in 1994.

LACK OF MONEY AND ELECTORAL FAILURE

If money doesn't guarantee electoral success, the lack of money almost always translates into an electoral defeat. Most candidates who are outspent are not as fortunate as Ken Bentsen, whose political lineage assured a high level of name recognition, or Michael Patrick Flanigan, whose opponent was faced with a multicount federal indictment. Minority leader Richard Gephardt, for example, outspent his Republican opponent by almost $2.5 million during the 1994 elections and by nearly $2.6 million during the 1996 elections, despite the fact that neither opponent had prior political experience. Gephardt's spending habits are not an anomaly in House elections. In 1994, Norman Mineta (Democratic, California) spent $1,009,947, while his Republican opponent spent only $13,759.

Republicans have been equally guilty of campaign excess. In 1994, Dan Burton (Republican, Indiana) spent $455,095 despite facing an opponent who spent no money and was able to garner only 23 percent of the vote. Similarly, Dennis Hastert (Republican, Illinois) spent $696,217 against an opponent who spent only $54,330 and received a mere 24 percent of the vote. In 1996, Republican leaders Dick Armey (Republican, Texas) and Tom Delay (Republican, Texas) each spent more than $1.6 million, while their opposition spent $56,094 and $28,383, respectively. In all fairness, many party leaders (such as Gephardt, Armey, and Delay) raise money to distribute to other candidates in more competitive districts. Yet, if these examples exaggerate the size of the gap in spending, they also illustrate the norm in House elections: a well-funded incumbent versus an underfunded challenger.

OPEN-SEAT ELECTIONS

Though congressional elections are often discussed in terms of incumbency, they are also about political parties and, especially, about partisan control of the legislative chamber. Because the majority party, by definition, controls a larger share of the seats, the incumbency advantage frequently translates into an advantage for the majority party. Hopes for gaining control of the legislative chamber focus primarily, though not exclusively, on open-seat elections. Without the specter of incumbency, open seats provide political parties with their best opportunities for gaining legislative seats (Gaddie 1995a). Open-seat elections also provide the best opportunity for strategic politicians seeking elected office. R. Keith Gaddie (1997) observes that, since 1966, the majority of new representatives won election in an open-seat contest. As a consequence, open-seat elections are generally competitive in terms of candidates' prior experience and campaign spending.

While the literature on the impact of candidate spending in open-seat elections is relatively sparse, money is clearly important in these contests regardless of whether the candidate is a Democrat or a Republican and of which party controls the presidency (Gaddie 1995a, 1995b, 1997; Gaddie and Mott 1997; Abramowitz 1991b). As in incumbency-contested elections, money does not appear to buy electoral success in open-seat elections—outspending an opponent is no guarantee of electoral success, though it does appear to help. At a minimum, candidates have to raise at least enough money to run a competitive campaign, generally estimated at around $500,000.

In 1994, Republican hopes for regaining majority control of the House of Representatives were bolstered by an unusually large number of retirements by Democratic incumbents. Throughout the 1980s, Democrats maintained control of the House at least in part by fielding more politically experienced, better-funded candidates in open-seat elections (Gaddie 1995a; Jacobson 1990a). In 1994, Republicans not only recruited more experienced candidates to contest these open-seat elections, they also made sure these candidate were adequately funded (Gaddie 1995b).

If Democratic retirements created opportunities for Republicans in 1994, they hindered Democratic chances for retaking the House in 1996. Faced with the loss of majority control for the first time in more than forty years, a large number of Democrats chose to retire at the end of the 104th Congress. Democrats were forced to defend a large number of open seats in what should have been a strong Democratic year. As a result, Republican gains in open-seat elections helped minimize the political damage of a national Democratic tide (Gaddie and Mott 1997).

To summarize the literature on money and electoral outcomes, we return to Gary Jacobson's dictum: Money is a necessary but not sufficient condition for electoral success in congressional campaigns. In other words, money helps to determine whether or not elections will be competitive, but it provides no guarantees as to the winner. The system of campaign finance that has developed in House elections benefits incumbents because it places an undue burden on potential challengers while simultaneously allowing incumbents to maintain permanent fund-raising organizations. In partisan terms, the advantage in fund-raising enjoyed by incumbents translates into a partisan advantage for the majority party.

MONEY, COMPETITION, AND CAMPAIGN FINANCE REFORM

While there is considerable debate in the academic literature regarding the electoral effects of candidate campaign expenditures, it is generally accepted that money is an important though not determining ingredient in congressional campaigns. But how might altering the rules of the campaign finance game impact competition in congressional elections? If one accepts the premise that incumbent spending matters very little, while challenger spending matters a great deal, the futility of spending limits becomes obvious: spending limits would limit the most effective electoral tool available to challengers (Jacobson 1980; Sorauf 1992; Smith 1995). Basing their views at least in part on this logic, critics of reform, such as Mitch McConnell (Republican, Kentucky), label campaign finance legislation "incumbency protection acts."

Not everyone, however, accepts the premise that incumbent spending is ineffectual (Green and Krasno 1988; Goidel and Gross 1994). For scholars, political activists, and even politicians who conclude that incumbent spending has a significant impact on electoral outcomes, the adverse consequences of spending limits are less obvious. In fact, these works generally conclude that, at least under certain scenarios, spending limits would enhance rather than diminish electoral competition. In addition, once public financing is coupled with spending limits, the effect of reform on the electoral process becomes even less clear. For example, while it is generally agreed that providing public financing would benefit challengers, it is unclear whether the benefits of providing public subsidies would outweigh the potential costs of spending limits.

It is also unclear how campaign finance reform proposals might affect the partisan balance of Congress and, by extension, outcomes in open-seat contests. The most relevant research on this question, conducted by Ruth Jones (1981) on the implications of public financing at the state level, reaches a somewhat ambiguous conclusion but argues that, overall, public funding is probably more beneficial to the minority party. Other research on state legislative public financing also renders a mixed verdict regarding the effectiveness of public funding (see, for example, Alexander 1992). Herbert E. Alexander, Eugene R. Goss, and Jeffrey A. Schwartz (1992), for example, note that "with some exceptions, public financing of state elections has not significantly affected the campaign process," though they attribute the limited effect of public financing to the insufficient funds provided by the respective states (see also Malbin and Gais 1998).

In an attempt to gain a fuller understanding of how reform proposals might affect the partisan balance of Congress, as well as the level of competition in congressional elections, we conducted regression-based simulations estimating the likely outcome of the 1994 and 1996 congressional elections under a variety of reform scenarios. While research at the state level is instructive and informs our understanding of the role of money in the electoral process, simulations have the advantage of allowing one to estimate how variations in public funding proposals and spending limits might affect electoral outcomes. For example, Alexander, Goss, and Schwartz (1992) conclude that state public financing schemes are frequently ineffective because the state fails to provide adequate public funding to legislative candidates. But what is adequate public funding? Simulations help to provide a reasonable, if uncertain, estimate of how various levels of public funding in combination with spending limits might affect electoral competition.

While the statistical procedure is quite complex, the logic of a regression-based simulation is relatively straightforward. For example, a small business owner seeking to maximize monthly profit margins might consider how changing from one supplier to another might impact the cost of operating her business. Whether this business owner is using a computer-based program or calculating figures on a legal pad, she is essentially conducting a simulation. In a similar vein, a college student who goes out five nights a week during the fall semester and manages to receive a 2.1 grade point average might decide that he could receive a 3.0 (or better) if he went out only three nights a week in future semesters. Perhaps without even recognizing it, this student is engaging in the same sort of logic that underlies regression-based simulations.

Because simulations are generally aimed at predicting future or hypothetical events, there is always uncertainty associated with these predictions. For example, it is assumed that the student who decides to limit himself to three nights of partying per week will actually study on the nights he stays in. If he watches television instead, his grade point average is unlikely to improve and may even decline. The same is true regarding simulations designed to estimate the likely effect of campaign reform proposals. If the assumptions underlying the simulations are incorrect, predictions based on these simulations are likely to be incorrect as well.[2]

One central assumption made in conducting these simulations is that the relationship between candidates' spending and their percentage of the vote at the district level should remain the same even if some version of campaign finance reform were to be enacted. An implication of this assumption is that we can use an estimate of the impact of candidate spending on the district-level percentage of the vote to gauge the likely effects of campaign reform on electoral outcomes in 1994 and 1996. A second, related, assumption is that the district-level percentage of the vote is primarily a function of incumbency, the partisan leanings of the district, nonincumbent candidate quality, and candidate spending. If either of these assumptions proves to be incorrect, the results of the simulations will be incorrect as well. (See appendix A for a fuller discussion of the simulations. Other assumptions, too numerous to cover here, were made in the choice of statistical model and estimation technique.)

In an attempt to consider the fullest possible range of campaign finance reform scenarios, we conducted simulations assuming the following:

1. Spending limits alone without any form of public financing, ranging from $100,000 to $1 million.

2. Matching funds, in which candidate spending is matched on a dollar-for-dollar basis up to a prescribed limit, ranging from $100,000 to $1million.
3. Full public financing, in which candidates are assumed to have spent an equal amount of money up to a prescribed limit, ranging from $100,000 to $1 million.
4. Partial public funding involving a public subsidy, ranging from $100,000 to $300,000, in combination with spending limits, ranging from $400,000 to $1 million.

Though spending limits without any form of accompanying public financing were ruled unconstitutional in the case of *Buckley v. Valeo* (1976), this scenario is included in the analysis because it helps to illustrate the likely effects of campaign finance reform on electoral competition. Before considering the results of the simulations, we begin by examining our estimates of the impact of candidate spending on electoral outcomes. In table 4.1, we present the estimated impact of $100,000 in campaign spending on the Democratic percentage of the vote according to candidate type. (The full regression models can be found in appendix A.)

As can be seen in table 4.1, nonincumbent spending matters much more than does incumbent spending. With regard to the partisan effects of candidate campaign spending, neither party appears to have much of an advantage in terms of the effect of nonincumbent candidate spending. Nonincumbent candidates gained about 16 percent of the vote for each additional $100,000 spent in 1994, and 18–20 percent for each $100,000 spent in 1996. One implication of this pattern is that "good" election years are, apparently, created not by a greater effectiveness of one party's spending but by the successful fund-raising efforts of the party's nonincumbent candidates (Jacobson and Kernell 1983).

The effectiveness of incumbent spending, on the other hand, appears to vary both by party and by election year. Spending by Republican incumbents was more effective in both the 1994 and the 1996 elections than

Table 4.1　Estimated Effect of $100,000 in Candidate Spending on Democratic Percentage of the Vote, 1994 and 1996

Candidate Making Expenditure	1994	1996
Democratic nonincumbent	+15.8	19.7
Republican nonincumbent	-15.5	-18.3
Democratic incumbent	-1.5	+3.9
Republican incumbent	-5.7	-8.3

spending by Democratic incumbents. Moreover, spending by both Democratic and Republican incumbents appeared to be more effective in 1996 than in 1994, perhaps reflecting the general dissatisfaction characterizing the 1994 elections and the greater level of contentment characterizing 1996. Republican incumbent spending was particularly effective in 1996, yielding just over 8 percent of the district-level vote for each $100,000 spent. Using these estimates, we can consider the likely effect of various campaign finance reform scenarios on electoral competition.[3] We begin with the most straightforward reform proposal: spending limits without any accompanying form of public financing.

Spending Limits

As can be seen in figure 4.1, in 1994, spending limits would have had the effect feared by most opponents of campaign finance reform. That is, had spending limits been imposed before the 1994 elections, Republicans would have won fewer Democratic seats. In fact, only with limits set as a high as $1 million would Republican victories in 1994 have approached the number of victories predicted assuming no change in existing election laws. The results also indicate, however, that Republicans would have still

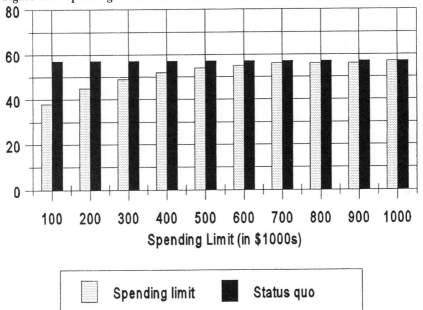

Figure 4.1   Spending Limits and Predicted Democratic Seat Loss, 1994

been a good bet to take control of the House with limits set as low as $300,000. While the general pattern of findings tends to support the argument that spending limits would have limited the number of Republican victories in 1994, it appears unlikely that spending limits, except at very low levels, would have kept the House in Democratic control.

To better illustrate the effects of spending limits on partisan competition, consider Ohio's Sixth Congressional District. During the 1994 elections, the Republican challenger, Frank Cremeans, outspent and narrowly defeated the Democratic incumbent, Ted Strickland. Atypical of most challengers, Cremeans spent more than $1 million, while his Democratic opponent spent just over $530,000. So how would Cremeans have fared had spending limits been enacted before 1994? It depends. According to these estimates, spending limits set lower than $700,000 would have led to the reelection of Democratic incumbent Ted Strickland. With spending limits set at or greater than $700,000, Cremeans would have been the predicted winner.[4]

If spending limits apparently hinder the success of high-spending challengers, their effects on challengers outspent by the incumbent are less clear. In Indiana's Ninth Congressional District, for example, Democratic incumbent Lee Hamilton was held to 52 percent of the vote by Republican State Senator Jean Leising; this was Hamilton's poorest showing in his thirty-year congressional career. According to the results of our model, spending limits set below $300,000 would have added to Hamilton's margin of victory. Spending limits at or greater than $300,000, however, would have had little or no impact on the outcome or the margin of victory. More typical congressional elections in which the challenger spends less than $100,000 are unlikely to be affected at all.

In 1996, spending limits would have had a similar effect, though in 1996, the Democrats would have been the disadvantaged party. As can be seen in figure 4.2, spending limits would have either reduced or had no effect on the number of seats predicted to be gained by the Democratic Party. With limits set at $100,000–$400,000, Democrats would have been expected to gain one to four fewer seats. Spending limits set at $500,000 or above, however, would have had no effect on the number of seats gained by the Democratic Party. Taken in the context of the findings from 1994, one might be tempted to conclude that the enactment of spending limits would limit the success of the minority party. Based on prior research (Gross, Shields, and Goidel 1997), however, we conclude that spending limits, without some accompanying form of public financing, would most likely limit the success of the party favored by short-term electoral forces.

The effect of spending limits on electoral competition in 1996 is perhaps best illustrated by reconsidering Ohio's Sixth Congressional District, in which Republican freshman Frank Cremeans faced former Democratic in-

Figure 4.2   Spending Limits and Predicted Democratic Seat Gain, 1996

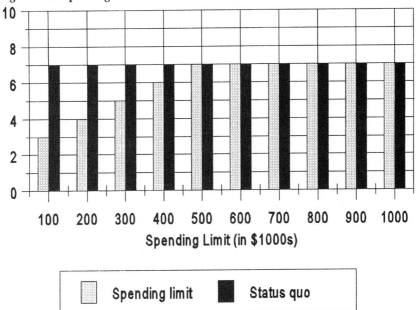

cumbent Ted Strickland in a rematch of their 1994 campaign. As in 1994, Cremeans outspent his Democratic opponent ($1,786,582 to $714,172), though neither candidate had much trouble raising or spending money.[5] Unlike 1994, however, this time around the Democratic candidate, buoyed by national partisan tides, was able to win the election. Would spending limits have protected Cremeans' brief tenure as the Republican representative from Ohio's Sixth District? According to the simulations, spending limits set below $700,000 would have resulted in a Cremeans' victory. Spending limits set at $800,000 or $900,000, however, would have marginally improved Strickland's chances at retaking the district.

Overall, spending limits pose little threat to candidates, most often challengers, who already spend less than the limit. For example, spending limits set at $600,000 would curtail the spending of about 15–20 percent of all challengers but would limit the spending of more than 30 percent of incumbents running for reelection. As a result, to the extent that spending limits require some modification of campaign behavior, it is incumbents rather than challengers who are most likely to be affected. While spending limits might have some impact in high-spending, competitive elections, it is unclear whether they would actually change the outcome of many elections. Assuming spending limits in the $600,000–$800,000 range, two well-funded campaigns, and a highly competitive election decided by 2–3 percent of the vote, the predicted effects of spending limits are generally quite small, often so close to 50 percent that most observers would hesitate to predict a winner. As a result, while the effects are in the expected direction, they are considerably less dire than critics often assume.

Matching Funds

If spending limits would have limited Republican victories in 1994, the effects of matching funds are less clear. As can be seen in figure 4.3, with limits set at relatively low levels, Republican victories would have been significantly reduced. As was the case with spending limits, however, even with matching funds at relatively low levels, Republicans would still have probably taken control of the House. With higher levels of matching funds, Republicans would have actually benefited from some form of public financing. For example, according to our estimates, Republicans would have won additional House seats had matching funds been set at least at $400,000. With matching funds and limits set at $800,000, Republicans would have won an estimated ten additional seats during the 1994 elections.

But what does this mean in terms of individual races? Consider again the

Figure 4.3   Matching Funds and Predicted Democratic Seat Loss, 1994

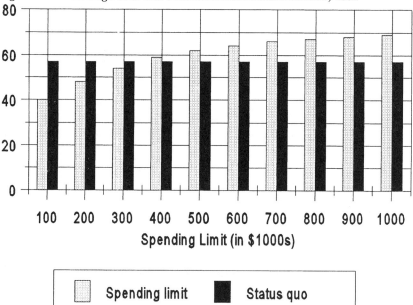

race between Republican challenger Jean Leising and Democratic incumbent Lee Hamilton in Indiana's Ninth Congressional District. After the election, Leising publicly criticized the Republican Party for devoting resources to other races believed to be more competitive, resources Leising believed would have made a critical difference in her failed election bid. Was she right? According to the results of our model, had a system of matching funds been in place, Leising might have very well knocked off the incumbent four years before his announced retirement. For example, with matching funds provided on a dollar-for-dollar basis and limits set at $600,000, Leising would have been able to increase her spending to $483,708 and would have been predicted to win with nearly 52 percent of the vote.

A similar story can be told regarding the effect of matching funds on the 1996 House elections. As can be seen in figure 4.4, with matching funds set at as low as $100,000, Democrats would have been expected to gain two fewer House seats. With matching funds set at $300,000 or higher, however, Democrats would have been expected to gain from one to four additional seats. While the gains would not have been large enough to regain control of the House of Representatives, the pattern is relatively clear. Matching funds in combination with spending limits benefit the minority party,

Figure 4.4 Matching Funds and Predicted Democratic Seat Gain, 1996

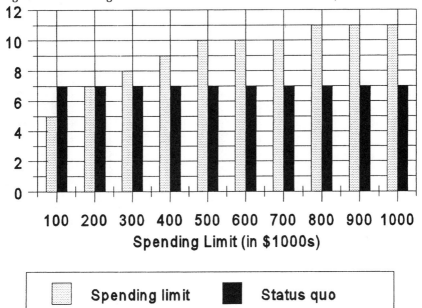

though the effects appear to be contingent upon the level of matching funds and the electoral context (that is, the election year).

Full Public Financing

The effect of full public financing on the 1994 elections would have been similar in nature to the effect of matching funds, though the overall effect is magnified a bit. Even with full public financing, competition would have been diminished if spending limits had been set at relatively low levels: according to figure 4.5, at less than $200,000. If public financing had gone beyond these relatively low levels, however, Republican candidates would have benefited tremendously. According to our estimates, if full public financing had been set at $400,000, Republicans would have gained an additional thirteen House seats in 1994. If full public financing had been set at $600,000, Republicans would have gained an additional twenty-one House seats. For candidates such as Jean Leising, who was able to raise some money on her own ($241,854), the positive effects of public financing would have been very similar to the estimated effects of matching funds. For example, in a hypothetical reform scenario in which both candidates received $600,000 in public funding, Jean Leising would have garnered 52 percent of the vote in her race against Democrat incumbent Lee Hamilton.

Figure 4.5   Full Public Financing and Predicted Democratic Seat Loss, 1994

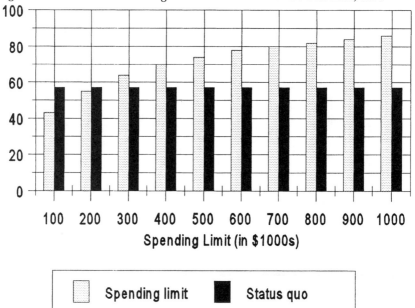

The real beneficiaries of public financing, however, would have been candidates like Republican Dennis Newinski, who raised only $93,457 in his bid to replace Democratic incumbent Bruce Vento in Minnesota's Fourth Congressional District. Despite being outspent by more than $230,000, and running in a district with a decided Democratic tilt, Newinski was able to hold incumbent Bruce Vento to the lowest winning percentage of his career. Under a system of public financing, Newinski would have significantly improved his chances of upsetting the incumbent, though in a district that leans heavily Democratic, the challenger would have still have faced an uphill battle. Interestingly, both Newinski and Leising ran again in 1996. While each candidate was significantly better funded than in 1994, both lost by a wider margin than in their previous, relatively underfunded campaign.[6] For some observers, such a result reemphasizes a point made earlier in this chapter: in congressional elections, money isn't everything. It also illustrates an additional point about congressional campaign finance: the market is relatively slow in adapting to changes in its external environment. Money became more accessible to Leising and Newinski only after they proved to be credible opponents, but by that time it was too late; the electoral environment no longer favored Republican challengers.

Similar to the estimated effects in 1994, had full public financing been in place before the 1996 elections, the minority party (in this case the Democrats) would have benefited tremendously (see figure 4.6). Even with full public financing set as low as $100,000, Democrats would have been expected to gain three additional seats. At higher levels of funding, Democratic gains would have increased. Had full public financing supported House candidates up to a limit of $500,000, Democrats would have been expected to gain sixteen additional House seats. For example, in Iowa's Second District, Democratic challenger Donna Smith spent just under $70,000, at least $600,000 less than the Republican incumbent Jim Nussle, yet garnered 46 percent of the vote. With a system of full public financing in place and subsidies as low as $300,000, Smith would have been expected to win the district. At the aggregate level, with full public financing set as low as $300,000, Democrats would have been predicted to pick up enough seats to retake majority control of the House of Representatives. As this example illustrates, full public financing, except when it is set at relatively low levels, serves to strengthen the minority party's electoral prospects.

Partial Public Funding

Perhaps the most interesting results of this analysis are based on assumptions of partial public financing that most resemble the version of campaign finance reform that failed to become law in the 104th and 105th Congresses. The results of our analysis indicate that campaign finance re-

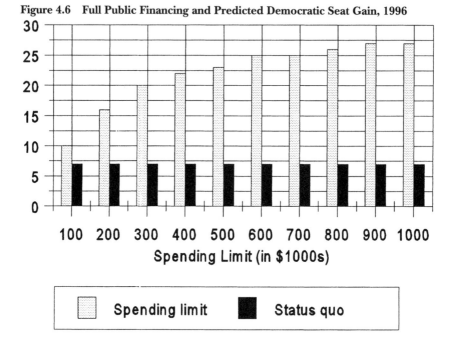

Figure 4.6   Full Public Financing and Predicted Democratic Seat Gain, 1996

form that involves public grants (or vouchers) in coordination with spending limits would have significantly increased the number of Republicans elected in 1994 and the number of Democrats elected in 1996. As with the other versions of reform, partial public funding serves to enhance the electoral prospects of the minority party.

Looking first at the results from 1994, in each of the scenarios considered we estimate that Republicans would have gained additional seats had campaign finance reform been in place before the 1994 elections (see figure 4.7). For example, in the version of campaign finance reform that most resembles the version considered by the House in 1993, vouchers of $200,000 and spending limits of $600,000, the simulations indicate that Republicans would have won an additional fourteen House seats. Even with lower limits ($400,000) and more modest vouchers ($100,000), the number of Republican victories would have slightly increased. Similar results were obtained from the 1996 elections (figure 4.8). As in 1994, the minority party would have benefited from the imposition of partial public financing. The 1996 results differ from the 1994 results, however, in that the imposition of spending limits appear to have little effect on the expected number of seats won by the Democratic Party. For example, Democrats would have been expected to win five additional seats with a $100,000 pub-

Figure 4.7   Partial Public Financing and Predicted Democratic Seat Loss, 1994

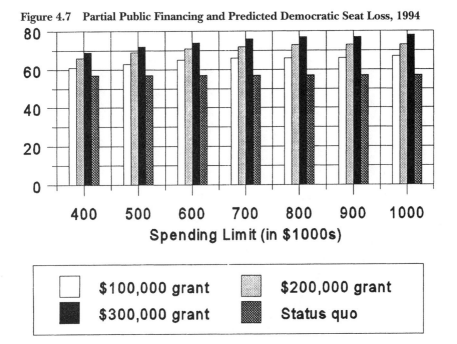

lic subsidy, sixteen to seventeen seats with a $200,000 subsidy, and twenty seats with a $300,000 public subsidy, regardless of whether spending limits were set as low as $400,000 or as high as $1 million.

In 1994, Republican challengers such as Jean Leising in Indiana's Ninth District and Dennis Newinski in Minnesota's Fourth District would have benefited tremendously had such a system been in place, while in 1996, Democratic challengers such as Donna Smith in Iowa's Second District would have benefited. Being less dependent on a campaign finance market that reacts slowly to changes in the electoral environment, public funding provides candidates with the ability to wage a campaign without having to first convince potential contributors that they have a viable candidacy. For challengers in tune with electoral tides but politically not well connected, public funding would serve as a valuable resource as well as an enticement to run. Yet, even in races in which the challenger remains a likely loser, the level of competition would increase significantly, enhancing the democratic process and perhaps even the quality of representation.

Summary of Results

Overall, the results indicate that spending limits would have potentially limited the number of seats won by the minority party in both 1994 and 1996.

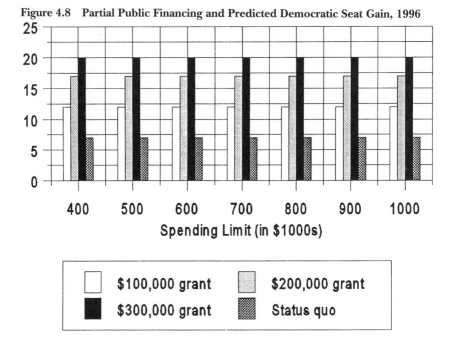

Figure 4.8   Partial Public Financing and Predicted Democratic Seat Gain, 1996

Prior research including an analysis of the 1992 congressional elections, however, indicates that any adverse consequences of spending limits, without some form of accompanying public financing, will be felt more by the party advantaged by short-term political tides (Gross, Shields, and Goidel 1997). Spending limits in combination with some form of public financing, however, would significantly enhance the electoral prospects of the minority party. Except at very low levels, Republican candidates would have benefited had a system of matching funds or public financing been in place before the 1994 elections, while Democrats would have benefited from some form of public financing in 1996.

CONCLUSION

Before 1994, Republicans feared that the implementation of campaign finance reform would inhibit their ability to gain control of the House of Representatives. While the increased fund-raising success of Republican challengers and the overall increase in campaign spending during the 1993–94 election cycle would seem to provide supportive evidence, our analysis indicates that campaign finance reform would not have significantly limited the number of seats won by the Republican party in 1994 and may have actually resulted in an increase in the number of seats won. Ironically, Republicans may have had more reason to fear campaign finance reform after gaining majority control of the House of Representatives than during their forty years in exile as the House minority. In this respect, our results indicate that, at least under reform scenarios involving significant public financing provisions, Republicans may well have lost majority control of the House of Representatives. More broadly, the results of our analysis tend to support the state-level research of Ruth Jones (1981), which notes that, on balance, public financing should benefit the minority party.

In an electoral system in which challengers find it difficult to raise the funding necessary to mount a serious campaign against an incumbent, the minority party is necessarily disadvantaged. One consequence of the strength of incumbency in House elections is that hopes for significant party gains rest primarily on those seats left open by opposition party retirements (Gaddie 1995a, 1995b). Absent a large number of majority party retirements (as was the case in 1994), the potential of the minority party to make substantial gains in the House elections is necessarily limited. Moreover, ill-timed retirements from the minority party (as in 1996) may have the inadvertent effect of making the task of recapturing the House that much more difficult.

Having finally overcome the obstacles created by their minority party status and having weathered the 1996 elections, Republicans should now be in a position to reap the benefits of their majority party status. Writing in the wake of the 1994 midterm elections, Theodore J. Eismeier and Philip H. Pollock (1996, 95) observed that "Democratic survivors will probably be able to fund adequately their 1996 campaigns. But it will require more hustling, an unappealing prospect that may urge some into retirement. Between defending incumbents and attempting to win back seats lost in 1994, the resources of labor PACs will be stretched very thin. Even with the support of labor PACs, Democrats have lagged behind Republicans in money for challengers. . . . Republican incumbents may become entrenched, and money to defeat them, or for that matter to defend Democratic incumbents, more and more scarce."

These observations proved prophetic, though perhaps less so than one might have suspected in the immediate aftermath of the 1994 elections. The fact that 1996 turned out to be a "good" Democratic year probably served to soften the blow of losing majority control of the House of Representatives (Jacobson 1997a). CNN Correspondent Brooks Jackson (1997, 252), for example, observes that "the change [in PAC contributions] was profound. In past elections PACs had given far more to Democratic congressional candidates overall. . . . But in the 1995–1996 election cycle PACs were giving more to Republicans."

For Democrats, the failure to act on campaign finance reform when they were in the majority and controlled the presidency may have been incredibly shortsighted.[7] As we demonstrate in this chapter, campaign finance reform would not, in all likelihood, have halted the Republican takeover of the House in 1994. In fact, it may have added Democratic casualities to the Republican Revolution, though the enactment of reform may also have facilitated Democratic efforts at recapturing the House in 1996.

Overall, a system of campaign financing that places challengers at a disadvantage also places the minority party at a disadvantage. In many ways, the obstacles confronting Democrats as the minority party are the same as those that confront Republicans. Even when Democrats controlled Congress, the proliferation of business-oriented political action committees, both in number and in total contributions, created a system that should have theoretically benefited the Republican Party. Democratic incumbents were able to adapt and prosper under this system of campaign financing, but they benefited only as long as they could remain in the majority. Now as the minority party, Democratic Party fund-raising should be significantly undermined, as should their ability to win back control of the House of Representatives.

NOTES

1. Research also indicates that retirements result from "progressive ambition" in which incumbent House members run for higher office (generally a Senate seat) as well as from changes in retirement benefits (Hall and Houweling 1995; Groseclose and Krehbiel 1994; Rohde 1979; Black 1972; Schlesinger 1966).

2. One particularly compelling problem involves what economists refer to as the Lucas critique. In terms of campaign finance reform, the Lucas critique refers to the manner in which strategic political actors will attempt to anticipate changes in the law and adapt their behavior accordingly. For example, faced with spending limits, incumbents may spend more time shaking hands and less money on television ads. However, while it is clear that strategic politicians will react to changes in the campaign finance laws, it is less clear as to how these actions will affect estimates of the likely impact of campaign reform.

3. Competition can be defined in numerous ways. In the analysis that follows, we focus on competition in terms of the number of seats won or lost by the minority party rather than on the percentage of the vote or margin of victory for the winning candidate.

4. Predictions of victory or defeat are of individual congressional elections and do not take into account the uncertainty of the estimate. In this example, the point estimates are almost within one standard error of the 50 percent win-or-lose criterion.

5. Strickland also benefited from a labor sponsored-issue advocacy campaign.

6. Newinski spent $315,410 for his 1996 election; Leising, $451,475.

7. Of course, Democrats were operating in the context of having held majority-party status for forty years and were not planning on losing majority status in 1994. Without the knowledge that they would lose majority party status, their incentives for reforming the system were marginal at best.

Chapter Five

The Question of Voter Turnout, Part I

The legitimacy of democratic government is based, at least in part, on the consent of the governed. While citizens may express their consent through other avenues of participation—and arguably, by not participating at all—the most obvious means of expressing one's consent is by turning out to vote on election day. Beyond simply expressing a preference between competing candidacies and parties, citizen participation reinforces the legitimacy upon which the political system is itself based. For this reason, classic democratic theory has long held that high levels of citizen participation are a sign of a healthy democracy (Pateman 1970).

Yet, by this standard, democracy in the United States is woefully inadequate. Since 1972, voter turnout in presidential elections has fluctuated between 49 and 55 percent of the voting-age population. Turnout in nonpresidential, midterm election years is even lower, averaging 36–40 percent of the eligible electorate. When compared to other Western democracies, the United States consistently ranks at or near the bottom in terms of the percentage of citizens casting a ballot (see, for example, Teixeira 1992). During the May 1997 parliamentary elections in Great Britain, for example, 71 percent of the eligible electorate turned out to vote. Although this was the lowest voter turnout in a British election since 1935, it was more than 20 percentage points higher than turnout in the 1996 U.S. presidential election.

At least as troubling as low voter participation rates has been a long-term trend toward declining voter participation in U.S. elections (see figure 5.1). According to Walter Dean Burnham (1970), voter turnout in the United States has been on a steady decline since the Progressive reforms of the 1890s limited the effectiveness of party mobilization efforts. In the late nineteenth century, turnout rates of more than 80 percent were not uncommon in presidential elections. By 1972, turnout rates had fallen below 60 percent in presidential election years. As Frances Fox Piven and Richard A. Cloward (1988, 6) observe, "by World War I, turnout rates had fallen to

Figure 5.1   Voter Turnout in Presidential Elections, 1960–1996

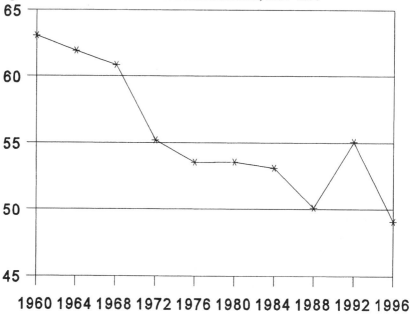

Source: FEC data.

half the eligible electorate and, despite some vacillations, they have never recovered." During the 1960 presidential election between John F. Kennedy and Richard M. Nixon, one of the closest presidential elections in recent history, 63 percent of the eligible electorate turned out to vote. By comparison, in the 1996 election featuring Bill Clinton and Bob Dole, a majority of the eligible electorate opted out of the electoral process for the first time since 1924. Overall, with the exception of 1992, turnout in presidential elections has been on a consistent decline since the 1960s.

A similar though less precipitous decline has occurred in midterm elections over the same time period. In 1962, 47 percent of the eligible electorate turned out to vote in an election in which Democrats lost only four seats in the House of Representatives. By comparison, during the much-heralded Republican Revolution in 1994, only 39 percent of the eligible electorate voted in an election in which Democrats lost fifty-two House seats. Still, turnout in 1994 was a slight improvement over previous midterm elections, in which turnout sagged to 36 percent (see figure 5.2).

DOES NONVOTING MATTER?

If voter turnout in U.S. national elections is low, it is reasonable to ask whether this low voter turnout matters. Does nonparticipation affect the

Figure 5.2   Voter Turnout in Midterm Elections, 1962–1994

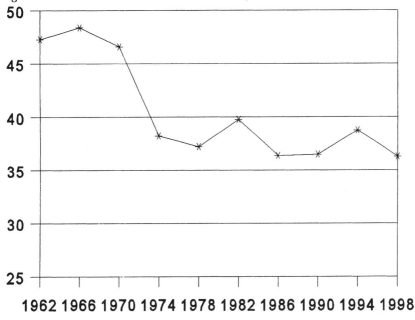

Source: FEC data.

type of leaders who are elected or, consequently, the type of policies that are enacted? Whether (and how) nonvoting actually affects the political system has been the subject of considerable academic debate. Beginning with the seminal work of Anthony Downs (1957), many observers of American politics have argued that nonvoting is a defensible, rational act. By applying the principle of economic rationality to individual voting decisions, Downs argues that the costs of voting nearly always outweigh the benefits. As a result, individual citizens have an incentive to remain uninvolved and, by extension, apathetic and ignorant about public affairs.

If nonvoting is defensible from a theoretical perspective, it is also defensible from a practical standpoint. First, a number of studies looking at attitudinal differences indicate that nonvoters and voters tend to have similar candidate and policy preferences (Gant and Lyons 1993; Bennett and Resnick 1990; Wolfinger and Rosenstone 1980; De Nardo 1980; Shaffer 1982; but see also Petrocik 1987; Radcliff 1994). Consequently, these studies conclude, nonvoting probably has little effect on who wins and who loses an election and, as a result, has little effect on public policy outcomes.[1] As Ruy A. Teixeira (1992, 87) observes in his review of this literature, "changing the outcome of an election by expanding the voting pool is far more difficult than is generally believed."

Second, pointing to the downfall of the Weimer Republic in pre-World War II Germany, many analysts note that high levels of voter participation are generally associated with greater political and social instability. In this respect, it is argued that nonvoters are not only less educated and less informed than voters, they are also less supportive of democratic values (but see Bennett and Resnick 1990 for contradictory evidence). As a result, the decision of this segment of the eligible electorate to opt out of the electoral process may arguably serve to further democratic governance. On a related note, it is also argued that nonvoting indicates satisfaction with the status quo. If voters were genuinely dissatisfied, they would use the electoral process to express their dissatisfaction with current government policies. Rather than indicating a crisis of democracy, substantial percentages of nonvoters may instead indicate a relatively healthy polity free of the sort of contentious, divisive issues that attract citizens to the polls. During partisan realignments, which tend to coincide with economic, political, and social crises, the cleavages dividing political party coalitions are redefined. Political participation increases and becomes more intense during these periods of political upheaval. Lacking such divisive and contentious issues, periods of "normal" politics are much less conducive to citizen participation (Key 1955; Burnham 1970; Clubb, Flanigan, and Zinglae 1990).

For various reasons, we reject arguments that nonvoting is either inconsequential or desirable. First, even if voters and nonvoters prefer the same candidate, they are clearly distinct in their preferences. Voters, after all, feel strongly enough about their candidate preference to actually cast a ballot. Voters and nonvoters also differ in other important ways. Voters tend to be more educated and to have higher incomes and longer and more enduring ties to the community. As Piven and Cloward (1988, 4) explain, "the active American electorate overrepresents those who have more, and underrepresents those who have less." Is it reasonable to assume that an electorate biased in favor of the middle and upper classes will represent the interest of the working class? Probably not. Piven and Cloward argue that the class biases of the active electorate provided the political support necessary for the dismantling of the welfare state in the 1980s and, presumably, for the continued public support of welfare reform in the 1990s. Kim Quaile Hill, Jan E. Leighley, and Angela Hinton-Andersson (1995; see also Hill and Leighley 1992) provide more systematic evidence of a connection between the class biases of the active electorate and public policy by demonstrating that state spending on social welfare programs is significantly higher in states with more highly mobilized lower-class citizens.

Generational politics also attest to the implications of a biased electorate. It is hardly coincidental that elderly Americans participate at higher rates than younger Americans and also receive a larger share of federal benefits. "The success of the elderly in protecting their government benefits in an era of belt-tightening," Sydney Verba, Kay Lehman Schlozman, and Henry E. Brady (1995, 31) write, "is frequently attributed to the American Association of Retired Persons and to high rates of participation, especially electoral turnout, among senior citizens." Nor, according to Verba, Schlozman, and Brady (1995) is it a coincidence that government services provided to African Americans improved as their opportunities for participation increased following the passage of the Voting Rights Act of 1965 (Button 1989; Keech 1968). Overall, participation matters because participants are more likely to have their demands heard and responded to by elected officials than are nonparticipants. Evidence that nonvoters would have supported the same candidates as voters, and perhaps by an even larger margin, hardly detracts from this statement. Nonvoters in 1996 chose not to participate because they lacked sufficient motivation to do so. While for some nonvoters the lack of motivation may be attributed to a general satisfaction with the status quo, many others failed to participate because of a more pervasive dissatisfaction with the candidates and, more broadly, with the electoral process.

CITIZEN DISSATISFACTION AND VOTER TURNOUT

In a 1993 study, Lyn Ragsdale and Gerold G. Rusk examine the amount of attention that nonvoters paid to the 1990 midterm Senate elections. According to the results of the study, a full 41 percent of nonvoters were informed about the election, paid more attention to news reports about the campaign than did the average voter, and had well-developed, structured opinions about the candidates. Yet these informed nonvoters opted out of the electoral process because they evaluated both major party candidates negatively. As this study points out, for at least a substantial subset of nonvoters, the decision to vote and the decision about whom to vote for go hand in hand. As a result, looking at the candidate preferences of nonvoters after the election may not be very revealing. These nonvoters may marginally prefer one candidate to the other but decide not to participate because they find neither of the available candidates sufficiently attractive.

The nature of contemporary politics, with its emphasis on style over substance and negative campaigning over positive, may further dampen individual motivation to participate in the electoral process. As Ragsdale and Rusk (1993, 745) observe, "nonvoters are not fools. Many people observe the campaign as if they were going to vote, even if they do not." Negative campaigning, undoubtedly, has a great deal to do with nonvoter (and voter) dissatisfaction with political candidates. "Campaign messages," these authors write, "may actually be keeping some people away from the polls" (745). More systematic support of this theme is offered by Stephen

Ansolabehere and colleagues (1994), who present convincing experimental evidence that negative advertising decreases individual intentions to participate in an election, while negative campaign environments coincide with decreased aggregate turnout and increased voter roll-off in Senate elections.[2] As Ansolabehere and colleagues (829) observe, "Campaigns have also turned increasingly hostile and ugly. More often than not, candidates criticize, discredit, or belittle their opponents rather than promoting their own ideas and programs. In the 1988 and 1990 campaigns, a survey of campaign advertising . . . found that attack advertisements had become the norm rather than the exception."

Campaigns are not the only source of negative information about political candidates. Thomas Patterson (1996) observes that media coverage of presidential campaigns has become increasingly negative as well. Nor is negativity limited to presidential campaigns; it also includes Congress, congressional leaders, and political parties. As Patterson (18) observes, "The media's bad news tendency has heightened Americans' disillusionment with their political leaders and institutions. Congress has perhaps fared the worst. A relentless stream of negative stories about congressional scandal, rivalry, conflict, and self-interest since the 1970s has helped to drive Congress's approval rating to historical lows."

The recognition that media coverage of political campaigns and political institutions may erode the public's sense of civic responsibility has not been lost on journalists. The Civic Journalism Movement reflects an attempt on the part of journalists to cover public affairs in a way that connects (or reconnects) citizens with government. Jan Schaffer (1997) of the Pew Center for Civic Journalism notes, "The journalists' goal is to treat readers and viewers not as window dressing or passive spectators but as meaningful participants in important issues, as meaningful as the elites and the experts the journalists so often quote." Whether the Civic Journalism Movement can ignite citizen interest and participation in politics is not entirely clear. Yet it is noteworthy that journalists and communication scholars, like political scientists, recognize the potential connection between negativity in campaigns and citizen participation.

INDIVIDUAL AND SYSTEMIC CAUSES OF LOW VOTER TURNOUT

While there seems to be a growing recognition that campaigns can influence citizen participation, the literature on voter turnout has, in the past, focused almost exclusively on factors unrelated to politics. As recently as 1993, Steven J. Rosenstone and John Mark Hansen (1993, 3) lamented that "the reigning theories of participation in American politics, amazing as it may seem, do not have much to say about politics. Instead, they trace activism to the characteristics of individual American citizens, to their educations, their incomes, and their efficacy." In this respect, research on voter turnout tends to focus on two related questions: Why is voter turnout so low in the United States? And why has turnout declined over time?

Research on the first question tends to focus overwhelmingly on the effects of individual social economic status (SES), particularly education, and state-level registration requirements. First, with regard to education, it is generally agreed that, at least in the United States, education is the single best predictor of individual participation. In other Western democracies, the connection between education and voter turnout is less clear, a fact frequently attributed to the absence of a socialist political party in the United States (Powell 1986). Unfortunately, while education and other socioeconomic variables are, empirically, well connected to participation decisions, the theoretical connection has, at least until quite recently, been relatively weak. As Verba, Schlozman, and Brady (1995) observe, "The strengths of the SES model are in its empirical power to predict activity and in the political relevance of the groups upon which it is based. . . . However, the SES model is weak in its theoretical underpinnings. It fails to provide a coherent rationale for the connection between the explanatory socioeconomic variables and participation."

While education appears to facilitate voter turnout in U.S. elections, registration requirements serve to depress voter participation. Studies repeatedly demonstrate that states with more stringent registration requirements have lower voter turnout.[3] One striking difference between the United States and other Western democracies is the amount of initiative required of U.S. citizens to register to vote. Comparatively speaking, other Western democracies assume greater responsibility for voter registration, whereas registration in the United States has been largely left to the individual. Recognizing this, a number of scholars note that it is unsurprising that U.S. voter turnout lags behind voter turnout in these other nations (Wolfinger and Rosenstone 1980; Powell 1986). Some scholars, in fact, go so far as to argue that stringent registration requirements reflect an intent on the part of political elites to keep economically marginal voters from participating in the electoral process (see, for example, Piven and Cloward 1988).

If education and registration requirements appear to provide powerful explanations of individual voting decisions, they fail altogether as explanations of the decline in voter turnout. In recent decades, both education and registration requirements have changed in ways that should have resulted in increased voter participation. Yet, as education has increased and registration requirements have weakened, voter turnout continues to decline. In terms of registration requirements, one need look no further than the 1996 presidential elections for compelling evidence that lessened registration requirements provide no guarantee of increased turnout. By the

1996 presidential elections, many states had implemented motor voter legislation (the National Voter Registration Act), allowing individuals to register to vote while obtaining a driver's license or federal government benefits. According to one estimate, the motor voter act added 12 million new voters to the registration rolls for the 1996 elections. Yet, when all was said and done, voter turnout in 1996 declined to its lowest level since 1924.[4]

But if education and registration requirements fail to explain the decline in voter turnout over time, what does? Early explanations of the decline in electoral participation focused on psychological factors such as efficacy and trust. A study by Paul R. Abramson and John H. Aldrich (1982), for example, attributes the bulk of the decline in turnout to a decline in the belief that government is responsive to individuals and their needs. More recently, Teixeira (1987, 1992) has argued that the historical decline in turnout is attributable primarily to a decline in voter motivation created, by and large, from an individual sense of disconnectedness from the political system. Maintaining the focus on the lack of voter motivation, other explanations place greater emphasis on the political environment in which participation takes place. Rosenstone and Hansen (1993) argue that the historical decline in turnout is best explained by the failure of political parties to mobilize voters (on the importance of mobilization, see also Jackson 1993, 1997; Weilhouwer and Lockerbie 1994; Huckfeldt and Sprague 1992).

Emphasizing the importance of elite mobilization efforts, many scholars argue that reductions in campaign spending would likely result in fewer individuals mobilized and recruited into political activity (see, for example, Teixeira 1996). In this respect, higher spending and more competitive elections are generally associated with increased voter turnout (Caldeira and Patterson 1982; Patterson and Caldeira 1983; Caldeira, Patterson, and Markko 1985; Gilliam 1985; Cox and Munger 1989; Berch 1993; Jackson 1993, 1996a, 1996b, 1997). Consequently, critics of reform maintain, attempts to limit campaign spending would serve to depress voter turnout. Teixeira (1996, 14) observes that "it seems quite clear that spending limits would hurt, not help, voter turnout. Empirically, higher spending is associated with higher turnout, so lowering spending should logically depress turnout."

If the evidence seems clear that turnout is associated with higher spending and more competitive elections, the conclusion that campaign reform would necessarily reduce voter turnout, even reform that drastically reduces candidate spending, is considerably less certain. Though Teixeira (1996) argues against campaign spending limits, he also notes that findings that higher campaign spending is associated with higher turnout levels

> leave a number of questions unanswered. Chief among them is whether more
> spending and more competition promote turnout in an undifferentiated way,

or whether certain types of spending and competitiveness are particularly effective in generating higher turnout. The latter seems more plausible, since spending and competitiveness have their effects through campaign activities that mobilize individual voters, who, in turn, seem likely to react with different levels of enthusiasm to different activities (for example, party canvassing versus negative campaign advertising). If this is true, the maximum effect on turnout is likely to be obtained when a high level of spending is combined with a particular mix of campaign activities.

In other words, while campaign spending may be a potentially effective means of mobilization, several other forms of political recruitment may serve as even more powerful mobilization agents. For example, television advertisements are a very broad and indirect method of recruiting citizens, compared to more direct and personal contact from a political party official. In addition, there is mounting evidence that many forms of negative television advertising decrease, rather than promote, individual-level turnout decisions (Ansolabehere et al. 1994). More broadly, it is argued that the professionalization of politics, particularly with its reliance on television as the primary means of communicating with voters, has led individual citizens to view politics as a spectator sport, thus decreasing their willingness to participate in the political process (Becker and Preston 1970; Miller, Goldenberg, and Erbring 1979; McLeod, Ward, and Tancill 1965; Noelle-Neumann 1993; Flanigan and Zingale 1991, 22). Overall, it is hard to escape the conclusion that "campaigns can be either mobilizing or demobilizing events, *depending upon the nature of the messages they generate*" but not on the money that they spend (Ansolabehere et al. 1994, 829; emphasis in original).

Finally, there is substantial evidence that a significant amount of candidate resources are spent in areas and on items that have little to do with increasing citizen participation or, for that matter, contacting voters (Morris and Gamache 1994; Fritz and Morris 1992). This is particularly true of spending by incumbents intended to maintain a permanent campaign organization in nonelection years. Along these lines, recent studies indicate that challenger spending is a more effective stimulus of aggregate voter turnout than incumbent spending both in statewide elections (Jackson 1997) and in House elections (Goidel and Shields 1994). Unfortunately, at least from the standpoint of voter participation, most of the money spent in House races is incumbent spending and, as a result, has little impact on voter turnout. While campaign spending may be an important mobilization factor in congressional elections, there are several reasons to expect that reforms intended to reduce the amount of money spent in congressional races will not substantially reduce participation in electoral politics.

CAMPAIGN FINANCE REFORM AND VOTER TURNOUT

Voter turnout varies considerably across congressional districts as well as from one election to the next. The most widely noted swings in voter turnout are the traditional midterm decline in voter turnout and its corresponding surge in presidential election years. Early theories attempted to connect these biannual fluctuations in voter turnout with partisan seat change in Congress (Campbell 1960). More recent research either questions the impact of these fluctuations on turnout altogether (Wolfinger, Rosenstone, and McIntosh 1981), or has significantly revised the original theory (Campbell 1993).[5]

While most scholarly attention focuses on fluctuations in turnout from one election to the next, considerably less attention is devoted to the often dramatic fluctuations across congressional districts within a given election year (but see Gilliam 1985; Caldeira, Patterson, and Markko 1985). For example, while district-level turnout during the 1994 midterm elections averaged just under 40 percent in contested elections, overall turnout ranged from just under 16 percent to just over 59 percent. Aggregate district-level turnout was lowest in Texas's Twenty-ninth District, where just under 16 percent of voters turned out to reelect Democratic incumbent Gene Green with 73 percent of the two-party vote. As is the case with many low-turnout districts, Texas's Twenty-ninth District is composed of mainly minority voters, has a relatively low percentage of college-educated residents, and was not very competitive during 1994.[6] At the opposite end of the spectrum, district-level turnout was highest in Minnesota's Sixth District, which showcased a highly competitive, open-seat election in which the winner prevailed by less than 600 votes. Concurrent statewide elections for an open Senate seat and a contested gubernatorial reelection campaign undoubtedly boosted turnout in Minnesota, as well.

Though one might suspect that district-level turnout is more uniform during presidential election years, this is simply not the case. While district-level turnout averaged just under 50 percent during the 1996 presidential elections, approximately 10 percentage points higher than in 1994, turnout ranged from 15 to 77 percent of the eligible electorate.[7] As in 1994, turnout was highest in Minnesota's Sixth Congressional District in an election featuring a rematch between the 1994 contestants, incumbent Democrat Bill Luther and Republican challenger Tad Jude. Compared to the highly competitive 1994 election, which Luther won by less than 600 votes, the 1996 election was won by the incumbent with a relatively comfortable 56 percent of the vote. As in 1994, the lower end of the turnout spectrum was occupied by a district in which most of the electorate are members of a minority. In California's Thirty-third District, only 15 percent of the eligible electorate voted in a highly noncompetitive election won by the Democratic incumbent.

While these examples are illustrative, it is not entirely clear how important electoral competitiveness and campaign spending are to aggregate turnout rates. While Minnesota's Sixth District topped the list of high turnout districts both in 1994 and 1996, other districts in Minnesota with much more lopsided races had voter turnout only marginally lower than in the Sixth District. For example, in Minnesota's Third Congressional District, voter turnout neared 59 percent during the 1994 midterm election, despite an election in which the incumbent garnered 73 percent of the two-party vote.

While voters at least occasionally turn out for lopsided races, they can also fail to turn out for some relatively high-spending, competitive elections. Perhaps no single district better illustrates this fact across the 1994 and 1996 election cycles than California's Forty-second Congressional District. In 1994, despite an election in which Democratic incumbent George Brown won by only 2 percentage points and in which total candidate spending was just under $800,000 (more than $300,000 of which was challenger spending), district-level voter turnout was barely over 30 percent of the eligible electorate. In 1996, with incumbent George Brown running for election to his seventeenth congressional term, total spending increased to more than $1.4 million dollars. The challenger in the race, Republican Linda Wilde, spent $685,623—nearly half of total candidate spending. Despite the high levels of campaign spending and an election decided by less than a thousand votes, voter turnout was a dismal 27 percent, 3 percentage points lower than during the 1994 midterm election.

As these examples illustrate, the relationship between candidate spending and voter turnout is not entirely clear. In some districts, voter turnout is high despite lopsided, low-spending House races. In other districts, voter turnout remains low despite the presence of competitive, high-spending congressional campaigns. While campaign spending may stimulate voter turnout, the effects of spending on turnout, at least in House races, are best characterized as limited. Yet, if this true, what are the implications for arguments that campaign finance reform reduces voter participation?

To answer this question, it is necessary to first develop a more precise estimate of the effect of candidate campaign spending on voter turnout. To accomplish this, statistical analyses were conducted on turnout and spending data from the 1994 and 1996 House elections. Based on these analyses, we computed the effect of an additional $100,000 in spending on district-level voter turnout. In doing so, we controlled for other relevant factors, including district-level education and other important district-level demographic and political factors. (The full regression models as well as a description of the results can be found in appendix B.) In table 5.1, we present results based on these analyses.

As can be seen in table 5.1, the direct effects of candidate spending on voter turnout are actually quite small and vary considerably from one election year to the next. The largest effects of candidate spending on voter turnout were observed for Democratic open-seat candidates in 1994. Yet, even with this high-end estimate, it would require more than $200,000 in candidate spending to increase voter turnout by a single percentage point. In addition, while challenger spending exerts a consistent positive effect on voter turnout (Jackson 1997, 1993), the effects are substantively quite marginal.[8] Even under the best conditions, challengers would need to spend approximately $500,000 to increase voter turnout by 1 percentage point.

The limited effect of candidate spending is made even more clear when one considers computer-based simulations designed to estimate the likely effects of campaign finance reform on voter participation (see chapter 3 for a complete description of the simulations). As in chapter 3, we consider the likely effects of four reform scenarios: (1) spending limits ranging from $100,000 to $1 million, (2) matching funds with spending limits ranging from $100,000 to $1 million, (3) full public financing ranging from $100,000 to $1 million, and (4) partial public funding, including public subsidies, ranging from $100,000 to $300,000, with spending limits ranging from $400,000 to $1 million. We begin by considering the likely effects of spending limits on aggregate voter turnout.

As can be seen in figures 5.3 and 5.4, spending limits without some form of accompanying public financing would, on average, reduce districtwide

Table 5.1   Estimated Effect of $100,000 in Candidate Spending on District-level Voter Turnout

Candidate	1994	1996
All Democrats	+0.13	-0.04
All Republicans	-0.01	+0.15
Democratic incumbents	+0.05	-0.10
Republican incumbents	-0.05	+0.06
Democratic challengers	+0.10	+0.17
Republican challengers	+0.18	+0.21
Democratic open-seat candidates	+0.45	-0.13
Republican open-seat candidates	-0.12	-0.06

Note: Cell entries are the estimated effect of candidate spending on the percentage of votes cast divided by the voting age population.

Figure 5.3   Spending Limits and Aggregate Voter Turnout, 1994

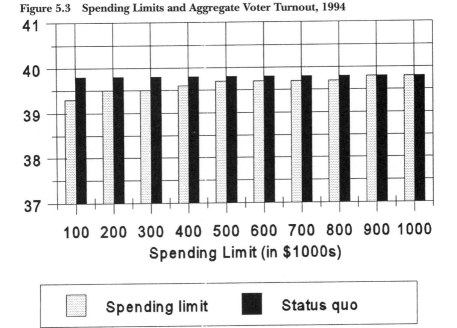

turnout in House elections. However, the effect would be minuscule. Limiting spending to $100,000 per candidate, the most restrictive scenario considered, would result in an estimated reduction in voter turnout of 0.4 percentage point in 1994 and 0.6 percentage point in 1996. Or put differently, in a district in which 200,000 citizens actually voted during the 1994 elections, all things being equal, we would expect a rather draconian $100,000 spending limit to reduce overall turnout by a mere 800 voters. In 1996, the same $100,000 spending limit would be only slightly more damaging, reducing turnout by 1,200 voters. With spending limits set at higher levels, the decline in voter turnout due to spending limits becomes even more modest. With spending limits set at $600,000, for example, turnout would be expected to decline only 0.1 percentage point in 1994 and 0.2 percentage point in 1996.

Taking a relatively extreme example, consider Washington's Fifth Congressional District during the 1994 elections in which incumbent House Speaker Thomas Foley was defeated by 2 percentage points of the vote. In this election, total spending topped $3 million, while 54 percent of the voting age population turned out to vote. But would spending limits have reduced voter turnout? If each candidate had been limited to $100,000, voter turnout would have declined only 2.8 percentage points, enough to alter

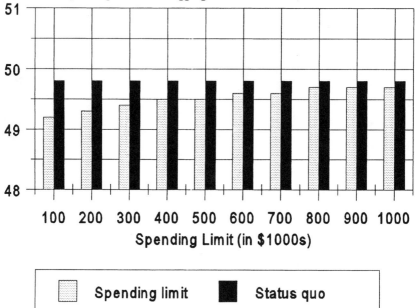

Figure 5.4   **Spending Limits and Aggregate Voter Turnout, 1996**

the outcome of the election only if nearly all of these potential nonvoters opted for the Republican challenger George Nethercutt. Had spending limits been set at $600,000, turnout would have been expected to decline by only 1.6 percentage points.

In a more typical district, the estimated effects of spending limits are considerably smaller. For example, in 1994 in Utah's Third Congressional District, Democratic incumbent Bill Orton defeated Republican challenger Dixie Thompson by 19 percentage points. Total spending (including spending by a third-party candidate) in the election was just over $400,000, while 44 percent of the eligible electorate turned out to vote. In this race, spending limits of $100,000 would have reduced voter turnout by an estimated 0.1 percentage point. While spending limits might decrease voter participation, the effect can, at best, be described as limited, and in most scenarios the effect would be more accurately described as negligible.

If spending limits appear to slightly decrease voter turnout, the results presented in figures 5.5 and 5.6 indicate that the effects of matching funds on district-level participation are less clear. According to the results of the 1994 midterm elections, it appears that with relatively low limits, matching funds would have decreased voter turnout; at moderate levels, there would have been no effect; and at higher levels, matching funds would have

Figure 5.5   Matching Funds and Aggregate Voter Turnout, 1994

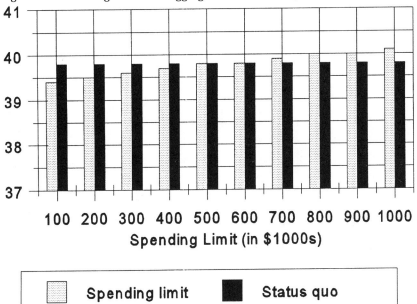

slightly increased voter turnout. The simulations from 1996 largely conform to this general pattern with one notable exception. In 1996, it would have required a higher level of matching funds before predicted turnout equaled or surpassed turnout that assumed no change in campaign finance laws. Overall, as was the case with spending limits, the estimated effect of matching funds on district participation appears rather minuscule. Matching funds up to $1 million, for example, would increase district-level voter turnout, on average, by only 0.3 percentage point in 1994 and by only 0.2 percentage point in 1996.

In figures 5.7 and 5.8, we present the results of the simulations designed to estimate the likely effects of full public financing. As can be seen in figure 5.7, except at relatively low levels, full public financing would likely increase district-level voter turnout. According to our estimates, in 1994, full public financing at $300,000 and less would have slightly decreased district turnout, while public financing at $400,000 and more would have slightly increased district turnout. In 1996, voter turnout would have been marginally less had public financing been less than $600,000 but would have marginally increased with public financing of $700,000 or more. As one would expect, higher levels of public financing are associated with higher voter turnout. Even in a scenario in which both candidates are assumed to have

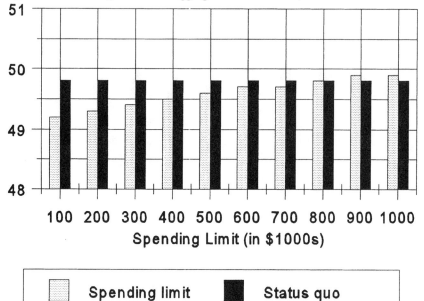

Figure 5.6   Matching Funds and Aggregate Voter Turnout, 1996

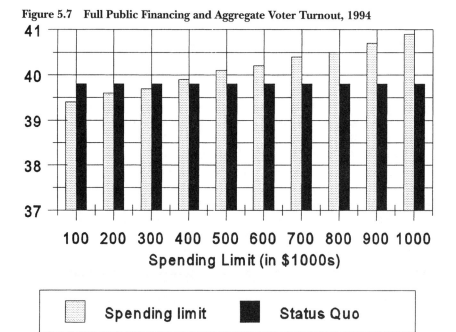

Figure 5.7   Full Public Financing and Aggregate Voter Turnout, 1994

Figure 5.8 Full Public Financing and Aggregate Voter Turnout, 1996

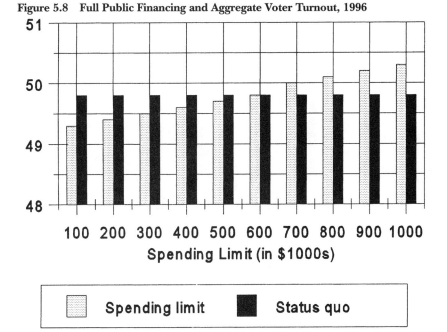

spent $1 million, however, voter turnout would, on average, be estimated to increase by only 1.1 percentage points in 1994 and 0.5 percentage point in 1996. For example, in 1994 in Colorado's First Congressional District, incumbent Democrat Patricia Schroeder defeated Republican challenger William Eggert by 20 percentage points. Shroeder also outspent her Republican opponent by nearly $200,000 in an election in which total spending was just over $325,000 and turnout was 36.5 percent of the voting-age population. Had full public financing been in place prior to the election, with public subsidies of $600,000, turnout would have been expected to increase by a single percentage point. With public subsidies of $1 million, voter turnout would have been expected to increase by just under 2 percentage points.

In our final scenario, we consider more realistic reform proposals, including public subsidies of $100,000–$300,000 and limits ranging from $400,000 to $1 million. The results are presented in figures 5.9 and 5.10. In 1994, as figure 5.9 illustrates, each of the reform proposals involving public grants is estimated to have increased voter turnout. However, as with the other reform proposals, the estimated effect on voter turnout is not very substantial. In fact, according to our estimates, the highest increase in turnout, associated with a public grant of $300,000 and no accompanying

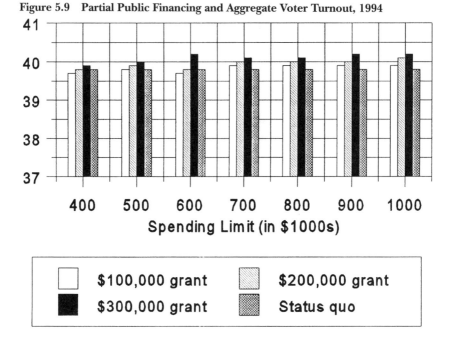

Figure 5.9 Partial Public Financing and Aggregate Voter Turnout, 1994

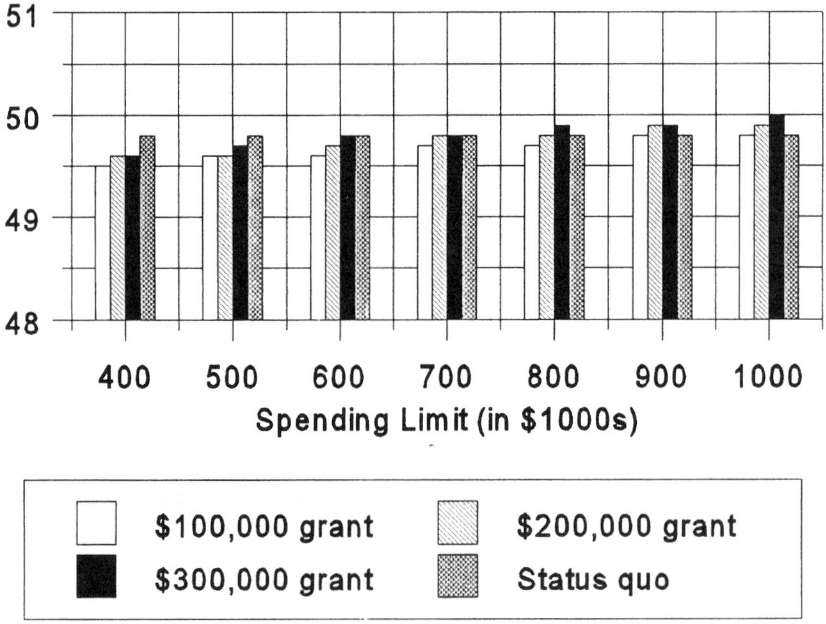

Figure 5.10 Partial Public Financing and Aggregate Voter Turnout, 1996

spending limits, would increase voter turnout by just 0.5 percentage point. Using Colorado's First Congressional District as an example, in such a scenario voter turnout would have been expected to increase by only 0.6 percentage point.

Overall, the results indicate that both reformers and critics may be misled if they believe that campaign finance reform will have much of an effect on voter participation. Restrictive limits may marginally reduce district-level voter turnout, but the effect may be best described as marginal. Similarly, public funding of campaigns may increase voter participation, but it would be misleading to suggest that voter participation rates would be greatly improved if public funding were provided or if spending in House races were limited. If reform is to increase (or decrease) level of voter participation in House elections, it will have to do so by some means other than by simply altering the absolute levels of spending in congressional campaigns. More than likely, to increase voter participation one would have to alter the nature of congressional campaigns, not simply the volume of money spent.

CONCLUSION

Low voter participation continues to be the embarrassment of American democracy. The 1996 elections, in which less than 50 percent of the eligible electorate bothered casting a ballot despite the addition of millions of voters through lessened registration requirements, are simply the latest symptom of a larger democratic malaise infecting the U.S. polity. While political scientists and other analysts have proven to be skilled in diagnostics, they have been less skilled in providing cures. Pointing to the empirical link between campaign spending and voter participation, scholars have argued that any form of public financing that involves spending limits would adversely impact citizen participation. In this chapter, we attempt to explain why such a view is, at best, misguided. While campaign spending may stimulate voter turnout, there is little reason to believe that increases in spending will automatically trigger increases in voter participation. As has been noted in recent research, the mobilizing effects of candidate campaign spending are largely contingent upon (1) the nature of the message (Ansolabehere et al. 1994), (2) the source of the spending; that is, incumbent versus challenger spending (Jackson 1993, 1997), and (3) the electoral context (Jackson 1997). Based on the evidence presented in this chapter, there is little reason to believe that campaign finance reform would significantly reduce aggregate district voter turnout.

The evidence also provides little reason to believe that reform would work to reconnect citizens to the political process. In this respect, reforms involving various versions of public financing appear to have only a marginal positive impact on aggregate voter participation rates. Yet there are at least a couple of reasons to be optimistic about the potential of significant campaign finance reform to enhance voter participation. First, as Verba, Schlozman, and Brady (1995, 531) observe, the "puzzle of participation" may reflect the increasing importance of money as a political resource. As these authors write, "it seems clear that making financial contributions has assumed greater prominence in the mix of citizen activities. Among activities, contributing is far from the most rewarding; compared with other activists, contributors garner relatively few gratifications, especially of the social sort, and are less likely to feel that what they did had an impact. . . . At the same time, the increasing importance of contributing as a form of participation is likely to feed public dissatisfaction with politics." A system of campaign finance based in large part on special interest money may also fuel public cynicism and distrust of political institutions, which in turn adversely affects citizen participation.

Second, campaign spending may be a poor substitute for actual mobilization efforts. Incumbents, in particular, are prone to engage in campaign spending that has little connection to communicating with, or mobilizing, voters (Morris and Gamache 1994; Fritz and Morris 1992). As a result, mobilization efforts may provide a potentially effective means of reconnecting citizens to the political process, even if the effect of campaign spending appears to be relatively marginal. In chapter 6, we explore this possibility further by examining the effect of various forms of political mobilization on individual participation decisions.

NOTES

1. Jack H. Nagel and John E. McNulty (1996) contend that the conventional wisdom that higher turnout helps Democratic candidates was true outside the South prior to 1964 but that since 1964 the effects of turnout on electoral outcomes have been insignificant.

2. Voter roll-off is defined as the difference between the percentage of voters casting a ballot for president and the percentage casting a ballot for the Senate.

3. Raymond E. Wolfinger and Steven J. Rosenstone (1980), for example, estimate that voter turnout would increase by 10 percent if all registration requirements were removed.

4. In 1924, turnout of eligible voters was 48.90 percent; in 1996, it was 49.03 percent.

5. The revisions to the theory hold that absolute levels of turnout are less important than how short-term national political trends shape the participation rates of partisan adherents and the vote choice of independent voters. According to James

Campbell (1991), partisans advantaged by short-term national trends turn out at higher rates than partisans disadvantaged by these trends.

6. While the general election was relatively noncompetitive, the primary was more closely contested. Green won the primary with only 55 percent of the vote.

7. In 1994, the standard deviation was 7.94, while in 1996 it was 9.69.

8. While the effects are consistently positive, they are not consistently significant at the .05 level.

Chapter Six

The Question of Voter Turnout, Part II

In the previous chapter, we argue that changes in the current system of campaign financing would only marginally affect aggregate, districtwide voter turnout. Overall, even drastic changes in campaign finance laws appear to have little substantive effect on the total number of people voting across congressional districts. Recall, however, that scholars frequently argue that campaign mobilization efforts by candidates and political parties are an important factor in generating greater voter turnout. But how can voter mobilization efforts be important if candidate spending only marginally affects voter participation rates? Surely, mobilization efforts, even if these efforts rely primarily on campaign volunteers, cost candidates and political parties something. The answer to the question lies in understanding the different ways that candidates and political parties seek to mobilize individual voters. Candidate spending does not automatically translate into a mobilization effort. Nor for that matter are all forms of mobilization equally effective at stimulating individual participation. To make this latter point as clear as possible, we begin by considering the difference between old-style, machine politics and new-style, electronic politics.

OLD-STYLE POLITICS AND THE PARTY MACHINE

At one point in American history political parties were very efficient at persuading people to vote. Political parties were well organized, well funded, and relevant to the everyday lives of the American people. Voting records from the late 1800s show that turnout rates in presidential elections were much higher than today due in large part to the effective mobilization efforts of political parties. For example, in his classic account of the Daley party machine in Chicago, the late Mike Royko (1971, 91) observed that the party machine "cracked the whip and the vote poured out. The blacks went in, pulled the lever, came out, and got their chickens. The Skid Row

107

winos, shaky with the bars being closed for the election, came out and got their bottles of muscatel. The elderly were marched wheezing out of their nursing homes, the low-income whites were watched by the precinct captains as they left for work in the morning and reminded that they had to stop at the polling place. . . . It wasn't a landslide, but the 100,000 vote spread was decisive. The machine had delivered as expected."

As the quotation by Royko graphically illustrates, party organizations effectively mobilized the electorate by providing citizens with real, tangible rewards in return for their participation. Even in the absence of outright vote buying, party organizations were expected to get people to the polls. During the golden age of party organizations, machines "controlled campaigns for public office—they held rallies, did door to door canvassing, and got the voters to the polls" (Sorauf 1992, 25). But the party mobilization efforts did more than simply get out the vote; they also connected citizens to the political system. As Joel Silbey (1997, 13–14) observes, "in addition to providing mediating, disciplining, and expressive functions, as important as each was, parties established an intimate relationship between the voters and the political process, between individual persons and the leadership at every level. In a society devoid of large-scale and intrusive institutions of national authority, parties brought people and the political system together. . . . As a result of these activities, parties successfully mobilized an expanding electorate. Turnout at the polls on succeeding election days soared to heights rarely seen before, and never with such constancy and regularity."

In fact, the present discontent with American politics, Silbey believes, has its roots in the decline of political parties beginning in the Progressive era in the 1890s. As Silbey (24) contends, "voters found themselves cut off from those institutions that had effectively organized and directed their behavior." Progressives attacked political party organizations as corrupt institutions that limited effective citizen participation. The Progressives, in this respect, envisioned a cleaner political world in which citizens would participate without coercion or material inducement. While Progressive charges of corruption were accurate, eliminating party machine corruption also eliminated many of the material incentives driving individual participation. More broadly, by reducing party incentives to devote scarce resources to get-out-the-vote campaigns, they ultimately severed personal relationships between citizens and the political process.

NEW-STYLE POLITICS AND THE INFORMATION AGE

While the description of politics as controlled by party machines may be overstated (Sorauf 1992), it is beyond question that political parties play less of a role in electoral politics than they did in the past. An equally unassailable proposition is that politics has become increasingly professionalized. As Herbert E. Alexander (1992, 161) observes, "Even candidates for state legislatures and city councils now hire pollsters, direct mail consultants, and fund-raisers."

Increasingly, campaigns are media-oriented affairs with little interest in direct, personal communication with voters. Writing about Michael Huffington's 1994 California Senate campaign, W. Lance Bennett (1996, 15) notes that "win or lose, the campaign stands as an exemplar of the contemporary consultant's chapter and verse: keep voters and reporters at maximum distance and administer a measured daily dosage of commercial imagery that pushes the fear buttons against the opponent, while offering the candidate as a safe, even amorphous alternative." While one might take issue with Bennett's description of the Huffington campaign, the increased professionalization of politics as well as the media-centered nature of subpresidential campaigns are beyond dispute. Though the process was gradual rather than abrupt, in the wake of television, politics changed from something people participated in to something people watched. This view is expressed by Stephen Ansolabehere, Roy Behr, and Shanto Iyengar (1993, 1) in their introduction to *The Media Game*, in which the authors observe that "once upon a time politicians communicated directly with their constituents. They gave speeches—directly to those they governed. They delivered their messages personally, through newspapers controlled by their political parties, or leaflets passed out by their supporters. They met and spoke directly with the citizens they represented. . . . That day no longer exists. Politicians still give speeches, but few Americans listen to them. Members of Congress still send out vast amounts of information and newsletters (at the taxpayers' expense), but few constituents bother to read them."

Political parties, which once served a primary role in the electoral process as an intermediary between voters and governing institutions, increasingly play a secondary, service role. Instead of mobilizing voters, parties direct the bulk of their efforts at mobilizing contributors to finance increasingly expensive, media-oriented political campaigns. Despite their ability to adapt to the new electoral environment, political parties have had only limited success in transferring their fund-raising abilities into some semblance of control over the electoral process. In part, this is because political parties have ridden on the crest of a rising tide of campaign money. They did not create the tide, nor do they control it. At times, however, the parties have been able to use this wave of money to serve partisan, political, and organizational interests.

In terms of their mobilization efforts, contemporary political parties are much more strategic in their get-out-the-vote appeals. In fact, according to

Steven J. Rosenstone and John Mark Hansen (1993), since the late 1950s political parties have become much more efficient in their mobilization and recruitment efforts. As these authors observe, "Constrained by limited money, limited time, and finite other resources, [the parties] target their efforts and time their efforts carefully. Anxious to involve the greatest number of the right people with the least amount of expense, they mobilize people who are known to them, who are well placed in social networks, whose actions are effective, and who are likely to act" (162). In this respect, party mobilization efforts in the 1990s differ dramatically from party mobilization efforts in previous time periods. In contemporary politics, political parties find themselves struggling with limited resources and time. Consequently, contemporary political parties are much less able to mobilize large segments of the population into political activity. In addition, mobilization efforts are becoming more and more focused on mass appeals through television and radio announcements rather than personal and direct contact. As a result of these changes, only about one in four Americans are contacted directly by either the Democratic or the Republican Party during a typical American election (ibid.).

Despite the changes in the process of party mobilization over time, one constant remains: direct personal contact by political party officials is often sufficient to mobilize people into the political process. According to Rosenstone and Hansen (1993, 161), "The bottom line . . . is very simple. People participate in electoral politics because someone encourages or inspires them to take part."

POLITICAL MOBILIZATION AND INDIVIDUAL PARTICIPATION

Recall from the previous chapter that many scholars argue that the reason for such low voter turnout in America is best explained by the failure of political parties to mobilize voters (Rosenstone and Hansen 1993). Of course, mobilization may take several different forms. For example, direct mobilization (such as personal contact) could take the form of simply giving a constituent a phone call to remind him or her about the election or, perhaps, even providing transportation for someone who might otherwise be unable to get to the polls. On the other hand, mobilization may be indirect, such as mass appeals through television commercials, radio speeches, or press releases. A fundamental difference between direct and indirect mobilization is that direct mobilization makes a specific effort toward a particular individual or household while indirect mobilization makes blanket appeals to many constituents simultaneously.

From a campaign standpoint, indirect mobilization (such as press releases or television commercials) may be a more efficient means of reaching constituents—especially in the sense that they permit candidates to reach many people concurrently. Moreover, if candidates and those directing their campaigns behave rationally, they will invest fewer resources (and therefore, less interest) in direct voter mobilization. In this respect, the task of the modern professional campaign is not to generate the highest turnout possible but to ensure that their candidate receives a plurality of the vote. In other words, the collective good of a participatory democracy is often sacrificed for the short-term candidate and party self-interest in winning elective office. As a result, parties and candidates generally focus their mobilization efforts on indirect but cost-efficient means of communication that, ideally, serve the dual purpose of mobilizing supporters while also converting existing voters.

Yet, if these indirect methods of mobilization (that is, mass appeals) are more cost-effective in terms of percentage of vote, they are less effective than direct mobilization (personal contact) at stimulating participation. Rosenstone and Hansen (1993) demonstrate that people who are personally contacted by a political party or candidate are much more likely to vote in the next election than are those individuals who are not contacted. Peter W. Weilhouwer and Brad Lockerbie (1994) show evidence that the effects of direct personal contact may, in fact, be growing in recent years. As people have lost trust in government officials and have begun to feel more out of touch with Washington, a personal contact from a political party official may be just enough of a boost to motivate people to take part in the election. As we explore in chapter 7, personal contacts may also have more enduring effects on political participation by forging the basis of a psychological attachment between citizens and government.

While many voters may have strong and enduring attachments to political parties, rendering party contact a powerful form of mobilization, contact from political candidates themselves may also be sufficient to entice citizens into the electoral arena (Verba, Schlozman, and Brady 1995). Since contact by political parties and candidates are personal and direct appeals for participation, they are very likely to have a comparatively large influence in mobilizing political participation. In addition, because candidates and parties are likely to contact citizens in a strategic manner, by recruiting those people who are likely supporters or people who are likely participants, contact by these political actors is likely to be successful (Rosenstone and Hansen 1993; Verba, Schlozman, and Brady 1995).

Despite these arguments, some scholars argue that indirect mobilization (mass appeals) also increases the probability that individuals will turn out and vote (Caldeira, Patterson, and Markko 1985; Jackson 1993, 1996a, 1996b, 1997; Goidel and Shields 1994). These studies often simply use the amount of campaign spending by a candidate as an indication of the candidate's overall mobilization efforts. While the overall amount of spending by a particular candidate includes money spent on both direct and indirect mobilization, the assumption is that most of this money was strategically spent on indirect mobilization (or mass appeals) such as television spots or radio ads. Based on such analyses, scholars argue that reductions in campaign spending would likely result in fewer individuals mobilized and recruited into political activity (Teixeira 1996).

Nevertheless, there are several reasons to expect campaign spending to be less important than direct (personal) mobilization for increasing voter turnout. First, campaign money spent on television advertisements is a very broad and indirect method of recruiting citizens compared to more direct personal contact from a political party official—who may remind citizens of the personal importance of the election, the issues involved and at stake in the election, and even assistance in reaching voting sites. Second, there is mounting evidence that many forms of negative television advertising decrease, rather than promote, individual-level turnout decisions (Ansolabehere et al. 1994). And third, there is substantial evidence that a great deal of candidate resources are spent in areas and on items that do little to increase citizen participation, such as campaign office furniture (Morris and Gamache 1994; Fritz and Morris 1992).

INDIVIDUAL PARTICIPATION

While the arguments based on aggregate district-level data in the previous chapter provide convincing evidence that the effects of mobilization efforts are contingent on both type of candidate spending and candidate partisanship, the data are limited in their ability to show how different forms of campaign mobilization efforts influence individual voting decisions. More specifically, aggregate district-level data do not permit us to test the relative importance of direct versus indirect mobilization efforts for specific individuals. To examine which form of mobilization—direct personal contact versus indirect mass appeals—has the greatest impact on the probability that a particular citizen will vote, we combined the 1994 and 1996 National Election Studies surveys with campaign finance data from each congressional district.

One of the shortcomings with previous research on political participation is the inconsistency in the way scholars measure campaign mobilization. In fact, most previous studies do not differentiate between direct and indirect forms of mobilization. Some research measures campaign mobilization efforts in terms of direct candidate and party contact (Weilhouwer and Lockerbie 1994; Rosenstone and Hansen 1993), while other works rely on more indirect measures such as candidate spending or electoral competitiveness (Jackson 1993, 1997). Either approach has its shortcomings.

Relying solely on candidate or party contact fails to indicate how the general campaign environment might affect voter participation. Relying solely on aggregate measures such as campaign spending and electoral competitiveness, on the other hand, fails to account for individual differences in exposure to campaign messages. Moreover, by analyzing the effects of only selected indicators of campaign mobilization, past research is limited in its ability to provide a clear indication of the relative importance of direct versus indirect mobilization efforts.

In the remaining sections of this chapter, we consider the effects of indirect and direct mobilization efforts on individual decisions to vote and on individual decisions to participate in the political process in some manner other than voting, including whether an individual attempted to persuade someone concerning their vote; wore a political button; attended a political meeting; worked for a political party or candidate; discussed politics with family or friends; or gave money to a political party, candidate, or group. In our attempt to estimate the effects of campaign spending and contact on individual participation decisions, we take into account other factors generally associated with participation decisions (age, education, registration requirements, and so on). A complete description of the model and the statistical analysis is provided in appendix C. For ease of presentation, however, we present the results graphically.

Participation in the 1994 Republican Revolution

Figures 6.1 and 6.2 show the effects of Democratic and Republican candidate spending and voter contact on the probability that an individual voted during the 1994 congressional elections. There is a tremendous difference between the probabilities that an individual voted depending on whether that person was contacted, either by a candidate or by the party. In fact, the average person in 1994 had a very good probability of voting if he or she were contacted and a rather low probability of voting if he or she were not contacted. Direct contact is a highly effective means for stimulating voter participation, particularly during a midterm election year.

But what about candidate spending? If we look at the entire range of spending, we see that there is little payoff for spending large amounts of money—at least in terms of stimulating individual participation. In fact, there was very little change in the probability that the average person voted in the 1994 elections, whether a candidate spent $10,000 or more than $2 million. Apparently, increasing candidate spending is simply not a very effective means of increasing individual participation. During the "Republican year" of 1994, while spending by Republican candidates did increase the probability that the average person would vote during the 1994 elections, the effects were very small: the probability of voting ranges from .37

Figure 6.1   Effect of Democratic Candidate Spending on Individual Voter Turnout, 1994

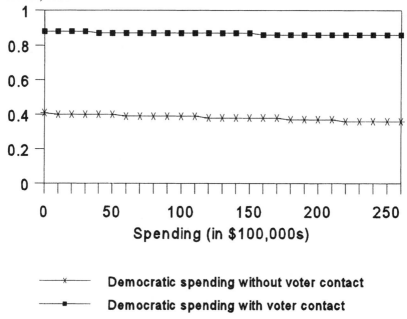

when the Republican candidate spent nothing to .58 when the Republican candidate spent just under $5 million. In other words, in 1994 it took nearly $5 million to raise the probability of voting for the average person from .38 to .58. Comparatively, even in a scenario in which the Republican candidate spent only $1,000, if the average person was personally contacted, the probability that this person would vote was .86.

Moving beyond voting, we see very similar patterns in figures 6.3 and 6.4, which depict the effects of spending and contact on the probability that the average person in 1994 engaged in any political activity other than voting. Again, the main point to be taken from these figures is that direct mobilization in the form of personal contact from a political party or a political candidate greatly increased the probability that the average person became politically active during the 1994 elections. The effects of campaign spending had comparatively meager influences on increasing the probability that the average person participated in the 1994 elections.[1]

The 1996 Status Quo Election

The results of the 1996 election provide even more conclusive evidence that the effects of campaign spending are not nearly as important as candi-

Figure 6.2   Effect of Republican Candidate Spending on Individual Voter Turnout, 1994

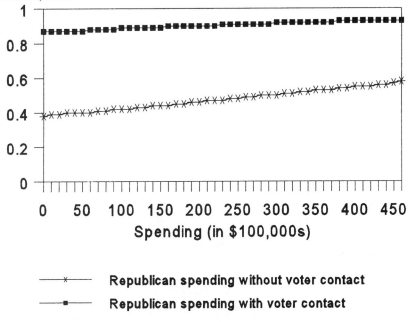

Republican spending without voter contact

Republican spending with voter contact

date and political party contact as agents of individual mobilization. Figures 6.5 and 6.6 depict the effects of spending and contact on the probability of voter turnout for the average person in the 1996 election. In some ways, the results are similar to those in the 1994 elections. The effects of candidate and political party contact substantially increased the probability that the average person voted in the 1996 elections. Close comparison of these figures with the figures for the 1994 election, however, reveals that the average person had a greater probability of voting in 1996 at every level of campaign spending. In other words, during a presidential election, the average person is more likely to vote than during a midterm election. The hype and drama of the presidential election year were apparently enough to boost the probability of voter turnout regardless of any other factor.

The effects of congressional campaign spending during the 1996 presidential election year were actually negative—though statistically insignificant. According to figure 6.5, the average person who was not contacted by a political party or candidate had about an .81 probability of voting if the Democratic candidate spent $1,000 but a probability of .73 if the Democratic candidate spent $2,500,000. Similar results are shown in figure 6.6, illustrating the effects of Republican spending.

Figure 6.3 Effect of Democratic Candidate Spending on Other Voter Political Activity, 1994

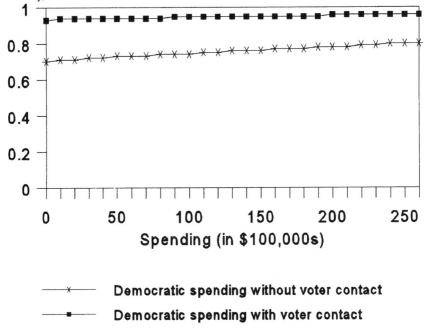

Figures 6.7 and 6.8 illustrate the effects of contact and candidate spending on political participation other than voting. Again, candidate spending had little impact on the probability that the average person engaged in any political act beyond voting. More direct forms of political mobilization, such as candidate and political party contact, had a much greater impact on increased probability of participation beyond voting than did congressional campaign spending. To put these results into perspective, consider that even if congressional campaign spending was more than $4 million, the predicted probability of political activity for the average person in 1996 was still not as high as if the person had been personally contacted by a political party or candidate.

To place these results into perspective, consider the 1996 election in Indiana's Ninth Congressional District featuring a rematch between incumbent Lee Hamilton and challenger Jean Leising. If we look specifically at the average voter in the race in which both candidates spent nearly $600,000, the average person had a probability of .79 of participating in the election if they were not personally contacted. If, however, the average person was personally contacted and both candidates spent only $100,000, the probability that they would have participated in the election was .93.

Figure 6.4   Effect of Republican Candidate Spending on Other Voter Political Activity, 1994

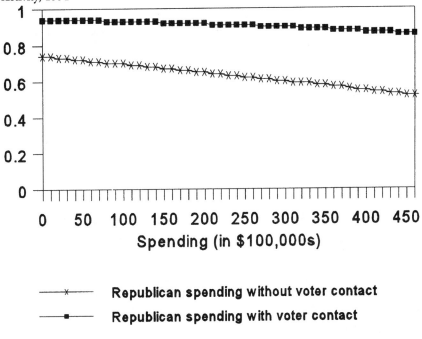

---×--- **Republican spending without voter contact**

---■--- **Republican spending with voter contact**

As this example illustrates, in terms of individual participation, candidate expenditures matter much less than party or candidate contact.

CONCLUSION

In this chapter, we present evidence that direct mobilization efforts (personal contact from a party or a candidate) have a much more profound effect on individual participation than indirect forms (that is, simply measured as overall campaign spending). To the extent that reform is geared toward increasing voter participation, the answer seems clear. Increasing personal contact between citizens and political parties and candidates serves as a powerful stimulus for individual participation. While such efforts may cost money, money alone is insufficient to increase voter participation. In fact, simply increasing the amount of money flowing into political campaigns is as likely to reduce as to increase voter participation. Increased campaign spending may only add fuel to public perceptions that politics is corrupt, that money buys political influence, and that elections are for sale

Figure 6.5   Effect of Democratic Candidate Spending on Individual Voter Turnout, 1996

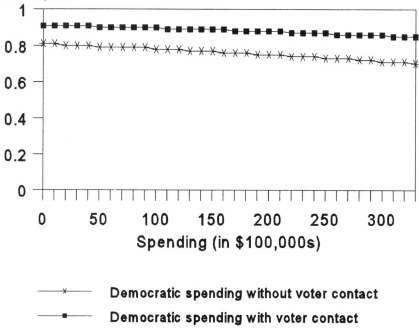

Spending (in $100,000s)

―――×――― **Democratic spending without voter contact**
―――■――― **Democratic spending with voter contact**

to the highest bidder. Whether these perceptions are accurate is largely irrelevant; the perception of corruption is real, as is the cynicism it fuels.[2]

Given the professional nature of modern campaigns, there is little reason to believe that more money will translate into greater contact between citizens and elected officials. Effective media campaigns, particularly negative campaigns, win elections, even if they fail to generate citizen participation. Put simply, in the world of professional politics, the short-term interest in winning elections is considerably more important than long-term attachments to the political system. Unless increased spending by candidates is spent largely (or exclusively) on direct mobilization efforts (a highly dubious assumption), there appears to be little reason to expect increased participation resulting from increased candidate expenditures.

NOTES

1. The effects are very similar if we look at the total spending rather than breaking spending down into the Republican and Democratic categories.

2. There is an irony in the view that perceptions of corruption drive down voter

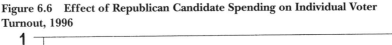

Figure 6.6   Effect of Republican Candidate Spending on Individual Voter Turnout, 1996

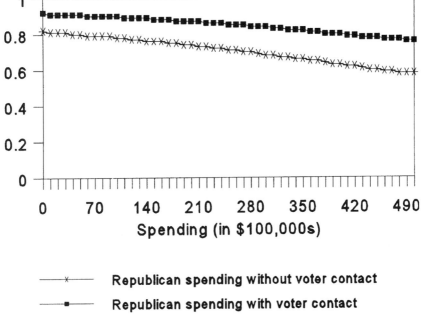

participation. Historically, the corrupt, party-centered eras of American politics have also been eras of intense citizen participation. Corruption, at least those forms directed at individual citizens, such as vote buying, may serve to enhance citizen participation. The corruption in contemporary politics drives down participation because it is elite centered and institutionalized (Sabato and Simpson 1996).

Figure 6.7   Effect of Democratic Candidate Spending on Other Voter Political
Activity, 1996

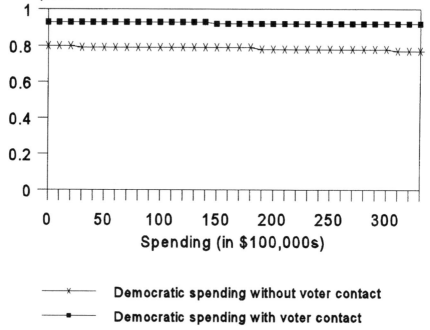

Figure 6.8   Effect of Republican Candidate Spending on Other Voter Political Activity, 1996

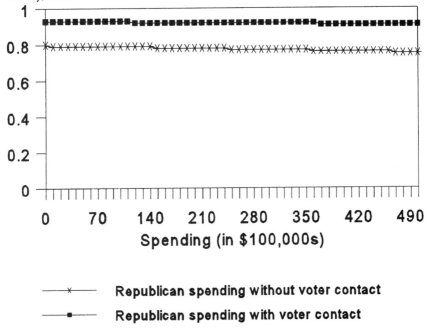

Chapter Seven

Democracy and Citizen Involvement

Campaign Spending and Cognitive Engagement

Nothing strikes the student of public opinion and democracy more forcefully than the paucity of information most people possess about politics.

—John A. Ferejohn

One of the most widely noted characteristics of United States House elections involves the dearth of information that most citizens possess when casting ballots for congressional candidates. In 1994, for example, only 22 percent of respondents were able to recall the name of the challenger in a contested House race (Jacobson 1997b). While respondents were more successful in recalling (and recognizing) incumbent and open-seat candidates, the amount of information voters possess in the average House election can be described as minimal, at best (see, for example, Jacobson 1997b; Mann 1978; Abramowitz 1980; Hinckley 1980). According to Michael X. Delli Carpini and Scott Keeter (1996, 70), only 25 percent of Americans in 1991 knew the length of a Senate term, while only 48 percent of Americans with a high school diploma (but no further education) were able to place congressional candidates on a liberal or conservative scale (190). The paucity of information that most Americans possess about fundamental aspects of American politics is, indeed, quite low. Consider the following description of the informational levels of the America polity:

> The most commonly known fact about George Bush's opinions while he was president was that he hated broccoli. During the 1992 presidential campaign 89 percent of the public knew that Vice President Quayle was feuding with the television character Murphy Brown, but only 19 percent could characterize Bill Clinton's record on the environment. Also, during that campaign 86 percent of the public knew that the Bushs' dog was named Millie, yet only 15 percent knew that both presidential candidates supported the death penalty.

Judge Wapner (host of the television series *The People's Court*) was identified by more people than were Chief Justices Burger or Rehnquist. More people know John Lennon than Karl Marx, or know Bill Cosby than either of their U.S. Senators. More people know who said "What's up Doc," "Hi Yo Silver," or "Come up and see me sometime" than "Give me liberty or give me death," "The only thing we have to fear is fear itself," or "Speak softly and carry a big stick." More people knew that Pete Rose was accused of gambling than could name any of the five U.S. senators accused of unethical conduct in the savings and loan scandal (Delli Carpini and Keeter 1996, 101).

Such findings concerning how little the average citizens knows (or cares) about politics have caused great concern among some political scientists, who doubt if such poorly informed citizens can fully perform their democratic obligations. Can citizens hold elected officials accountable for their actions if they do not even know who the officials are? If the people are not aware of what political elites are doing, can elites do whatever they want? If a representative lies to constituents, will constituents ever know? Such questions cause great concern for anyone who cares about democracy in America and the future of American politics.

CAN GOVERNMENT STILL FUNCTION WITHOUT INFORMED CITIZENS?

A Positive Answer from Heuristic Models

From the standpoint of democratic theory, scholars have found some relief in arguments that, through the use of voting cues and other heuristics, citizens are able to make reasonable decisions without much information (see, for example, Ferejohn and Kuklinski 1990; Page and Shapiro 1992; Popkin 1991; Sniderman, Brody, and Tetlock 1991). In other words, while the average citizen may not know what Bill Clinton's position is on, say, the environment, citizens can rely on their knowledge that Bill Clinton is a Democrat and then infer Clinton's issue opinion. This process may be fraught with mistakes, and citizen inferences may be incorrect, but many scholars argue that decisions based on inferences are not necessarily decisions made out of complete ignorance.

One interesting and important distinction made in this literature is between "on-line" and "memory-based" decision-making strategies. According to the on-line perspective, citizens may make relatively informed voting decisions with limited accessible information by maintaining on-line, or impression-driven, evaluations of political candidates but discarding more detailed candidate- and issue-oriented information (Lodge, McGraw, and

Stroh 1989; Lodge, Steenbergen, and Brau 1995). Despite mounds of survey evidence chronicling the informational deficiencies of the average voter (see, for example, Delli Carpini and Keeter 1991, 1996), this perspective holds that the average voter ultimately makes relatively sound and rational electoral decisions (Ferejohn and Kuklinski 1990; Fiorina 1990). In other words, this perspective argues that people keep a current and up-to-date tally of whether or not they "like/hate" or "approve/disapprove" of a particular policy or candidate. Each time the person receives new information concerning this policy or candidate, the tally is updated. More often than not, the specific piece of information used to update the overall evaluation is discarded from memory.

For example, suppose that a woman learns from a friend, or from a television speech, or from the nightly news, that Bill Clinton is strongly in favor of reforming health care in America. The woman may then update her "running evaluation" of Bill Clinton with this new information. If she agrees with Clinton's position, then her evaluation of him becomes more positive. According to this perspective, the updated, and now more positive, evaluation of Bill Clinton will remain in her long-term memory, but the specific information about Bill Clinton's health care policy position may or may not be stored in her long-term memory. If the woman does not believe that this specific information is necessary to memorize, she simply discards the specific information about the health care issue. If the woman is asked several months later about Bill Clinton's positions on health care, she may or may not remember. After all, the relevant update she learned from this specific information was efficiently stored in a running evaluation of Clinton, which is current and accurate.

Of course, such theories of information processing do not "save" democracy. The result is still a very poorly informed citizenry making decisions based on inferences and heuristics that may or may not be entirely accurate. While the models of on-line thinking make a convincing argument that citizens may be rational actors who efficiently store some information in summary form while tossing out the specifics, it does not prevent abuses by elites, who may attempt to misinform or mislead citizens relying on highly subjective heuristics. As Delli Carpini and Ketter argue (1996, 53), "In the end, the real value of the heuristic model [of decision making] is in demonstrating that a citizen need not know everything about a particular issue to reach a decision of some kind. It also points to the kind of proximate information that citizens can and do use in making certain kinds of decisions. However, demonstrating that certain heuristics are used is not the same as demonstrating that they are the best—or even modestly effective—decision rules. Nor does it eliminate the value of an informed citizenry."

An Answer Based on Elite Behavior

Research along a slightly different vein argues that the decision-making efforts of the average voter are facilitated by the actions of elite, strategic, political actors. According to Gary C. Jacobson and Samuel Kernell (1983), the actions of strategic actors, such as potential candidates and contributors, help to provide a mechanism of collective accountability (see also Jacobson 1989) even if voters remain relatively uninformed. According to this literature, higher quality candidates run when incumbent candidates are vulnerable to electoral defeat (see, for example, Krasno 1994; Krasno and Green 1988; Bond, Covington, and Fleisher 1985; Bianco 1984). As a result, incumbent officeholders are held accountable, at least by politically sophisticated elites, even if the average citizen has very little knowledge about their performance in office.

While these arguments may ease concerns that government in America can still function without an extremely informed citizenry, such a process is hardly optimal. In fact, taken to the extreme, it is a system in which only a few highly sophisticated people act on behalf of the entire polity, serve as the primary representatives of the polity, and serve as the only pool of future political leaders. Can such an elitist system be accurately called a democratic government? Of course, there are many perspectives on what democracy means, entails, and expects, but a democracy by only a few sophisticated and enlightened people is not the democracy typically equated with universal suffrage, political involvement, or government by and for the people (see Delli Carpini and Keeter 1996 for more on this topic).

Empirical Answers

In the most comprehensive treatment to date of the role of political knowledge in democratic government and American politics, Delli Carpini and Keeter (1996, 269) conclude that while the overall levels of political knowledge among the American public are dramatically low, "they are high enough among some segments of the population, and on some topics, to foster optimism about democratic possibilities." However, their optimism concerning the future of American democracy is somewhat tempered by the troubling nature of the socioeconomic class biases associated with political knowledge—the most knowledgeable citizens are those with the most money, education, and resources. In the end they conclude, "The fundamental question is not if the American system is democratic, but how democratic it is and for whom. In the end . . . for citizens who are the most informed, democracy works much as intended, while for those who are the most uninformed, democracy is a tragedy or a farce" (60). Ultimately, then, we are left with a system of government that works, either through citizens using heuristics or through strategic elite behavior, but it is far from what most people would expect from democratic governance. Further, given the large biases across levels of political sophistication among people in America, we are left with the question of whether the levels of political awareness in America can be improved.

CAN CITIZEN INFORMATION ABOUT POLITICS BE INCREASED?

If the literature is relatively successful in explaining how the system continues to work despite an uninformed electorate, it is less successful in explaining the variation in information levels over time and across electoral contexts. The few investigations that have been done focus largely on (1) individual rather than political explanations of election and candidate specific information (but see Franklin 1991; Dalager 1996); (2) behavioral differences between informed and uninformed citizens (Luskin and Globetti 1996; Bartels 1996); or (3) neutral political knowledge rather than election and candidate-specific learning (Zaller 1992; but see Delli Carpini and Keeter 1996). Perhaps even more surprising is that considerably less emphasis has been placed on how the electoral process may affect the amount of information that citizens possess about politics as well as their attentiveness to and motivation for acquiring new information.

A Review of the Literature

Research examining individual information in House elections generally focuses either on individual characteristics (that is, education) that lead people to be more informed about the electoral process or on candidate spending—under the assumption that greater spending leads to a more informed electorate. Both approaches, we believe, are flawed. First, while personal characteristics provide a powerful explanation of individual information levels, they cannot explain changes in information about candidates over time or across electoral contexts. As Robert Huckfeldt and John Sprague (1990, 23) observe, "The success of information transmission depends fundamentally upon the motivation of the receiver, and motivation responds to the systematic dynamic of politics and social structure." Individual explanations of political information are essentially apolitical. More-educated respondents are more informed about the candidates and issues in an election, while less-educated respondents are less informed. While it may seem that the only solution to an uninformed electorate is more education, such a statement does not appear to be supported by the evidence. Despite an increasingly educated citizenry, and despite technological advances that make information more readily accessible, information about politics appears to be either decreasing or staying at the same level (Jacobson 1997b; Bennett 1988, 1995; but see also Dalton 1996).

Second, within the congressional election literature, it is often assumed that spending is equated with increased voter information. In this respect, studies routinely demonstrate that increased spending is associated with greater candidate familiarity (see, for example, Jacobson 1997b; Mann 1978; Abramowitz 1980; Hinckley 1980). Along similar lines, research into political advertising finds that citizens learn more from political ads than they do from television news (Brians and Wattenberg 1996; Patterson and McClure 1976). Taken together, these findings have led to the conclusion that limiting spending in congressional elections would ultimately lower the amount of information possessed by the average voter. This is a refrain that is also heard among politicians, such as Newt Gingrich, who complain that the electoral process suffers not when too much money is spent on elections but when not enough money is spent. The relationship between candidate spending and citizen information is not, however, as simple as one might assume. While it is true that, at the individual level, candidate familiarity is associated with candidate spending, at the aggregate level, increases in candidate spending are not associated with increases in candidate familiarity over time (Jacobson 1997b, 94). In any specific election, and given any specific person (that is, the individual level), increases in campaign spending are likely to increase candidate familiarity. However, looking not at a specific individual but at the national average (that is, the aggregate level), as campaign spending has drastically risen since the 1950s, there has not been an increase over the same period among the American public in either their familiarity with candidates or their political sophistication.

In addition, while political ads may increase information about candidates, they may also obscure information or distort the record of an opponent. As Stephen Ansolabehere and colleagues (1994, 829) note, "campaigns can be either mobilizing or demobilizing events, *depending on the nature of the messages they generate.*" Extending this logic, if negative messages demobilize citizen participation, they may also lessen an individual's receptivity to and motivation for acquiring new information about the candidates in a given election. Along these lines, Charles H. Franklin (1991) observes that, depending on candidate campaign strategy, campaigns can either clarify or obscure candidate issue stances in U.S. Senate elections. "The extent to which elections help voters clarify their perceptions of the candidates thus rests substantially on the candidates' political judgments about effective electoral strategy . . . we cannot rely on competitive elections alone to produce an informed electorate" (1210).

Finally, according to Anthony Downs (1957), rational candidates will move toward the position of the median voter in hopes of winning electoral support. Other research indicates that candidates may have incentives to moderate policy stances or to make policy stances intentionally ambiguous (Wright and Berkman 1986; Page 1978; Shepsle 1972; but see also Enelow and Hinich 1981; Bartels 1986). From the standpoint of the average citizen, candidate spending may increase candidate recognition and may even clarify candidate issue positions, but it is just as likely to blur ideological differences between candidates. As a result, increased candidate spending may confuse rather than enlighten voters. More recent research by Jon K. Dalager (1996, 496) on voter information in Senate elections notes that "the level of campaign spending produced a surprising result. . . . As campaigns spend *less* money, the voters are more likely to know what issues are important in the campaign. . . . The increase in messages may simply increase the voters' degree of confusion over which issues were mentioned in the campaign."

Theoretically, this result fits nicely with information-processing, or heuristic decision-making, strategies. In low-spending races, citizens may make assumptions or inferences about where candidates stand based simply on political heuristics such as their partisan affiliation. Without access to any countervailing information, citizens may, for example, assume that Democratic candidates are more liberal and Republican candidates more conservative—perhaps even more so than they really are. In higher-spending races, citizens may be exposed to candidate-specific information that calls into question the use of partisan heuristics. In fact, in some races, constituents may be bombarded with some or all of the following: negative advertisements, character attacks, specific appeals on political issues, appeals to religious beliefs, and appeals to geographic or demographic relationships. As a result, they may have greater overall information, but much of it may be confusing, irrelevant, misleading, or simply lies. The result is that more information may actually serve to cloud constituent decisions.

Overall, works that argue that increased candidate spending translates into a more informed electorate assume an overly simplistic model of political communication. They assume that increased spending uniformly translates into greater information about candidates and issues in the political environment, which then somehow filters into the decision making of individual voters. This supply-side theory of political information assumes that by increasing the supply of information, political knowledge and sophistication will increase correspondingly. As Ansolabehere and colleagues (1994) argue, however, campaign money spent on negative advertising is likely to demobilize, frustrate, and alienate citizens. But what within the political context drives voters to seek new information about elections and candidates?

Direct Political Mobilization and Increased Involvement

As discussed in previous chapters, the political participation literature has increasingly stressed the importance of political mobilization (Verba,

Schlozman, and Brady 1995; Rosenstone and Hansen 1993; Jackson 1993; Weilhouwer and Lockerbie 1994). Just as mobilization efforts are required to increase voter participation in election campaigns, "cognitive mobilization" efforts may be necessary to increase political information.[1] Moreover, just as research on voter mobilization has found that one of the most effective forms of increasing voter participation involves some form of personal contact by the candidates or the political parties (Verba, Schlozman, and Brady 1995; Rosenstone and Hansen 1993), the most effective cognitive mobilization should involve some form of personal contact. According to Steven J. Rosenstone and John Mark Hansen (1993, 174, 177),

> contact with political parties promotes participation by several different routes. Contact with party workers, perhaps, reshapes people's perception and changes people's attitudes about the parties, the candidates, the election, and the efficacy of political action. By this line of reasoning, party appeals for support deepen citizens' affection for the parties and their candidates. They elevate voters' concern about the outcome of the election. They frame people's perceptions about the closeness of elections and the need for personal involvement. They enhance citizens' belief in their own political efficacy. Mobilization by political parties, in this view, works indirectly. It fosters perceptions and beliefs that promote political involvement. . . . Party mobilization is a powerful inducement to participation in electoral politics. By subsidizing information and by creating social connections, political campaigns lower the costs and increase the benefits of voting, persuading, volunteering, and contributing.

In summary, while some argue that candidate spending may increase an individual's familiarity with House candidates, there are several reasons to expect that some forms of campaign spending, especially those spent on negative campaign advertisements, are likely to have just the opposite effect.

INFORMATION, INTEREST, AND CANDIDATE SPENDING, 1994 AND 1996

If candidate spending truly informs and engages individual citizens in the electoral process, we would expect citizens in congressional districts with higher levels of candidate spending to be (1) more informed about the congressional candidates, (2) more interested in the election, (3) more concerned about the election outcome, (4) more attentive to media reports regarding the election, and (5) better able to make ideological distinctions between congressional candidates. To test these hypotheses, we constructed several statistical models controlling for the effects of all other variables found to be relevant in past research (for example, education, income, strength of partisan affiliation). For readers interested in examining these results more closely, the full statistical models may be found in appendix D.

In tables 7.1 and 7.2, we present a summary of the findings regarding the effects of campaign spending and direct mobilization on the various indicators of "cognitive mobilization" in both the 1994 and 1996 congressional elections.[2] Each of the numbers in the table represents the impact of spending more money (table 7.1), or of being contacted (table 7.2), controlling for the effects of other variables included in the model. In other words, these numbers give us a way to compare the impact on cognitive engagement of candidate spending and party contact. The asterisks next to the coefficients indicate statistical significance. For our purposes, statistical significance means simply that we are willing to bet, based on established probabilities, that the relationship is not a result of sampling error, some other element, or chance.

Looking first at table 7.1, we see that in most cases the coefficients are not accompanied by asterisks and are not statistically significant in terms of their effects. In other words, the statistical analysis tells us that, with a few notable exceptions, campaign spending had little discernible impact on the cognitive engagement of these survey respondents. There are, however, some exceptions. In 1994, candidate spending was associated with greater candidate familiarity, regardless of the source. Both incumbents and challengers became more familiar to voters as they spent more money during the 1994 elections. In 1996, increased spending by incumbents apparently had little influence on incumbent familiarity, while increased spending by challengers in 1996 appears to have increased both incumbent and challenger familiarity.

Other significant effects of candidate spending in both 1994 and 1996 are shown in table 7.1, but these effects are negative, indicating that spending adversely affected individual cognitive engagement in the electoral process. In 1994, for example, the more the challenger spent, the more difficult it became for citizens to make ideological distinctions between candidates. In other words, increased challenger spending may have confused rather than enlightened voters. Similarly, in 1996, while challenger spending was associated with increased confidence that respondents were correctly placing challengers along an ideological continuum, it was also associated with a decrease in confidence regarding the placement of incumbents. Overall, in both 1994 and in 1996, candidate spending apparently increased candidate familiarity but may have blurred ideological distinctions between candidates. As a result, while candidate spending may have increased the information available, it may also have increased the information costs required to make an informed decision.

Looking now at table 7.2, we see the effects of direct mobilization on individual-level cognitive engagement. First, note that direct contact had a significant impact in many more instances than did campaign spending. Second, note that none of the coefficients in table 7.2 are negative. This

Table 7.1 Effects of Incumbent and Challenger Spending on Measures of Voters' Cognitive Engagement, 1994 and 1996

Dependent Variable	Incumbent Spending	Challenger Spending
1994		
Familiarity with incumbent	.10 *	-.005
Familiarity with challenger	.04	.21 ***
Concern about the outcome of a race involving an incumbent and a challenger	-.01	-.04
Interest in the campaign involving an incumbent and a challenger	-.05	-.01
Media attention to campaign involving an incumbent and a challenger	-.002	-.09
Ideological distance involving an incumbent and a challenger	.11	-.11**
Certainty of ideology of incumbent	.02	-.02
Certainty of ideology of challenger	-.11*	.07*
1996		
Familiarity with incumbent	-.016	.043**
Familiarity with challenger	-.009	.126***
Ideological distance involving an incumbent and a challenger	.786*	-.048
Certainty of ideology of incumbent	.009	-.049*
Certainty of ideology of challenger	-.007	.059**

$*p < .10; **p < .05; ***p .01.$

Table 7.2 Effects of Party and Candidate Contact on Measures of Voters' Cognitive Engagement, 1994 and 1996

Dependent Variable	Political Party Contact	Candidate Contact
1994		
Familiarity with incumbent	.15 ***	.93 ***
Familiarity with challenger	.29 ***	.17 **
Concern about outcome of a race involving an incumbent and a challenger	.24***	.44***
Interest in the campaign involving an incumbent and a challenger	.18***	.21***
Media attention to campaign involving an incumbent and a challenger	.08	.05
Ideological distance involving an incumbent and a challenger	.05	1.07***
Certainty of Ideology of incumbent	.18***	.34 ***
Certainty of ideology of challenger	.16**	.03
1996		
Familiarity with incumbent	.13***	----
Familiarity with challenger	.09	----
Ideological distance involving an incumbent and a challenger	1.46***	----
Certainty of ideology of incumbent	.25***	----
Certainty of ideology of challenger	.16**	----

$**p < .05; ***p < .01.$

means that at no time in either 1994 or 1996 did these measures of direct mobilization have a negative effect on respondents' interest in the campaign, ability to recognize the incumbent or challenger, or certainty in placing candidates on an ideological scale.

Overall, tables 7.1 and 7.2 demonstrate that while campaign spending had some modest positive effects during 1994 and 1996, it also had some modest negative effects. On the other hand, candidate and party contact had substantial positive effects in both 1994 and 1996 and apparently influenced many more aspects of cognitive engagement. In 1994, direct contact by a political candidate or party significantly increased respondents' interest in the congressional race, respondents' certainty about their ability to accurately place the candidates' on ideological scales, and respondents' concern about the outcome of the congressional race.

While these tables provide us with some idea of the different impacts of candidate spending versus direct mobilization, graphic displays of these variables provide even greater insight into how spending and contact influence voters. Rather than present a figure for each coefficient in the tables, we limit our remaining discussion to a few illustrative examples: candidate familiarity, individual certainty in placing candidates along an ideological continuum, and concern about the election outcome. We should note, however, that the figures for the other coefficients presented in the tables are similar to those presented below; we omit them only for purposes of brevity.

Candidate Familiarity

Depicted in figures 7.1 and 7.2 are the effects of incumbent spending, challenger spending, and direct mobilization efforts on respondents' familiarity with the incumbent in 1994. The scenario presented in these and the following figures is based on the average respondent in 1994 and the statistical models presented in appendix D. In figures 7.1 and 7.2 the horizontal axis represents the amount of money that a candidate spent in 1994 and the vertical axis is the degree of familiarity with the incumbent candidate. Note that in 1994, as in most races, incumbent candidates spent much more money than did challengers.

The first important finding is that the degree of familiarity with the incumbent candidates is greatly increased if the average respondent is contacted, regardless of how much money either candidate spent on the race. For example, the average respondent was more likely to be familiar with the incumbent candidate if they were contacted and the incumbent spent only $50,000 than if they were not contacted and the incumbent spent more than $5 million. Put simply, the average respondent was more familiar with the incumbent candidate if they were contacted regardless of how

Figure 7.1 Incumbent Spending and Respondent Familiarity with Incumbent, 1994

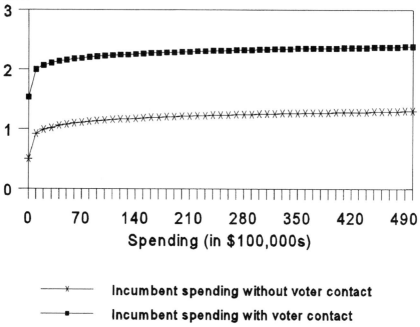

much money the incumbent candidate spent, even if the incumbent spent several million dollars.

The results presented in figures 7.3 and 7.4 show similar effects for familiarity with the challenger. These figures again show that the average respondent in 1994 was more influenced by direct mobilization than candidate spending. According to these estimates, we would expect that the average respondent in 1994 would be just as familiar with the challenger in the following two situations: (1) if the respondent was contacted and the challenger spent $500,000 or (2) if the respondent was not contacted and the challenger spent well over $3 million. As one would suspect, challengers become much more familiar to voters as their spending increases. The effects, however, were negligible when compared to the effects of direct mobilization.

Ideological Certainty

In figures 7.5 through 7.8 we present the effects of spending and contact on the certainty of the average respondent's placement of incumbent and challenger candidates in 1994. In figures 7.5 and 7.6, for example, we see

Figure 7.2 Challenger Spending and Respondent Familiarity with Incumbent, 1994

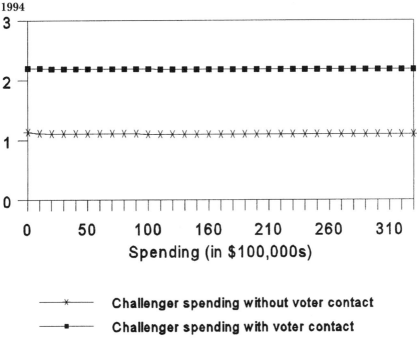

Challenger spending without voter contact

Challenger spending with voter contact

that direct mobilization through political contact increases the certainty of the average respondents' ideological placement of the incumbent candidate, while candidate spending, by either the incumbent (figure 7.5) or the challenger (figure 7.6) has little impact on incumbent ideological certainty. In fact, the lines in figures 7.5 and 7.6 are nearly flat, indicating that, as candidates spent more money in 1994, there was no discernible effect on the average respondent's ability to place the incumbent candidate on an ideological scale. It did not matter, for example, if the incumbent spent a few million dollars, the effects of spending were insignificant on the average respondent's certainty in placing the incumbent along an ideological continuum.

In contrast, respondents directly contacted by a political party or a political candidate were much more certain of the incumbent's ideological placement, regardless of whether the incumbent or challenger spent as little as $50,0000 or as much as $6 million (figures 7.7 and 7.8). The message should be clear. Direct mobilization in the form of party and candidate contact significantly increases the extent to which most citizens are familiar with the candidates in congressional races and increases the extent to which citizens are able to place the candidates on an ideological scale. Fur-

Figure 7.3   Incumbent Spending and Respondent Familiarity with Challenger, 1994

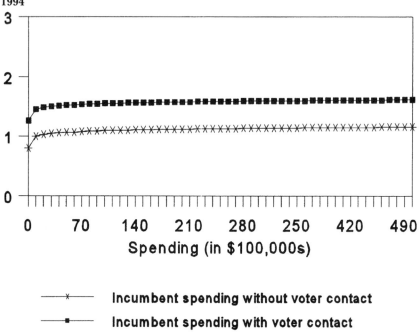

Incumbent spending without voter contact

Incumbent spending with voter contact

ther, direct mobilization appears to have a much greater effect than candidate spending. In fact, candidate spending may even have a negative effect. As illustrated, we see that the more money incumbents spent in 1994, the less certain respondents became in terms of the ideological placement of the challenger.

Concern about the Outcome

Finally, figures 7.9 and 7.10 present the effects of candidate spending versus direct mobilization on individual concern about the election outcome in 1994.[3] As the figures illustrate, as incumbent and challenger spending increased in 1994, citizen concern about the outcome of the election either remained the same or declined. On the other hand, citizens directly mobilized through political contact were much more concerned about the outcome of the election. Consider the following illustrative contrast: respondents in 1994 who were contacted, and in which total combined candidate spending was less than $100,000, were more likely to care about the outcome of the election than were respondents who were not contacted and in which total combined spending was nearly $10 million. Overall, it ap-

Figure 7.4   Challenger Spending and Respondent Familiarity with Challenger, 1994

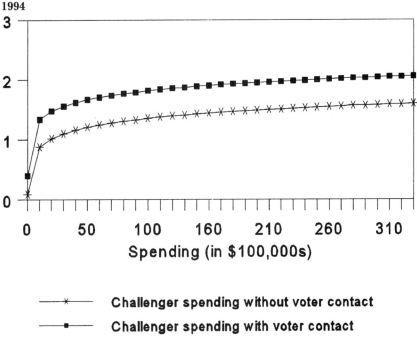

pears that citizen interest and concern depend more on the extent to which parties and candidates reach out and personally contact individuals than on the sheer amount of money the candidates spend.

CONCLUSION

Previous research has documented that greater candidate spending increases the supply of candidate information in the electoral environment, which may then translate into a more informed citizenry. The results of our analysis, however, indicate that this supply-side perspective of candidate campaign spending is, at best, incomplete. While increased candidate spending does increase candidate familiarity to some extent, it has either no effect or a negative effect on political interest, concern about the election outcome, and attentiveness to news reports about the campaign. As a result, exposure to high-spending House elections does little to connect citizens to the electoral process. In other words, in high-spending campaigns, citizens may be more familiar with the candidates, but they may care less, they may be less interested, they may pay less attention, and they

Figure 7.5   Incumbent Spending and Respondent Certainty about Incumbent Ideology, 1994

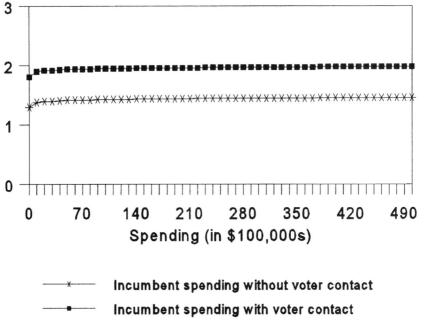

Spending (in $100,000s)

———×——— Incumbent spending without voter contact
———■——— Incumbent spending with voter contact

may be less certain or able to distinguish the ideological leaning of candidates. Moreover, in some races, spending may have the effect of blurring perceived ideological distances between candidates. Nor does candidate spending appear to make citizens any more certain in their ideological placements of candidates and, in some cases, may actually make citizens less certain.

Politicians, such as Newt Gingrich, who argue that more (rather than less) money needs to be spent in House elections so that voters can make more informed decisions are missing an important piece of the puzzle. More spending may increase candidate familiarity but will do little to connect citizens to the democratic process and may obscure rather than clarify candidates' stands on issues. Consistent with the literature on political mobilization, the results presented here indicate that political information and the motivation for acquiring new information (as measured by political interest and concern for the election outcome) are most effectively increased through candidate and party contact. In this respect, citizen interest in and concern about House elections has to be mobilized by campaigns just as active voter participation has to be mobilized.

While we do not have any evidence to speak directly to this question, we

Figure 7.6   Challenger Spending and Respondent Certainty about Incumbent Ideology, 1994

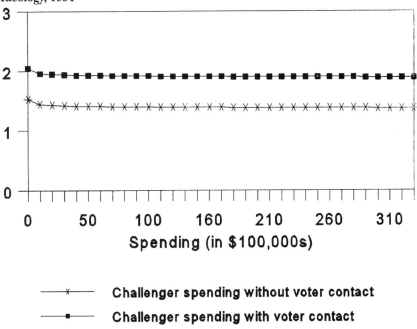

contend that the over-time decline in recall documented by Gary C. Jacobson (1997b, 94) reflects the candidate- and media-centered nature of contemporary American politics. With television and radio advertising (not to mention the internet), the potential to inform citizens about the political process has expanded exponentially in recent years. While our information capabilities have expanded, however, citizens have seen less and less of a connection between themselves and the political process. Part of this disconnectedness, we believe, has direct roots in the electoral process. As a result, higher spending campaigns, which theoretically should result in a more informed electorate, frequently serve to confuse rather than enlighten citizens.

NOTES

1. The term cognitive mobilization comes from Russell J. Dalton (1984).

2. For the purposes of summarizing the information, we present only the findings for incumbents and challengers. Readers can find the results based on candidate partisanship in appendix D.

3. A similar question was asked in 1996 but referred to the presidential election. As such, it is inappropriate for the purposes of this analysis.

Figure 7.7   Incumbent Spending and Respondent Certainty about Challenger Ideology, 1994

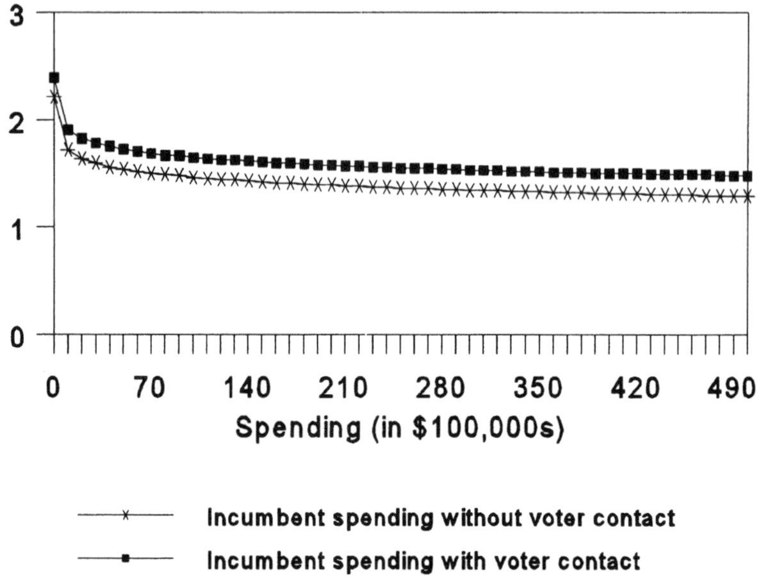

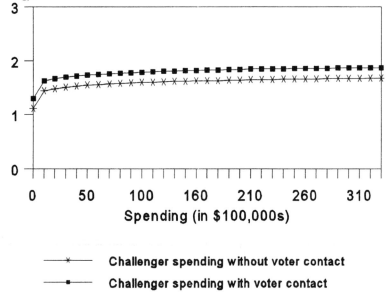

Figure 7.8   Challenger Spending and Respondent Certainty about Challenger Ideology, 1994

Figure 7.9   Incumbent Spending and Respondent Concern about Election Outcome, 1994

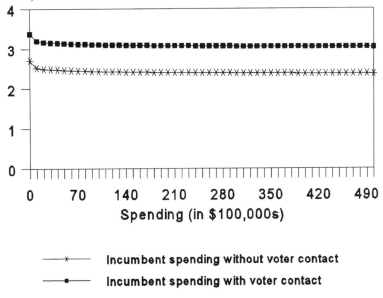

Figure 7.10   Challenger Spending and Respondent Concern about Election Outcome, 1994

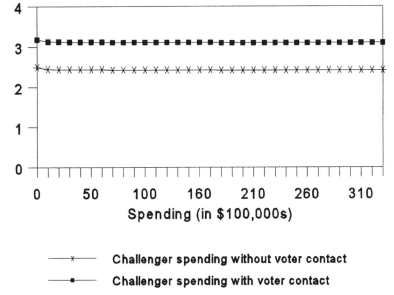

Chapter Eight

Loopholes in the Federal Election Campaign Act

At least until recent elections, it was not uncommon for campaign finance scholars to claim that one success of the 1971 Federal Election Campaign Act and its subsequent amendments was that it required disclosure of campaign expenditures and receipts. Despite other flaws, both real and imagined, campaign finance information was readily available to interested citizens, journalists, and academics. Frank Sorauf, for example, observed as recently as 1992 that "the sheer detail of the candidate, PAC, and party reports under the FECA has become a wonder of the democratic political world. Nowhere else do scholars and journalists find so much information about the funding of campaigns" (229).

By November 1996, even many defenders of the American system of campaign finance were acknowledging that the system was broken. Not only was interested money pouring into the electoral process at rates that alarmed even the system's most stalwart defenders, but also much of the money was unregulated and undisclosed. Encouraged by a Court ruling allowing parties to engage in unlimited independent expenditures, both parties aggressively tested the legal limits of FECA. The result was that more money was spent during the 1996 elections than during any election in American history. Because much of the spending was unregulated and beyond the reach of FECA's disclosure requirements, estimates of total spending during 1996 are, at best, educated guesses. At a minimum, it is estimated that more than $2 billion was spent during the 1996 election cycle, a figure more than $650 million above the total spent in 1992.[1]

Since its comprehensive amendments in 1974, FECA has stood like a dam, albeit not a particularly effective one, holding a river of campaign money at bay. Leaks in the dam were immediately obvious to most observers, but because many politicos and scholars argued that these leaks were not terribly important, they were ignored. Though there were scattered at-

143

tempts aimed at closing existing leaks, defenders of the status quo argued that, if successful, such efforts would result in new, perhaps larger and more dangerous leaks in different parts of the dam. In 1996, after two decades of leaking, however, the dam finally collapsed and money came pouring into presidential and congressional campaigns in amounts reminiscent of the pre-Watergate years. The regulatory regime created in the early 1970s, flimsy from the beginning, had finally collapsed under the weight of soft money, independent expenditures, and issue advocacy campaigns.

As the 1998 midterm elections approached, the limits on contributions and expenditures established by FECA became merely a facade. Individuals, corporations, political parties, and political action committees could now contribute and spend unlimited sums in an effort to affect electoral, or legislative, outcomes. As Brooks Jackson (1997, 225) notes, "Watching the hundreds of millions of dollars spent in the 1996 elections, citizens might be surprised to find that there were any laws limiting campaign finance at all. One business corporation gave nearly $2.2 million to the Republican Party, despite the fact that it had been illegal since 1907 for corporations to make any contribution in connection with a federal election."

In 1998, the primary impact of campaign finance laws involved how money was channeled into the electoral process. Candidate receipts in House elections were actually down slightly compared to 1996. The decline in candidate receipts, however, has to be placed in the context of an election with fewer open seats and fewer competitive districts and in which overall spending in House elections increased. House incumbents vastly outspent their opposition, and most (more than 98 percent) won reelection. In these races, money flowed into the electoral process through a variety of avenues, including issue advocacy campaigns and party soft money accounts. In this respect, party fund-raising was up significantly over the 1994 midterm election cycle. According to FEC reports, the Democratic Party increased its overall fund-raising by more than 40 percent, Republicans increased theirs by 16 percent. In terms of soft money, Democratic fund-raising increased 84 percent, Republican fund-raising increased 144 percent.[2] As Anthony J. Corrado observed, in the 1998 elections "we have unprecedented amounts of money being spent in federal elections and the least competitive elections in more than a decade."[3] Overall, if candidate fund-raising was down slightly in 1998, the flow of money into the electoral process continued unabated, much of it raised by the parties and spent in soft money issue campaigns.

SOFT MONEY AND ISSUE ADVOCACY

The Federal Election Campaign Act places relatively clear, unambiguous limits on individual contributions. Individuals are limited to $1,000 contributions per candidate per election, $5,000 to political action committees, and $20,000 to a political party, while total individual contributions are capped at $25,000 in a given election cycle. Despite these relatively clear limits, individual contributors routinely give six-figure, sometimes seven-figure, sums to favored parties and candidates. What is surprising is not that these limits are skirted but how easily and how often this is done—without raising any questions regarding the legality of the practice. In fact, skirting campaign finance limits is a practice that has been legally recognized and sanctioned by the Federal Election Commission and the Supreme Court.

How does an individual or a corporation contribute $1 million to a political party, despite relatively clear limits on individual contributions and a ban on direct corporate contributions? One answer is by contributing soft, as opposed to hard, money. The term *soft money* originated as a means for labor unions to distinguish between "hard" money spent directly in support of political candidates through contributions and "soft" money spent indirectly via voter registration drives and get-out-the-vote campaigns. In addition to this type of indirect candidate and party support, labor unions and corporations have also used soft money on internal communications to members and their families in support of (or opposition to) political candidates; and on the administrative overhead involved in creating and maintaining a political action committee.

Political party soft money, which has its origins in the 1979 amendments to the Federal Election Campaign Act, has been used for similar purposes, loosely defined as "party building." Following the 1976 presidential election, the first election paid for with public funding, there was a growing concern by both political parties that limits on candidate spending had inadvertently limited the amount of money devoted to grassroots, political party activities. Recognizing the potentially adverse consequences on citizen participation, the FECA was amended in 1979 to exclude certain types of contributions and expenditures from existing disclosure requirements and contribution limits. Specifically, the 1979 amendments allowed state and local political parties to spend unlimited amounts on certain types of campaign material (bumper stickers, yard signs, pins, and so on) and on voter registration and get-out-the-vote campaigns.

The 1979 amendments did not, however, open the door to unrestricted soft money fund-raising, à la 1996. As Anthony Corrado (1997a, 170) observes, "The 1979 revision thus did not create 'soft money'; it simply exempted any federal monies ('hard dollars') a party committee might spend on certain political activities from being considered a contribution under the law." The door to unlimited soft money was lifted instead by Federal Election Commission rulings allowing both state and national parties to distinguish between federal and nonfederal allocations of party money.

While campaign finance regulations differ from state to state, many states have more lenient contribution and expenditure limits than those at the national level governing federal elections. As a result, national parties, labor unions, and corporations can filter money to state parties for the presumed purpose of party building or in direct support of state and local candidates. The national parties can then raise and spend money to support nonfederal candidates and political parties subject to the much looser regulatory limitations that exist in the states. State and local parties can also use contributions that would be illegal if contributed directly to federal candidates (that is, direct corporate or labor union contributions) to fund joint federal/nonfederal activities as "long as they allocated their costs to reflect the federal and nonfederal shares of any costs incurred" (ibid., 172). Because there are generally more state and local candidates, soft money was used to cover the bulk of the costs associated with these activities.

In recent elections, the distinction between federal and nonfederal accounts has grown increasingly thin as has the distinction between soft and hard money. In this context, charges that Democrats turned soft money into hard money during the 1996 elections are hardly surprising. Both parties raise soft money with explicit appeals to contributors that such money will help the party in upcoming federal elections. Soft money can then be used to cover most of the party's infrastructure and administrative costs, freeing up hard money to be used for campaigning.

In a recent article, appropriately titled "Spinning Straw into Gold," Diana Dwyre (1996) details the process by which soft money raised by the national party ends up in federal campaigns. First, the national party raises money, primarily through large contributors, who make their checks payable to nonfederal party accounts. Second, the money is transferred to state and local parties in areas and regions where competitive elections are expected to take place. Third, the soft money transfer from the national party committee allows the state (or local) party to cover administrative overhead or make contributions to state and local candidates. This frees up hard money for direct (and legal) contributions to federal campaign accounts. Legally, state and local parties cannot simply transfer this national party soft money to federal candidates. With careful accounting procedures, however, soft money can cover costs that the state party would normally have to cover with hard dollars. This transfer of soft money allows the state party to make contributions to federal candidates that, in all probability, would not have been made otherwise.

Because there were no disclosure requirements until 1991, estimates of the total amount of soft money raised and spent during the 1980s are necessarily inexact. Still, it is clear that the use of political party soft money has grown considerably since its inception in 1980. In 1980, it is estimated that, combined, the two parties spent about $19.1 million in soft money. In 1992, the two parties spent $79.1 million in soft money. It was not until 1996, however, that the use of party soft money truly exploded (see figure 8.1). In 1996, the Democratic Party alone spent nearly $122 million, nearly four times the amount spent by Democrats in 1992. Not to be outdone, the Republican Party spent just under $150 million, nearly three times its 1992 total. While the impact of soft money on electoral outcomes, particularly in congressional campaigns, is unclear, the growth of soft money suggests that both parties believe soft money spending is important.

Admittedly, the growth of political party soft money may have some positive effects on the political system. First, it can be argued that by raising large sums of money through individual, union, and corporate contributors, the national parties have reasserted themselves as important players in federal elections. In this respect, the growth of soft money could, at least potentially, help to refocus electoral activity around political parties. Second, because soft money generally travels through state and local political parties, it may strengthen the traditionally weak bonds between the national party and its state and local affiliates. As a result, it can be argued that soft money has reinvigorated the American party system.

Any potential advantages created by the soft money loophole are, how-

Figure 8.1   Political Party Soft Money Expenditures (In Millions), 1992–1998

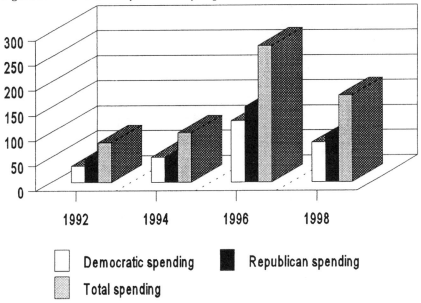

Source: FEC data.

ever, outweighed by its disadvantages. To the extent that the campaign finance reforms of the 1970s were aimed at reducing the influence of large
contributors, the prevalence of soft money in contemporary elections un-
dermines this goal. Fund-raising in the late 1970s and early 1980s was based
on direct-mail appeals to small contributors, leading Frank Sorauf (1992),
among others, to boast that "no other system of campaign funding any-
where in the world enjoys so broad a base of support. None even approaches it." Fund-raising efforts in the 1990s are directed at squeezing six-
and seven-figure contributions from individual and corporate donors. This
is not to suggest that parties no longer seek small contributions; they do.
But like any rational political actor, they devote the bulk of their resources
to the most lucrative return on their investment.

While soft money cannot, legally, be used to promote federal candidates,
as parties have been more creative in their use of soft money the line between soft and hard money has grown increasingly thin. In the 1996 election, much of party soft money was spent on issue advocacy ads. "In theory," Jackson (1997, 236) writes, "the ads merely discuss the issues of the
day, and were not technically contributions to a campaign. But the distinction was almost entirely academic." In fact, issue advocacy ads differ from
campaign ads in only one key respect: they cannot explicitly advocate electing (or defeating) a candidate. They can, however, attack an opposing candidate or promote a favored candidate.

With this avenue wide open, political parties raised and spent record
amounts of soft money in 1996. Much of this money went to "issue advocacy" advertisements that only marginally differed from campaign ads. The
bulk of the money went to the presidential candidates. The Democratic
National Committee began its issue advocacy campaigns in 1995, with ads
painting President Clinton as defending the public interest against the Republican Congress. In a similar vein, when the Dole campaign reached the
spending limits for the nominating phase of the presidential election, the
Republican National Committee helped to fill the gap with issue advocacy
ads funded entirely with soft money.

With the majority control of the House and Senate hanging in the balance, issue advocacy also made its way into congressional campaigns. Dwyre
(1997) reports that the Democratic Congressional Campaign Committee
transferred $8.4 million to state parties, which in turn spent the money on
issue advocacy ads in sixty marginal House districts. Not to be outdone, the
National Republican Campaign Committee spent more than $18 million
on issue advocacy ads in House campaigns, much of it directed to marginal
races. Typical of the issue advocacy ads is the following ad paid for by the
National Republican Senatorial Committee: "You work hard for your pay-
check, but liberal Paul Wellstone votes repeatedly against requiring welfare
recipients to work for their checks. Wellstone even votes for billions more

in welfare spending. That's wrong. Since Wellstone went to Congress, welfare spending is up 71 percent to $260 billion. Yet, Wellstone votes against workfare. Call liberal Paul Wellstone. Tell him he is wrong to spend billions more on welfare. Tell him to vote for the Governor's plan to replace welfare with workfare" (in Dwyre 1997, 17).

Other than imploring citizens to "Call liberal Paul Wellstone," the ad is indistinguishable from a campaign ad, particularly given that such ads are aired repeatedly during campaign season. Yet, because the ad does not explicitly call for the defeat of the incumbent, Senator Paul Wellstone, by the Supreme Court's definition, the ad involves issue advocacy rather than express or electoral advocacy. As a result, the ad can be paid for with direct, unlimited individual, corporate, or union contributions, contributions that are otherwise banned in federal elections.

INDEPENDENT EXPENDITURES AND ISSUE ADVOCACY

Political parties are not the only political organizations that exploit the issue advocacy loophole in existing laws. Political action committees also engage in expensive issue advocacy campaigns, presumably to influence both electoral and legislative outcomes. In 1996, the most notable and controversial interest group campaign was waged by the AFL-CIO, which spent more than $35 million in an effort to return the House to Democratic control. Despite the AFL-CIO's publicly stated objective of overturning the House majority, this $35 million effort was considered issue, rather than electoral, advocacy. As a result, the AFL-CIO campaign was not disclosed to the Federal Election Commission.

Technically, issue advocacy campaigns, which are not disclosed, can be distinguished from independent expenditures, which are disclosed. Independent expenditure campaigns are waged with the explicit purpose of electing or defeating a candidate for public office. Issue advocacy campaigns cannot, by definition, advocate the election or defeat of a candidate. Like the distinction between hard and soft money, the distinction between independent spending and issue advocacy is an artificial one. Both independent expenditures and issue advocacy campaigns arose out of the landmark case of *Buckley v. Valeo* (1976) in which the Supreme Court equates free speech with unlimited spending. In the majority opinion, the Court distinguishes between contribution limits, which are constitutional, and expenditure limits, which are not. Contribution limits, the Court reasoned, can be justified because they protect the integrity of the electoral process. Expenditure limits, however, have the primary effect of limiting political speech. As a result, they violate First Amendment free speech protections. Practically speaking, the ruling means that individuals and PACs can spend unlimited sums to defeat or elect a specific candidate, as long as the spending is independent of any political campaign.

The first widespread use of independent spending occurred in 1980, when the National Conservative PAC (NCPAC) targeted six liberal Democratic senators. Four were defeated, and NCPAC took much of the credit. In 1984, other PACs, hoping to emulate the success of NCPAC, spent millions in independent expenditures, but none were nearly as successful. In fact, in several instances, independent spending backfired on the candidate it was intended to help. Rather than the continuous growth in independent spending that might have been expected following the 1980 elections, the amount of independent spending has varied considerably from one election cycle to the next. In 1996, independent spending in House elections alone reached $4.8 million, the highest total ever for House races and over twice the 1994 total of $2.1 million (figure 8.2). Despite establishing the record amount of independent spending in 1996, in the average congressional race, independent spending is rarely a factor. In just under 30 percent of House elections in 1996, there was no reported independent spending; while in 50 percent of House races, total independent spending was less than $700.

Yet, if independent spending is largely absent from, or plays a minimal

Figure 8.2   Independent Expenditures in House Races (In Millions), 1978–1996

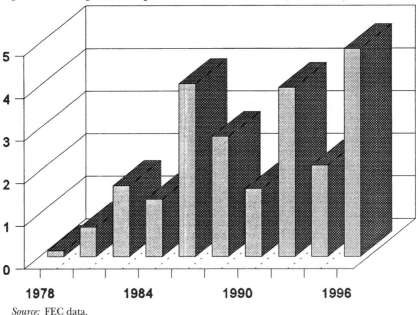

Source: FEC data.

role in, the average congressional race, it is potentially significant in at least some congressional districts. In Washington's Ninth Congressional District, incumbent Republican Randy Tate was challenged not only by Democrat Adam Smith but also by the $231,572 in independent spending aimed specifically at removing him from congressional office.[4] Nor was Tate the only incumbent to face serious independent spending campaigns. Though his effort to unseat Republican incumbent Helen Chenoweth in Idaho's First Congressional District fell short by two percentage points, Democratic challenger Dan Williams was aided by $239,085 in independent spending. In trying to regain North Carolina's Fourth Congressional District seat, Democrat David Price benefited from $118,274 spent independently to defeat Republican incumbent Fred Hieneman and $77,225 spent in support of Price's campaign.

While these examples are nowhere near exhaustive, they do illustrate the potentially important role that independent spending can play in congressional elections. Increasingly, however, groups or individuals wanting to influence electoral outcomes do so through issue advocacy rather than independent expenditures. As a result, the $4.8 million reported to the FEC as independent expenditures represents only a fraction of what political action committees and interest groups spent during the 1996 election cycle. Not only are these expenditures not subject to any limit, they are also undisclosed. As a result, it is impossible to gauge just how much money interest groups and political action committees spent trying to influence electoral outcomes in 1996.

Relying on figures provided by the AFL-CIO, Jackson (1997) estimates that the AFL-CIO spent approximately $630,000 on issue advocacy ads in Washington's Ninth Congressional District alone. In North Carolina's Fourth Congressional District, Jackson estimates that the AFL-CIO spent approximately $460,000. What is striking about these figures is that they represent the issue advocacy campaign of a single interest group. Undoubtedly, other groups also engaged in issue advocacy spending in these (and other) districts. As with party issue advocacy ads, the distinction between issue advocacy campaigns and electoral advocacy campaigns is extremely artificial. While the ads cannot explicitly advocate the election or defeat of a candidate, the campaign message from these ads is generally clear. For example, consider the following description of an issue advocacy ad aired in 1992 (Potter 1997, 233–34),

with a full color picture of candidate Bill Clinton's face superimposed on an American flag, which is blowing in the wind. Clinton is shown smiling and the ad appears to be complimentary. However, as the narrator begins to describe Clinton's alleged support of "radical" homosexual causes, Clinton's image dissolves into a black and white photographic negative. The negative darkens

Clinton's eyes and mouth, giving the candidate a sinister and threatening appearance. Simultaneously, the music accompanying the commercial changes from a single high pitched tone to a lower octave.

The commercial then presents a series of pictures depicting advocates of homosexual rights, apparently gay men and lesbians demonstrating at a political march. . . .

As scenes from the march continue, the narrator asks in rhetorical fashion, "Is this your vision for a better America?" Thereafter the image of the American flag reappears on the screen, but without the superimposed image of candidate Clinton. At the same time, the music changes back to the single high pitched tone. The narrator then states, "for more information on traditional family values, contact the Christian Action Network."

The message of the ad is unambiguously anti-Clinton, and there can be little doubt that the ad was aimed at affecting individual voting decisions. Yet, according to the Supreme Court, this particular ad is outside the reporting requirements of FECA because it involves issue rather than electoral advocacy.

PARTY INDEPENDENT SPENDING

Under the provisions of the Federal Election Campaign Act, political parties have been allowed to engage in coordinated expenditures since 1974. The term *coordinated expenditures* implies what to many observers seems to be obvious: political parties and candidates are, for better or worse, irretrievably linked. Coordinated expenditures allow parties to contribute public opinion polling and mass mailings, to pay the production costs of advertisements, and to engage in research for party candidates. However, such activity was limited to $10,000 in 1974 dollars in House campaigns and to two cents times the voting age population, up to a maximum of $20,000, in Senate campaigns. Unlike other contribution limits established by FECA, these coordinated expenditures were indexed to inflation.

In 1996, however, the question of whether party spending can be independent of a candidate's campaign was put to the Supreme Court. The Supreme Court ruled in the case of *Colorado Republican Federal Campaign Committee v. Federal Election Commission* (1996) that parties could engage in unlimited, independent spending. The result opened yet another avenue for money to pour into the electoral process. Republicans, for their part, immediately took advantage of the ruling, spending $10 million in independent party expenditures in 1996. Democrats were slower to adapt, but still managed to spend $1.5 million. The potential to spend unlimited hard dollars to affect federal election outcomes should, in the future, prove attractive to both parties. While both parties engaged in independent spending in 1996, the full impact of the *Colorado* ruling would not be felt until the 1998 midterm elections. By 1998, both parties had ample time to consider the implications of the ruling and how the ruling could be exploited for partisan political gain.

BUNDLING

The term *bundling* refers to political action committees collecting individual contributions that they then deliver in bulk to individual candidates. In 1996, with public and media attention devoted primarily to party soft money and issue advocacy campaigns, bundling hardly registered as a blip on the radar screen. Yet bundling continues as a practice by which political action committees skirt existing contribution limits. While each individual can contribute only $1,000 per candidate per election, the bundled contribution is much more substantial, presumably increasing the group's political access to, and influence over, the policy maker.

Bundling has been most successfully used by Emily's List. Emily's List, which is an acronym for "early money is like yeast," is defined as a political network designed with the specific purpose of electing pro-choice, Democratic women to Congress. It does so by collecting individual contributions and then bundling these contributions and giving them to selected candidates.

For liberal reformers, Emily's List presents something of a dilemma. Any reform designed to reduce or eliminate loopholes in existing campaign finance laws would also put Emily's List out of business. Yet reform efforts that ignore bundling, or that allow an exception for Emily's List, ring of hypocrisy. Added to the symbolic importance of Emily's List is its significant fund-raising clout. In both 1994 and 1996, Emily's List reigned as the single largest fund-raising organization in American politics. In 1994, Emily's List distributed more than $8.2 million to pro-choice women candidates; in 1996, the figure was more than $13.6 million. Despite the success of Emily's List in raising and distributing campaign dollars for the seemingly benign purpose of electing more women to Congress, bundling represents a successful effort at avoiding existing contribution limits.

CONCLUSION

Disclosure requirements, at least in theory, allow citizens to make informed judgments about the sources of candidate funding and any related conflict of interest. If, for example, a candidate receives a large contribution from the tobacco industry, the AFL-CIO, or the National Realtors Association, with full disclosure, citizens should be able to factor the appropriateness of the contribution into their voting decision. At least in theory, legislators who accept contributions from disfavored groups could then be voted out of office.

Rarely, however, has the practice of democracy lived up to its theoretical expectations. Citizens are woefully uninformed about the sources of candidate campaign finance, and attempts to be informed require herculean efforts. Tracking campaign contributions has proven a daunting task even for highly skilled academics and journalists. Even when contributions are fully disclosed, it is difficult (though not impossible) to account for the sources of candidate and party campaign funding. Contributors who wish to skirt contribution limits can easily do so using a variety of means, but most often they have done so through soft money contributions, independent expenditures, and now increasingly through issue advocacy campaigns.

That individual contributors, candidates, PACs, and parties attempted to stretch the limits of existing campaign finance laws in 1996 is hardly surprising. In every election since 1974, the limits established by the FECA have been stretched in some way. Seen in this light, the 1996 election was the logical outcome of a system in which enforcement is virtually absent and in which parties gain a strategic advantage by being the first to violate the spirit, if not the letter, of existing regulations.

What is perhaps surprising is how an electoral system once defined by candidate control over the electoral process is now a system in which candidate spending may be usurped by unregulated, and sometimes undisclosed, spending by interested political action committees and political parties. In a report entitled *New Realities, New Thinking,* a group of political scientists led by Herbert Alexander concludes that "whole new categories of players . . . now operate outside the rules set up for the system as it existed in 1974. And whole new categories of money . . . are unregulated, subject only to limited disclosure" (Citizens' Research Foundation 1997, 487). From the standpoint of democratic theory, control over spending is important because it implies control over the campaign message. At least in a few cases, the message bought by PAC and party spending was neither approved nor welcomed by the candidate it was intended to help. For example, freshman incumbent Phil English, from Pennsylvania's Twenty-first Congressional District, believed Republican ads attacking big labor hindered rather than enhanced his efforts at reelection. "If they had asked me," English said, "I would have told those guys that attacking big labor is not a particularly effective strategy in Erie" (Gugliotta and Chinoy, 1997). Even if the spending works as intended, however, it can still have negative consequences on the electoral process. Because campaign messages are not always within the control of the candidates, negative campaigning can occur even if the candidates themselves disavow it.

In Wisconsin's 1998 Senate race, Democratic incumbent Russell Feingold promised to abide by the limits set forth in the campaign finance reform legislation he cosponsored with Arizona Reublican John McCain. Feingold even asked that Democratic Party soft money ads not be aired on his behalf. His adherence to principle cost him a ten-to-fifteen-point lead in the polls and nearly cost him his Senate seat. His Republican opponent, Representative Mark Neumann, had no qualms about the millions of dollars in soft money being spent on his behalf. Although Feingold adhered to his own self-imposed limits, may of his supporters did not, including the AFL-CIO. For Feingold, adherence to principle meant being limited to only that money he could control as a candidate or at least influence through Democratic Party leadership. It also meant running the risk of losing a Senate seat. Faced with a similar choice, most candidates, even those with the best of intentions, are co-opted by a campaign finance system that scarcely limits campaign spending.

Overall, the changes in campaign financing in 1996 raise critical issues about candidate accountability. Political scientists have long described the electoral process as candidate centered. Many lament the candidate-centered nature of American politics because of the inherent difficulties citizens face in holding political parties accountable for policy outcomes. While the 1996 elections may represent the demise of candidate-centered politics, there is little cause to celebrate. The decline of candidate-centered elections (to the extent that there is a decline) has not resulted in a resurgence of party-centered elections. Instead, candidate-centered campaigns appear to have been replaced by politics without a center.

NOTES

1. This estimate is taken from Anthony Corrado (1997b) but is based only on disclosed candidate and party direct expenditures.

2. "Fundraising Escalates for Political Party Committees," FEC press release, October 27, 1998.

3. Quoted in Stone (1998), 2680.

4. This figure combines independent expenditures by nonparty committees and by individuals. In addition, Tate was aided by $194,341 in independent spending aimed at supporting his reelection.

Chapter Nine

Improving the Electoral Process through Campaign Finance Reform

The manner in which representatives are elected to public office is a central concern of democratic theory. At a minimum, for democracy to remain healthy, elections must be competitive, citizens must participate and be reasonably informed, and political debate must be open and relatively unrestrained. Unfortunately, the campaign finance system that currently governs congressional and presidential elections threatens the legitimacy of the electoral process because it values political contributions over grassroots political participation, incumbency and legislative access over electoral competition, and economic inequality over political equality.

Citizens may be largely uninformed and uninterested in politics, but they do know enough to realize that most contributors do not give a $500,000 contribution out of sense of civic duty. At a minimum, contributors expect that when they speak they will be heard, though it is also reasonable to assume that most expect something more tangible in return. The average citizen has no such guarantees. In fact, the average citizen has little reason to expect that his or her voice will be heard at all. And why should they? To the extent that the political process seeks their input it does so primarily through solicitations for political contributions or through media-generated marketing appeals aimed at manipulating mass voting decisions. Such a climate not only breeds cynicism, it nurtures its growth as well.

And why shouldn't voters be cynical? Political candidates and party officials aggressively raise money from large contributors based on explicit promises that such contributions will enhance their "political access" to key decision makers. In effect, the right of a citizen to petition the government for redress of grievances, which depends upon access to government officials, becomes a commodity to be bought and sold on the open market. Whether the context of the appeal is President Clinton requesting donations over White House coffees or the Speaker of the House asking for contributions at a Republican National Committee fund-raiser, the result is the same: access is bought and sold on a regular basis. Individuals who prove especially adept at selling access are either brought into the party leadership to raise money for other candidates or encouraged to run for higher office. After all, what is a stronger testament that a House member should be a senator, or that a senator or governor should be president, than their ability to raise millions of dollars in party money? Nothing is more valued or more clearly rewarded in the modern political climate.

Having said all of this, we must also acknowledge that money alone is not the root of all that ails the contemporary American polity. Other factors undoubtedly play a role as well, including the long-term decline (or transformation) of political parties and the rise of television as the dominant form of political interaction. Yet, if money is not the sole cause of the current discontent in American politics, it is certainly a major contributing factor. But what, if anything, can be done about it? In this chapter, we outline several criteria for evaluating the success of campaign finance reform. We then use these criteria to evaluate three general approaches to campaign finance reform: the do-little approach, the moderate (or incremental) approach, and the comprehensive approach. After discussing the various approaches, we then explain why significant campaign finance reform is unlikely in the short run but highly probable in the long run.

CRITERIA FOR EVALUATING CAMPAIGN FINANCE REFORM

There are many criteria that one might use to evaluate campaign finance reform. For example, a strong partisan might desire reforms that would give his or her political party a strategic political advantage. From our perspective, democratic theory suggests that, to be successful, reform must accomplish at least four major objectives.

First, reform must reduce the natural tensions between economic inequality and political quality. The American creed simultaneously values the principle of democratic equality (one person, one vote) and capitalism (the material accumulation of wealth). Politics and economics, however, have never been, nor is it likely that they ever can be, distinct realms of social activity. Put simply, economic inequalities create political inequalities. Undoubtedly, this has been true throughout U.S. political history. Yet it has also been true that at certain points in U.S. history the disparities between economic and political power have been blatant enough that reform was necessary to reestablish the legitimacy of the political system. We live in such an era. Public opinion polls routinely show that the public believes that special interests dominate the political process, that individual citizens like themselves have little say in Washington, and that politicians don't care what they think. Others argue that such perceptions are not grounded in reality. We tend to disagree, but it makes little difference, because it is perception itself that defines the legitimacy of a democratic political system.

Second, reform must increase electoral competitiveness. Healthy democracies engage in competitive elections. Incumbent success rates suggest that congressional elections are anything but competitive. While the incumbency advantage is rooted in more than money, the most significant threat to incumbency, other than a political scandal, is a well-funded challenger.

Third, reform should increase citizen participation and information, but at a minimum, it should do no harm in terms of reducing voter participation or increasing information costs.[1] Critics often argue that reform efforts that limit spending will also reduce political participation by lowering already dismally low levels of information. There is a kernel of truth here. Candidate spending has the potential to increase voter participation and information. Yet this potential is seldom realized. While higher-spending races have the potential of mobilizing a larger share of the electorate, they also add fuel to existing public cynicism.

Engaging citizens in the electoral process requires more than simply dumping additional revenues into candidate or party coffers; it involves reconnecting citizens to the electoral process in a direct, personal manner. For this, the answer seems clear: political parties need to be strengthened at the grass roots. As shown in earlier chapters, political information and mobilization are most effectively furthered through candidate and party contact. This has been a central role for political parties throughout much of American history.[2] Over the last few decades, however, parties have adapted to a changing electoral environment by increasing their fund-raising and service capacities. For many scholars, better-funded, more institutionalized party organizations are indicative of a strengthening of U.S. political parties that has been occurring at least since the 1980s. This may be true; but as of yet, strengthened political parties have meant little to the average citizen, who views such organizations with suspicion. An analogy to professional sports may be appropriate here: higher-paid athletes do not necessarily translate into a better game or greater fan support, nor do better-funded political parties translate into a stronger democracy.

Finally, reform should increase democratic accountability. Fundamental to the operation of the American democratic system is the principle that citizens can hold elected officials accountable for their actions in office through the periodic holding of open, fair, and competitive elections. Citizens need information about both candidates. Particular candidates or political parties should not be able to gain a significant strategic advantage in any set of elections because of large contributions from individual donors. And citizens must have an effective choice between at least two candidates. If one of the two candidates in an election remains unknown and with little or no money to mount an effective campaign, the election becomes a sham with no real electoral choice for the voter. Very simply, a financially capable loyal opposition is necessary before, during, and after elections to provide citizens with alternative perspectives on governing.

Now, when utilizing these four objectives as criteria for evaluating campaign finance reform, the student of politics must keep two additional points in mind. First, campaign finance reforms are doomed to failure if they are not vigorously enforced and if sanctions for noncompliance are insufficient. Second, reform of the campaign finance system is an ongoing process. As political actors adjust to any set of reforms, further reform efforts will likely be necessary to compensate for their actions.

As discussed in chapter 2, much of the history of campaign finance legislation is a history of noncompliance that resulted from lack of enforcement and minimal sanctions for violations of the law. Campaign finance legislation is much like any other law. The likelihood of compliance depends upon the benefits derived from violating the law, the likelihood that one will be convicted for violating the law, and the sanctions or penalties imposed for conviction. For example, there is little sense in posting speed limits on interstate highways if no one is ever going to be stopped for speeding. In this respect, the contrast between allegations of vote fraud and violations of campaign finance laws is instructive. Substantial evidence of buying votes or stuffing ballot boxes can result in election results being overturned or a special election being called. While the potential rewards of such activities are substantial enough that many individuals, candidates, parties, and interest groups continue to engage in vote fraud, the penalties for doing so are also substantial, as are enforcement efforts in most states. As a result, these activities have been greatly diminished over the last hundred years.

Today, individuals who violate campaign finance laws needn't worry too much about any significant repercussions. It is unlikely that they will be caught. Funding for the Federal Election Commission is routinely cut by Congress to ensure that its enforcement is something less than vigorous. In addition, the partisan makeup of the FEC almost ensures that only the most blatant offenses will be pursued. When high-profile cases of campaign finance abuse do come to light, such as with Newt Gingrich, Bill Clinton, Al Gore, and Haley Barber, it is often the result of partisan politics rather than regulatory enforcement. And since the advent of FECA in the 1970s, no federal election has ever been overturned because of violations of campaign finance regulations. In this respect, violations of federal campaign finance laws need to be taken at least as seriously as allegations of vote fraud.

It is also important to recognize that, for the foreseeable future, there is no final solution to campaign finance reform. Critics of reform often note the failures of past reform efforts in limiting campaign finance abuses as sure evidence that future efforts will also fail. Such cynicism may be justified, but it hardly merits inactivity. Nor is it a convincing defense of the status quo. If campaign finance reform efforts have to create a new, clean world for politics, they are certain to fail. Held to a similar standard, however, welfare reform is also certain to fail, as is any reform of the tax structure. Combining the rhetoric of reform and the skepticism of its critics often sets the bar too high. The result is that reform has to miraculously transform American democracy into a political Lake Wobegone: where all voters care, participate, and are informed; where all elections are about substantive issues; and where all candidates and contributors place the national interest above their self-interest. Yet in campaign finance as in all politics, there are no final solutions. Reform efforts will undoubtedly create unanticipated consequences, many of which may form the basis of future reform efforts. Moreover, even when reform is successful, success may very well prove fleeting.

The campaign finance reform efforts of the 1970s are instructive on this point. As critics correctly observe, changes in the campaign finance laws during the 1970s led to the proliferation (though not the creation) of political action committees. Political action committees are now routinely fingered as one of the principal villains of contemporary campaign finance. While the reform efforts intentionally legitimized PAC activity, the proliferation of PACs was clearly an unanticipated consequence of reform. Despite such unanticipated consequences, the reform efforts of the 1970s were not an unqualified failure. They were successful in limiting political contributions and candidate expenditures in presidential elections for at least a limited period of time. That smart politicians, lawyers, and contributors found ways around existing laws is easy to read as a sign of failure. It is also easy to read as an indication that more effective campaign finance legislation, with more rigorous enforcement, is needed.

Politics is vitally important because it is the process through which resources and values are allocated within society. Because politics is important, individuals with a stake in political outcomes will naturally attempt to bend the rules of the game in their favor. Over time, the political system itself becomes biased in favor of individuals who have been most successful in bending the rules of the game to their advantage. As a result, not only do these individuals frequently have more resources to influence the system, but the system also becomes more responsive to their interests. Unfortunately, there is no self-correcting mechanism within the political system, other than political reform, that can flush the system of such biases. Moreover, even when the system is flushed, many of the existing biases will remain, and those biases that were effectively reduced will eventually creep back into the system, though frequently in some new manifestation. The inevitability of bias does not, however, mean that we throw in the towel and accept the status quo. Instead, it means the reconciliation between the values of economic inequality and political equality must be continually confronted by political reformers. New rounds of reform will be required whenever the biases within the political system are severe enough that they threaten the legitimacy of the political system. Such is the status of the American polity in the late 1990s.

EVALUATING CAMPAIGN FINANCE PROPOSALS

If the laws that have governed campaign finance since the 1970s are no longer effective, what, if anything, can be done? To answer this question, we evaluate three general approaches to campaign finance reform: the do-little approach, the moderate approach, and the comprehensive approach. In this section, we discuss the merits of each approach, with particular attention to the criteria of reform we have just developed. Table 9.1 summarizes how each of the approaches to campaign finance reform can be evaluated in terms of the criteria developed in the beginning of this chapter.

The Do-Little Approach

To some extent, tensions between economic inequality and political equality are inevitable. Individuals with more of whatever society values naturally bring more weight to bear in the political process. Taken to its logical extreme, one can even envision a political system that is not entirely unlike Kurt Vonnegut's classic short story, "Harrison Bergeron." In the story, the title character is weighed down to compensate for his superior physical strength and subjected to intermediate piercing noises to compensate for his superior intelligence. All of this, of course, is done in the name of social equality.

Proponents of the do-little approach, aptly named after California Republican Richard Doolittle, envision comprehensive campaign finance reform as working in a similar fashion. Wealthy contributors, corporations, even labor unions would be handicapped by spending limits that effectively muzzle political expression. Rather than attempt to compensate for economic inequalities by handicapping the rich, advocates of this approach believe that the best hope for reform involves removing existing limits on contributions and spending while requiring full disclosure of all political contributions. To a certain degree, the logic is unassailable. Individuals are not born equal, nor can legislation create equality. Moreover, if we remove wealth as a source of inequality, we still have differences in intelligence, speaking ability, and so on. Are we going to legislate these inequalities away

Table 9.1   Summary Evaluation of Three Campaign Finance Reform Approaches

Reform Criteria	Do Little Approach	Moderate Approach	Comprehensive Approach
Tensions between economic inequality and political equality	No effect. Perceptions of corruption will continue to exist. Perceptions of corruption will increase if contribution limits are eliminated.	Modest effect. Includes limits on contributions from large contributors as well as a ban on soft money and political action committee contributions.	Strong effect. Removing private money should significantly reduce public perceptions that government is controlled by special interests.
Electoral competition	No effect. Elections will continue to be affected by moneyed interests and candidate appeals to those interests.	Modest effect. Free radio and TV time to candidates who abide by voluntary spending limits may increase electoral competition.	Strong effect. Providing challengers with money, even relatively modest amounts, should significantly increase competition in the average congressional election.
Voter turnout	No effect or a negative effect. Perceptions of corruption and government controlled by special interests will likely increase with potentially adverse consequences for voter participation.	Modest effect. Free radio and TV time to candidates could encourage participation by increasing electoral competition.	Modest to strong effect. Increased challenger funding should increase competition, while limiting spending should encourage other forms of election activity, including direct mobilization efforts.
Voter information	No effect or a negative effect. Increased distrust may decrease individual motivations for attending to political information.	Modest effect. Free radio and tv time should increase information particularly for lesser known candidates.	Modest to strong effect. Increased challenger spending should increase challenger name recognition and may also increase attentiveness to issues.
Democratic accountability	Some possible effect. Making information more accessible may improve accountability but the improvement is contingent on motivation of voters to find this information and use it in their voting decisions.	Modest effect. Eliminating soft money while limiting issue advocacy campaigns would limit the amount of undisclosed and unregulated money in congressional campaigns.	Strong effect. All money spent in an electoral campaign would be regulated and disclosed.

as well? And why is wealth singled out as a source of inequality when these other inequalities also clearly exist and impact the political system?

Short of redistributing income, it is unlikely that tensions between economic inequality and political equality will ever be fully resolved. And even if these inequalities were resolved, other inequalities would continue to bias the political system in favor of advantaged individuals and groups. Yet acknowledging the inevitably of inequality is not the same as acknowledging that such inequalities should be left unchecked and allowed to grow into an ever-increasing chasm between the politically powerful and the politically vulnerable. In any political system there are ways, both legal and corrupt, to transfer economic wealth into political power, which can then be used to further economic power. The question is not whether such inequalities can be eliminated, because they cannot, but whether a given political system, either implicitly or explicitly, legitimizes these inequalities.

In addition, the approach is also based on the flawed assumption that citizens will, first, inform themselves about the source of political contributions and, second, factor that information into their voting decisions. The logic is that full disclosure of contributions allows citizens to make informed choices on whether or not politicians are indeed "bought" by special interests. Provided there is full information, supporters contend that the electoral market is self-regulating and needs little interference from government.

While this model of citizen behavior is admirable from a theoretical standpoint, it is at best questionable from an empirical standpoint. First, it is unclear why anyone would expect that citizens who frequently lack the ability to name candidates for congressional office would go to the trouble of gathering information about political contributions, particularly if the overwhelming percentage of contributions are going to the incumbent. Second, other than candidates who are independently wealthy, any candidate with a chance of winning must rely on contributions, both from individuals and from PACs. Electoral choice may then be a decision between a candidate "bought" by BIPAC (Business and Industry Political Action Committee) versus a candidate "bought" by the AFL-CIO. Voters may learn that one candidate is more worker friendly while the other is more business friendly, but both candidates would appear to be equally corrupt. The effects of money on the political process are so pervasive that voters, even if they were to fully inform themselves about the source of contributions, can do little more than pick between a candidate who receives money from groups and individuals they like versus a candidate who receives money from groups and individuals they dislike. Except in rare instances, the only way to vote against the pervasive influence of money in the political process would be to abstain from participation.

Overall, the do-little approach fails to fulfill any of the criteria that we suggest as important for evaluating campaign finance reform. It will not reduce the natural tension between economic inequality and political equality. It is more likely to exacerbate the problem, as economic power is used to obtain political power that is then used to gain even more economic power, ad infinitum. It will not increase electoral competition and might even further reduce electoral competition. The asymmetric monetary advantages of incumbents over challengers will remain or actually increase. In addition, it is unlikely that the do-little approach would increase voter information or turnout. As we argue in this book, more spending in congressional elections usually does not result in greater voter information or higher voter turnout. The do-little approach might actually reduce these very phenomena, which ought to be encouraged, because a continued upward spiral in contributions and expenditures will continue to increase citizen mistrust and cynicism.

Finally, while one component of political accountability might be improved by the do-little approach, other components of accountability will remain unchanged or be diminished. If reporting and disclosure requirements are tightened and are expanded to cover soft money and independent expenditures, citizens will have more information available to hold governmental officials accountable. As stated earlier, this is contingent on the motivation of individual voters to find the information and to use it in their voting decisions. Other aspects of political accountability—electoral competition and voter information—will not improve under this approach. Most important, the do-little approach does nothing to address one of the fundamental problems underlying the current campaign finance system: in most congressional districts, the loyal opposition simply does not have enough money to communicate to the electorate its alternative perspectives on government. This is why the current system tends to advantage the majority party. Everything we know about the financing of congressional elections tells us that removing existing limits on contributions and spending simply will not, in general, overcome the problem of a financially incapable loyal opposition in congressional districts. Removing limits will, more than likely, make matters worse.

The Moderate Approach

The moderate, or incremental, approach to campaign finance reform generally include one or more of the following: (1) limits on campaign spending tied into provisions for free advertising time or moderate-sized public subsidies, (2) provisions for closing existing loopholes, such as soft money, issue advocacy, and bundling, and (3) strengthened enforcement of campaign finance regulations. Such approaches are based on the assumption that, while a complete overhaul of the campaign finance system may be unnecessary, without serious corrective surgery the current regime either is collapsing or, in light of 1996, has in fact collapsed. What distinguishes the moderate approach from more comprehensive reform efforts is that, while incremental reform attempts to correct for the most blatant abuses of the existing system, it leaves room for "interested" money to influence the political process. Both approaches assume that elections have become too expensive and that money has a distorting effect on policy outcomes.

The most visible example of moderate reform is the widely touted McCain-Feingold legislation, which, at least in its original form, included provisions for (1) banning soft money, political action committee contributions, and bundling, (2) limiting issue advocacy campaigns, (3) imposing voluntary spending limits on Senate and House campaigns in return for reduced or free advertising time, and (4) limiting out-of-state contributions and total contributions from large contributors. If passed, McCain-Feingold could address a number of the problems, including the growth of soft money and the masquerade of interest group and party electoral campaigns as issue advocacy. In addition, with provisions banning PAC contributions (or in case a ban is declared unconstitutional, significantly reducing PAC contribution limits), McCain-Feingold would address public perceptions that money buys political influence.

While the McCain-Feingold legislation is appealing on a number of counts, it also has its limitations. First, in allowing a continued role for private money, McCain-Feingold may address some of the more blatant abuses of the existing system, but it will also suffer from some of its faults. This perspective is perhaps best expressed by former New Jersey Senator Bill Bradley, who has observed that, "Money in politics is like ants in your kitchen: If you don't close all the holes, money will find a way out. And once money is in the system, it tends to corrupt politics in subtle and gross ways that laws simply cannot control."[3] The link between political contributions and access to political decision makers continues to be legitimized.

Second, as our analyses in previous chapters suggest, spending limits without public subsidies are not likely to increase electoral competition, nor are they likely to significantly decrease the financial advantages enjoyed by incumbents. Free media time may help challengers, but it is unlikely to be enough. In this respect, challengers need money not only for advertising but also to help create campaign organizations. Finally, the positive benefits of McCain-Feingold can be increased further by more comprehensive reform.

If we return once again to the criteria for evaluating campaign finance reform, McCain-Feingold would likely make modest improvements on all dimensions. A ban on soft money, political action committees, and money from large contributors and limits on independent expenditures would reduce the tensions between economic inequality and political equality. However, the continued role for private money would continue to legitimize these tensions. Free radio and TV time for candidates that abide by spending limits might increase voter information, voter turnout, and electoral competition. Any increase in electoral competition, however, will be limited unless candidates are provided with direct public subsidies that can be used to build campaign (and fund-raising) organizations. Otherwise, existing disparities in incumbent and challenger fund-raising will remain even if they are somewhat diminished. Finally, political accountability would be modestly improved as the amount of undisclosed and unregulated money in congressional elections is significantly decreased.

Having said this, one should not dismiss moderate approaches in their entirety. This is especially true compared to the alternative of the do-little approach. Reform proposals that simply ban soft money would do a great deal in terms of cleaning up the electoral process. Yet, as long as private, interested money is the foundation of political campaigns, perceptions of influence will persist. Moreover, the boundaries of the existing system will continue to expand as interested money finds new ways to "get into the kitchen."

The Comprehensive Approach

Overall, we are convinced that the optimal solution to the campaign finance problem in America is full public financing of congressional elections with provisions that would ban soft money and independent party expenditures and place McCain-Feingold-type limits on issue advocacy campaigns. There are a number of reasons that suggest the need for such comprehensive reform. First and foremost, by removing the specter of private money, full public financing of congressional elections removes, as completely as possible, the perception that money buys political influence. While we are not so optimistic as to assume that public financing will create a clean, new world for politics, public financing does more to reconcile the democratic value of the one person, one vote ideal with economic inequality than any other approach.

Second, while some academics and politicians have long derided public funding proposals as "incumbency protection acts" that would reduce electoral competition, the findings presented in the preceding chapters suggest that such a view is misinformed. Largely due to campaign funding practices, electoral politics in the United States is biased in favor of incumbents and the majority party. Public funding enhances the electoral prospects of challengers and of the minority party, thereby enhancing partisan competition.

Third, we reject the argument that many critics of full public financing make regarding the effects of public financing on citizen participation and information. Pointing to some academic studies demonstrating correlations between spending and voter turnout and between spending and candidate recognition, critics of reform argue that the end result of public financing would be less citizen participation and less citizen information. Upon closer inspection, however, such a view appears to be largely without merit. While spending can potentially increase citizen participation and information levels, there is little reason to believe that it normally does so. Higher spending is not a magic bullet that naturally leads to a more involved and informed electorate, nor is it necessarily true that reduced spending will lead to a less informed and less involved citizenry.

We recognize that campaign finance reform may not lead to a more informed and more involved citizenry. The central question is whether any positive effects that reform may have in reducing public cynicism and apathy will be outweighed by any negative effects that may arise from reducing candidate expenditures and, as a result, possibly limit candidate mobilization efforts. Our analyses indicate that this much is clear: arguments that reform would have dire consequences on citizen participation and information levels simply do not stand up to scrutiny.

Returning again to a consideration of the criteria for evaluating campaign finance reform, our best evidence suggests that only the comprehensive approach would have modest to strong positive effects for all of the criteria. Tensions between economic inequality and political equality would be strongly reduced as the influence of private money would be massively reduced. Removing private money would significantly reduce public perceptions that government is controlled by special interests. Voter information would likely increase, as increased challenger spending should increase challenger name recognition and attentiveness to issues on the part of citizens. As we establish in earlier chapters, providing challengers with money so they can actually run serious campaigns is likely to be the only way that one can significantly increase competition in congressional elections. Voter turnout would likely increase in such a setting, and political accountability would receive a major boost. Overall, almost all money spent during the electoral season would be regulated and disclosed; voter information would increase; elections would become more competitive; and in each congressional election there would be a loyal opposition financially capable of providing the citizen with alternative perspectives on governing.

Of course, much of this may be considered immaterial for the practical politician if Congress continues its stalemate over the issue of campaign finance reform. Given this scenario, it is important to conclude by considering the politics of reform and the reasons that we think that the reformist agenda will eventually succeed.

THE POLITICS OF REFORM

Given the current political climate and the behavior of Congress over the last several decades, one might conclude that our call for comprehensive reform instead of moderate reform is actually immaterial because the prospects for the implementation of either type of reform is near zero. For long-time observers of American politics, the failure of campaign finance reform efforts, following a presidential election with the most serious violations of campaign finance laws since Watergate, is hardly surprising. It was no less surprising when the 103rd Congress (1992–94) failed to enact campaign finance reform despite having a president who promised to sign the legislation. For Democrats, reform has always been easier to pass when it was assured of a veto by a Republican president. Nor was it surprising when, in 1995, the infamous handshake between Bill Clinton and Newt Gingrich not only failed to result in reform but never even resulted in a bipartisan commission to recommend solutions. Many cynics would simply argue that, while campaign finance reform rhetoric makes good politics, there are simply too many reasons why Congress is incapable of passing meaningful campaign finance reform.

First, there are serious partisan and ideological differences between Democrats and Republicans regarding both the nature of the problem and the acceptability of various solutions. As the party of smaller governments, Republicans are naturally inclined to oppose public funding of election campaigns. Mitch McConnell (Republican, Kentucky) illustrates this type of opposition to campaign finance reform. He is a staunch believer that such reform efforts involve the government in free speech issues, where the government does not rightfully belong. Other Republicans oppose reform for partisan as opposed to ideological reasons. Despite President Clinton's flouting of existing election laws, it is the Republicans who reign supreme as kings (and queens) of campaign fund-raising. As a result, limits on such activities may cut into a clear partisan advantage enjoyed by the Republican Party.

Second, many Democrats support election reform primarily so that they can lay claim to the "good government" mantle during election campaigns. Their interest in true reform, however, is often less than sincere. As a result, they may vote for reform on the floor, but they also count on Republican opposition, whether such opposition comes in the form of filibuster in the Senate or, as in 1992, a presidential veto.

Third, public opinion on the issue is permissive but not demanding, meaning that, although there is broad public support for reform, the issue is not highly salient to individual voting decisions. One might be tempted to conclude from opinion polls that politicians have not been responsive to public opinion on the issue of campaign finance reform. This is only partly true. Public opinion polls routinely show that the public favors some type of reform and that politics is dominated by special interests. It is considerably less clear as to whether public opinion would support full public financing, particularly once it is labeled "welfare for politicians" by opponents. More important, while public opinion polls show support for reform, they also show that campaign finance reform is not an issue that drives voting decisions for individual voters. The Republican Revolution of 1994, for example, followed a Republican-led Senate filibuster of campaign finance reform. Citizens may want the system cleaned up, but they are not demanding political action.

Finally, many would suggest that the *Buckley* decision and subsequent Court decisions establish a fundamental constitutional wall that prevents the implementation of any meaningful campaign finance reform. Senator McConnell has been the leading opponent of comprehensive campaign finance reform for a number of years. His strategy to stop such reform relies heavily upon the *Buckley* decision. Not only does it give him a theoretical justification for his opposition, it also has the practical appeal of suggesting that, even if comprehensive reform were desirable (which, according to him, it isn't), it makes no sense to pass legislation that the Supreme Court will declare unconstitutional. It is in many ways a compelling logic, and the *Buckley* decision is an important impediment to comprehensive campaign finance reform.

The reality of the political landscape does make the immediate prospects of comprehensive reform seem bleak. Yet we would argue that comprehensive campaign finance reform will eventually be passed into law. The current system is so scandalous and is deteriorating so quickly that the arguments in favor of reform become more compelling each year. The systemic problems in the current campaign finance system cannot simply be wished away, and ignoring them virtually guarantees they will reach crisis proportions. Even though Congress has failed to pass any meaningful campaign finance reform in recent memory, the political tide seems to be slowly moving toward reform efforts. In the last Congress, McCain-Feingold was stopped in the Senate through the use of a filibuster. When Newt Gingrich used parliamentary tactics to stop a vote on similar legislation in the House of Representatives, supporters successfully used the discharge petition to force House action. While this is certainly no guarantee of success, it is an indication that the tide may be turning on the issue of campaign finance reform at the federal level.

Campaign finance reform is proceeding even more rapidly at the state level. Twenty-four states already have some provision for public funding of state legislative campaigns. As laboratories of democracy, the states provide a testing ground for policy innovation. They can acquaint citizens and the politicos of the future with significant campaign reform, making similar efforts at the federal level appear less threatening.

Of course, without significant pressure from "outside the Beltway," reform is unlikely even if it appears to enjoy fairly wide public support in public opinion polls. As scandals continue to mount, the public becomes ever-more cynical and distrustful of the current campaign finance system. Throughout the history of the United States, corruption has bred public cynicism and mistrust until a major scandal has pushed the public beyond the breaking point and government was forced to reform itself. The current campaign finance system is no different. Eventually, a crisis will be so severe that the public will demand reform. For this reason, it is not a question of whether or not reform will eventually be passed. The question is whether we reform in the near future, when we can carefully reform in response to systemic problems, or whether we reform in a crisis atmosphere, when ill-advised reform efforts are more likely.

Finally, we suggest that the *Buckley* decision, while a significant impediment to reform, is not the insurmountable wall suggested by the critics of reform. First of all, we reject the rhetorical arguments by apologists, such as Senator McConnell, who equate money with free speech. Money is not speech. If you talk or write to someone encouraging them to vote for a candidate, you have broken no law. If you pay them to vote for a candidate, you have broken a law in every state in the Union. Second, we are uneasy with the Supreme Court's proposition that money used for campaign expenditures is a form of constitutionally protected expression. Limiting campaign expenditures does not limit speech itself but, rather, limits the amplification and dissemination of speech through the mass media. The Court's decision equating candidate expenditures with free speech guarantees access to the media and the amplification of speech to those who can afford it. Those who cannot afford such access may say whatever they want, but they will say it much more softly.

Finally, even if we did accept the rough equivalence between campaign expenditures and free expression, we argue that the Supreme Court is simply wrong in how it views the balance among constitutional rights in the *Buckley* decision. As in many civil rights questions, the Court often has to balance constitutional rights when evaluating electoral laws. Contribution limits, laws prohibiting vote buying, laws prohibiting the intimidation of voters, and regulations prohibiting electioneering near a voting booth have all been upheld by the Supreme Court as necessary to protect the integrity of the electoral process. We view the current campaign finance system as no less a threat to the integrity of federal elections.[4]

To have meaningful campaign finance reform, the *Buckley* decision needs to be reversed just as Supreme Court decisions that gave constitutional approval for slavery and segregation were eventually overturned. Appropriate Supreme Court appointments could be used to allow the Court to slowly modify *Buckley* or to simply reverse it, as the Supreme Court did with the *Plessy v. Ferguson* (1896) decision, which upheld segregation, through the *Brown v. Board of Education* ruling. The second alternative is to pass a constitutional amendment in an effort to overturn *Buckley*. Such an amendment has been introduced during recent sessions of Congress. *Buckley* is an impediment to meaningful campaign finance reform; but it is not an insurmountable obstacle.

Overall, the politics of reform ensure that reformist rhetoric will remain on the public agenda but that immediate reform is not likely. Republicans want to nail President Clinton and Vice President Gore for campaign finance violations, but they are largely uninterested in altering a system that favors these violations. While this doesn't excuse the Clinton-Gore indiscretions, it is reasonable to assume that had Bob Dole won the presidency in 1996, there would be no congressional or Justice Department investigations of campaign fund-raising practices. Democrats, on the other hand, claim to want reform but are more interested in portraying Republicans as puppets bought, owned, and controlled with corporate dollars. Democratic claims that the system is corrupt and in need of reform are true enough, but Democrats should at least acknowledge that they have played an important role in further corrupting the system.

Even if the immediate prospects for campaign finance reform seem slight, reform will eventually occur because the problems in the current system of campaign finance are so fundamental that citizens will eventually demand action. The status quo in campaign finance in the late 1990s is unacceptable. Large contributors, including individuals, corporations, and labor unions, dominate American politics in a manner reminiscent of the pre-Watergate era. Access is bought and sold on a continuous basis. Elections are largely uncompetitive, and citizens are increasingly withdrawn from politics and the electoral process. Without reform, the future promises more of the same: more aggressive pursuit of soft money by political parties and by party leadership, more lucrative spending on issue advocacy campaigns by parties and interest groups, increasingly uncompetitive elections as Republicans learn to fully exploit the advantages of their majority party status, and an electorate that increasingly sees politics as best left to those who can afford it. It is unlikely that campaign finance reform can cure all that ails the American electoral process, but this much is clear: without campaign finance reform, the political system will continue to lurch toward crisis.

NOTES

1. The phrase *do no harm* is from the Hippocratic oath and has been used by Michael J. Malbin and Thomas L. Gais (1998) as a standard for evaluating the effectiveness of state campaign finance laws.

2. More than fifty years ago E. E., Schattscheinder made the argument that "modern democracy is unthinkable save in terms of the parties" (1942, 1).

3. Quoted in "Aim for the Heart," *New Democrat*, May/June 1997.

4. A number of legal scholars agree that the Supreme Court is simply wrong in the *Buckley* decision (see, for example, Rosenkranz 1998; Levitt 1993).

Appendix A

The Statistical Basis for Chapter Four

The bulk of the analysis in chapter 4 is based on simulations of a number of hypothetical campaign finance reform scenarios. To conduct the simulations, it was first necessary to run a basic regression model. In the analysis, the Democratic percentage of the vote is seen as a function of candidate spending, incumbency, nonincumbent candidate quality, and the underlying partisan division of the district. Our unit of analysis is the aggregate, district-level, Democratic percentage of the vote per House election. Because a great deal of the literature is devoted to the important distinction between incumbent and challenger spending, interaction terms between incumbency and candidate spending are also included in the model (see, for example, Jacobson 1978, 1980, 1985, 1990b; Green and Krasno 1988). More formally, the model can be specified as follows:

$$\text{Dem\%} = a + b_1 (\text{Dem\$}) + b_2 (\text{Rep\$}) + b_3 (\text{Dinc}) + b_4 (\text{Rinc}) + b_5 (\text{DemQual}) + b_6 (\text{RepQual}) + b_7 (\text{Partisan}) + b_8 (\text{Dem\$ X Dinc}) + b_9 (\text{Rep\$ X Rinc}) + e.$$

Where

Dem% = the Democratic percentage of the vote;
Dem$ = the natural log of Democratic spending;
Rep$ = the natural log of Republican spending;
Dinc = Democratic incumbency, coded 1 if there is an incumbent Democrat, 0 otherwise;
Rinc = Republican incumbency, coded 1 if there is an incumbent Republican, 0 otherwise;
DemQual = candidate quality, a measure on a five-point scale, where 0 indicates no previous political experience, 1 indicates nonelective political experience, 2 indicates local political experience, 3 indicates

state legislative experience, and 4 indicates statewide experience or former representatives;

RepQual = a measure for Republican nonincumbent candidates that is identical to DemQual; and

Partisan = the underlying partisan division of the district as indicated by the percentage of the vote received by Clinton in 1992.

A couple of points are in order regarding the model. First, the model explicitly incorporates the distinction between incumbent and nonincumbent expenditures made in the previous literature (see, for example, Jacobson 1978, 1980, 1985, 1990b; Green and Krasno 1988). Second, the model taps the underlying partisan division of the district using previous presidential vote rather than previous congressional vote. Unlike the previous congressional vote, the previous presidential vote should not be as contaminated by the effects of congressional incumbency and, consequently, should give a better indication of the underlying partisan leanings of the district. Third, ordinary least squares is used to estimate the model.

While there is considerable debate regarding the appropriate estimator of a model that includes campaign spending, we decided to use OLS to estimate our model. In the previous literature, models that employ OLS are generally less supportive of campaign finance reform (see, for example, Jacobson 1980; Abramowitz 1991a), while models that employ more sophisticated estimation procedures are more supportive of reform (see, for example, Krasno and Green 1993; Green and Krasno 1988; Goidel and Gross 1996; Gerber 1998; Erikson and Palfrey 1998). For this reason, the results presented in this analysis should be biased in favor of the status quo and, by extension, against campaign reform. In addition, the purpose of this text is to forecast the number of Democrats expected to lose in a number of hypothetical reform scenarios. Our purpose is not to identify the number of incumbents expected to lose or to attribute causal responsibility to incumbent or challenger spending. Because we are primarily interested in forecasting rather than in making causal inferences, and because the previous literature indicates that OLS provides estimates that tend to be most supportive of the status quo, we believe that OLS is a suitable estimator for the purposes of this analysis.

On a final note, the previous literature is inconsistent in its treatment of spending as an endogenous variable. Some works assume that both incumbent and challenger spending are endogenous variables (Goidel and Gross 1994), while other works assume that only incumbent spending is endogenous (Green and Krasno 1988) or leave incumbent spending out of the model altogether (Abramowitz 1991a). The confusion surrounding questions of endogenous regressors and the simultaneity bias led Gary Jacobson (1990b) to conclude that the problem may itself be intractable. While we are more optimistic that these questions can be resolved, addressing these problems is beyond the scope of the current analysis (but see Goidel and Gross 1994).

Data for this analysis were collected on all contested elections in 1994 and 1996, though we limit the current analysis to those elections in which both the Republican and the Democratic candidate spent at least $500. The data on candidate spending, Democratic percentage of the vote, and incumbency were taken from *Politics in America* 1996 and Federal Election Commission 1995–96. Data on candidate quality were taken from the special editions of *Congressional Quarterly Weekly Report* devoted to the 1994 and 1996 congressional elections. The results of the initial regression analysis are displayed in table A.1.

As can be seen in table A.1, the model provides an impressive fit to the data across election years. Looking first at the results for the 1994 elections, both the *r*-square and the adjusted *r*-square indicate that the model explains nearly 88 percent of the variance in the Democratic party vote. With the exception of the variable tapping Democratic nonincumbent quality,

Table A.1   OLS Regression of Democratic Vote on Candidate Spending

Variable	1994 Estimate	1996 Estimate
Democratic spending	3.15 (.40)**	3.95 (.31)**
Republican spending	-3.19 (.29)**	-3.66 (.32)**
Democratic incumbent	51.32 (10.7)**	49.70 (10.47)**
Republican incumbent	-33.90 (14.7)*	-30.15 (11.35)**
Democratic quality	-.09 (.34)	.66 (.30)*
Republican quality	-.97 (.31)**	-.71 (.37)*
District partisanship	.38 (.03)**	.39 (.03)**
Democratic incumbent * Democratic spending	-3.44 (.80)**	-3.17 (.78)**
Republican incumbent * Republican spending	2.06 (1.10)*	2.02 (.83)*
Constant	30.31 (6.44)**	29.50 (5.83)**
r-square	.8796	.8998
Adjusted *r*-square	.8763	.8974

Note: Standard errors are in parentheses.
*$p < .05$; **$p < .01$.

every variable in the equation is statistically significant. While this nonfind-ing was unexpected given past research on the electoral importance of nonincumbent political experience (see, for example, Bond, Covington, and Fleisher 1985; Krasno and Green 1988; Jacobson 1989), given the anti-Democratic mood of the electorate in 1994, it is not altogether surprising. Also worth noting is the relatively high value for the coefficients associated with the variables tapping Democratic and Republican incumbency. While it may seem that these values are highly inflated, keep in mind that the main effect in this case indicates the value of incumbency for those incum-bents who spent no money in their reelection attempt. Since we would as-sume that these hypothetical incumbents were not challenged, the ex-pected vote should be near 100 percent.

The results based on the 1996 elections are very similar. As with the 1994 data, the model provides an impressive fit to the data explaining nearly 90 percent of the variance. Moreover, every variable included in the regres-sion model is statistically significant at the .05 level or greater. Finally, look-ing across election years, the coefficients for each of the variables are rela-tively stable, indicating that our estimates of the effects of candidate spending on the Democratic percentage of the vote are not peculiar to a given election year.

On the basis of these initial regression results, we ran simulations to esti-mate the likely effect of spending limits, matching funds, partial public fi-nancing, and full public financing on the electoral fortunes of Democratic congressional candidates. To estimate the effects of the respective spend-ing scenarios on the outcome of the 1994 and 1996 elections, we computed the aggregate number of Democrats predicted to lose based on a summa-tion of each individual probability that the Democratic candidate won the election (Gelman and King 1994; Goidel and Gross 1996). According to Andrew Gelman and Gary King (1994), the probability that the Democratic candidate won the election can be computed as follows:

$$\text{Prob (Democrat Wins)} = (Y^{\text{Pred}} - .50)/\text{SE}^{\text{Pred Y}}.$$

Summing these probabilities across congressional districts should then give a reasonable approximation of the number of Democrats expected to win or lose in a given election year.

In creating the hypothetical spending scenarios, we used a wide range of reform proposals and possible limits. For the simulations designed to esti-mate the effects of spending limits, we set any candidate spending greater than the designated limit equal to the limit. The designated limits ran from a low of $100,000 to a high of $1 million. For the simulations of matching funds, we first multiplied candidate spending by two; if this modified spending variable was greater than the designated limit, we truncated candidate spending to the limit. As in the analysis of spending limits, the limits ranged from $100,000 to $1 million. For the simulations of partial public financing, we first created a modified candidate spending variable by adding the value of the communication voucher; if this modified spending variable exceeded the designated limit, we then set it equal to the limit. The limits in this particular portion of the analysis ranged from $400,000 to $1 million, while the vouchers ranged from $100,000 to $300,000. Finally, for the simulations of full public financing, we set candidate spending equal to the designated limit ranging from $100,000 to $1 million.

To provide a baseline for comparing the results of the simulations, we first computed estimates of Democratic seat losses and gains for a model assuming no change in campaign finance laws. According to this baseline prediction, in 1994 the Democrats would have lost fifty-seven seats and in 1996 they would have gained seven seats had the elections conformed exactly to the expectations of our regression model. We should note that this baseline prediction slightly overpredicts the actual number of seats lost by the Democratic Party in 1994 and the number of seats gained by the Democratic Party in 1996.

Appendix B

The Statistical Basis for Chapter Five

The analysis presented in chapter 5 is derived from computer-based simulations estimating the likely effect of various versions of campaign finance reform on voter turnout. In the analysis, the dependent variable is defined as the number of votes cast during the election as a percentage of the total voting-age population in the district. Voter turnout is then seen as a function of various demographic and political factors. In terms of demographics, the regression model includes the percentage of the population with a college education, the percentage residing in rural areas, the percentage over sixty-five years of age, and the percentage of minorities in the district. In terms of political factors, the model includes the presence of a gubernatorial or senatorial election, the competitiveness of the House campaign, whether the incumbent was running for reelection, the closing date for voter registration, prior voter turnout, and Democratic and Republican spending. In our original analyses, we included logged, rather than untransformed, spending variables. Surprisingly, the results indicate that the untransformed candidate spending has a larger effect on voter turnout than does logged candidate spending. Because we are arguing that campaign spending has a much more limited effect on turnout than is assumed in the previous literature, we present the analysis using the untransformed spending variables. More formally, the model can be stated as follows:

Turnout = Prior Turnout + Education + Minority + Region + Rural + Age + Senate Race + Governor's Race + Competition + Democratic Spending + Republican Spending + Open Seat + Closing Date + e.

The results of this initial regression analysis are displayed in table B.1. As can be seen in the table, our model of district-level turnout does an impressive job of predicting aggregate turnout levels. Overall, the model explains 78 percent of the variance in district-level turnout in 1994 and 84 percent of the variance in 1996. In the analysis based on the 1994 data, the variables

Table B.1 Regression of Aggregate, District-Level Turnout

Variable	1996 Elections	1994 Elections
Prior turnout	.84 (.04)**	.65 (.04)**
Education	.06 (.03)*	.16 (.03)**
Minority	-.07 (.01)**	.02 (.02)
Region	2.4 (.68)**	-1.43 (.69)*
Rural	-.001 (.02)	.11 (.01)**
Age	.005 (.03)	.10 (.03)**
Senate race	2.0 (.46)**	2.76 (.54)**
Governor's race	3.6 (.65)**	3.0 (.50)**
Competition	.01 (.02)	-.018 (.016)
Democratic spending	-.004 (.005)	.013 (.006)*
Republican spending	.015 (.005)**	-.001 (.006)
Open seat	.48 (.65)	.49 (.60)
Closing date	-.05 (.02)*	-.02 (.02)
Constant	14.1 (2.1)**	-13.1 (2.9)**
Adjusted *r*-square	.84	.78

Note: Candidate spending is measured in $10,000. Standard errors are in parentheses.
$*p < .01$; $**p < .05$ (one-tailed test).

that one would suspect are mostly closely associated with aggregate turnout are in fact significant and in the expected direction. We find higher aggregate turnout is associated with higher previous turnout during the presidential election year, larger percentages of college-educated citizens, more rural congressional districts, larger percentages of citizens over the age of sixty-five, the presence of a statewide election, and non-Southern congressional districts. Despite Republican gains in 1994, Democratic rather than Republican spending is associated with higher voter turnout.

In 1996, with the stimulus of the presidential election, many of the demographic factors were less important as predictors of aggregate, district-level turnout. Of the demographic factors included in the model, the percentage of the district with a college education and the percentage of minorities within the district were statistically associated with voter turnout. In addition, as in 1994, the presence of a gubernatorial or senatorial election stimulated voter turnout in House campaigns. However, in 1996, it was Republican rather than Democratic spending that appeared to stimulate voter participation. Oddly, this is consistent with the 1994 results in that the party disadvantaged by short-term political trends appeared to be most effective in stimulating aggregate voter turnout.

Based on prior research, it seems likely that the effectiveness of campaign spending in stimulating voter participation depends, at least in part, on the electoral environment in which the election is taking place. Candidate spending, one would presume, should have a different effect depending on whether candidate spending reflects spending by an incumbent, a challenger, or a candidate for an open seat (Jackson 1993, 1997). To explore this possibility, we conducted an additional regression analysis, including interactive terms designed to test whether the effect of spending differs according to type of candidate. The equation for this analysis is specified as follows:

Turnout 94 = Equation 1 + Republican Incumbent + Democratic Incumbent + (Republican Spending × Republican Incumbent) + (Republican Spending × Democratic Incumbent) + (Democratic Spending × Democratic Incumbent) + (Democratic Spending × Republican Incumbent) + e.

The two variables indicating partisan affiliation and incumbency replace the open-seat variable used in the earlier analysis. Taken together, the base effects of the spending variables in combination with the interactive terms indicate the contingent effects of campaign spending on voter turnout. First, the base effects of the spending variables indicate the effect of spending by Republican and Democratic candidates in open-seat elections. Second, the interaction between Republican spending and Republican incumbency status indicates whether spending by Republican incumbents had a different effect on district-level voter participation than spending by Republican open-seat contestants. Similarly, the interaction between Democratic spending and Democratic incumbency status indicates whether spending by Democratic incumbents had a different impact on turnout than spending by Democratic open-seat contestants. Finally, whether there is a difference in the effect of spending by Republican and Democratic challengers can be determined by looking at the effects of the interactions between Republican spending and Democratic incumbency and Democratic spending and Republican incumbency, respectively.

The results presented in table B.2 indicate that the effects of campaign spending are highly contingent on type of candidate spending. In 1994, Republican campaign spending appeared to stimulate turnout only in those races in which a Republican challenger faced a Democratic incumbent. Spending by Republican incumbents and open-seat contestants during the 1994 elections appears to have had either no effect on aggregate turnout or a negative effect. For Democrats in 1994, it appears that higher levels of spending are associated only with higher turnout in open-seat races, while spending by both Democratic incumbents and challengers appears to have had a negligible effect. Overall, the results from 1994 indicate that the effect of candidate spending on voter turnout is contingent both

Table B.2   **Conditional Effects of Spending on Aggregate District-Level Turnout**

Variable	1996 Elections	1994 Elections
Prior turnout	.84 (.04)**	.65 (.04)**
Education	.06 (.03)*	.15 (.03)**
Minority	-.08 (.02)**	.02 (.02)
Region	2.5 (.68)**	-1.5 (.69)*
Rural	-.001 (.02)	.11 (.02)**
Age	-.002 (.03)	.11 (.03)**
Senate race	2.0 (.46)**	2.5 (.54)**
Governor's race	3.6 (.65)**	3.0 (.50)**
Competition	.01 (.02)	-.02 (.02)
Democratic spending	-.013 (.019)	.045 (.015)**
Republican spending	-.006 (.016)	-.012 (.009)
Republican incumbent	-2.3 (1.6)	4.39 (3.88)
Democratic incumbent	-1.8 (1.6)	3.47 (3.81)
Closing date	-.04 (.02)*	-.01(.03)
Republican spending * Republican incumbent	.012 (.017)	.0007 (.016)
Republican spending * Democratic incumbent	.027 (.021)	.030 (.014)*
Democratic spending * Democratic incumbent	.003 (.021)	-.040 (.017)**
Democratic spending * Republican incumbent	.030 (.020)	-.035 (.024)
Constant	16.5 (2.6)**	-16.1 (4.7)**
Adjusted *r*-square	.85	.78

Note: Candidate spending is measured in $10,000. Standard errors in parentheses.
$*p < .05; **p < .01$ (one-tailed test).

upon the type of candidate spending (incumbent versus challenger) and on candidate partisanship.

Looking at the results from 1996, however, we find no significant effects of campaign spending on voter turnout (table B.2). Unlike 1994, the effects of candidate spending in 1996 were apparently not contingent on candidate type or candidate partisanship. The result conforms with recent research indicating that, during presidential election years, spending in gubernatorial and senatorial campaigns fails to stimulate voter participation in statewide elections (Jackson 1997).

Because the results differ depending on whether the year was a midterm or a presidential election year, we used the results presented in table B.1 for simulating aggregate turnout in 1996 and the results presented in table B.2 for simulating turnout in 1994. In creating the hypothetical spending scenarios, we used the reform scenarios as outlined in appendix A.

Appendix C

The Statistical Basis for Chapter Six

The tables below show the logistic regression results used to create the figures in chapter 6. As shown in columns 1 and 2 of table C.1, candidate spending, regardless of whether it is measured as total spending or separated into Republican and Democratic spending, had an insignificant impact on the probability that an individual would participate in a congressional election, either through the simple act of voting or through other forms of participation.

Table C.1   Effect of Mobilization on Political Participation, 1994

Variable	Model 1: Vote	Model 2: Vote	Model 3: Other	Model 4: Other
Constant	-4.59 (.57)**	-4.62 (.67) **	-2.12 (.77) **	-2.12 (.77) **
South	-.25 (.15)	-.257 (.15)	.054 (.19)	.085 (.18)
Education	.37 (.05) **	.37 (.05) **	.45 (.07) **	.44 (.07) **
Family income	.05 (.01) **	.05 (.01) **	.027 (.015)	.027 (.015)
Age	.05 (.025) *	.05 (.015) *	.03 (.03)	.03 (.03)
Age squared	-.0002 (.0003)	-.0002 (.0003)	-.0003 (.0002)	-.0003 (.0003)
African American	-.12 (.25)	-.14 (.249)	.017 (.30)	.03 (.30)
Closing date	-.005 (.007)	-.005 (.007)	-.008 (.009)	-.008 (.009)
Senate race	.31 (.19)	.30 (.19)	-.39 (.25)	-.36 (.24)
Gubernatorial race	.28 (.17)	-.27 (.17)	-.08 (.19)	-.09 (.19)
Competitive election	.004 (.006)	.005 (.006)	.03 (.007) **	.03 (.007) **
Total spending	----	.000000027 (.00000015)	----	.000000027 (.00000018)
Republican candidate spending	.00000017 (.00000024)	----	-.00000022 (.00000028)	----
Democratic candidate spending	.00000007 (.00000019)	----	.0000002 (.00000025)	----
Candidate contact	.86 (.17) **	.86 (.17) **	.88 (.19) **	.89 (.19) **
Party contact	1.49 (.18) **	1.46 (.18) **	.90 (.24) **	.89 (.24) **
-2 log likelihood	1309.152	1309.762	965.0	966.221
Chi-square	360.745 **	360.135 **	164.508 **	163.287 **

Note: Cell entries are logit estimates. Standard errors are in parentheses.
$*p < .05; **p < .01$ (two-tailed test).

185

The same models estimated with the 1996 data are listed in table C.2. The 1996 survey respondents were not asked in separate questions whether they were contacted by a political party or candidate. Respondents were, however, asked if they had been contacted by a political party and then in a separate question asked if they were contacted by anyone else. We coded both variables in the 1996 analysis below, but only direct contact by the political party exerted any significant impact on the probability of political activity.

Finally, in table C.3, we include the descriptions for each variable used in the analysis.

Table C.2　Effect of Mobilization on Political Participation, 1996

Variable	Model 1: Vote	Model 2: Vote	Model 3: Other	Model 4: Other
Constant	-2.37***	-2.36***	-.616	-.618
South	-.134	-.139	.047	.054
Education	.444***	.444***	.418***	.419***
Family income	.061***	.061 ***	.025*	.025*
Age	.037	.036	.042*	.042*
Age squared	-.00003	-.00003	-.0004*	-.0004*
African American	.237	.242	-.007	-.015
Closing date	-.0008	-.0008	-.015	-.015
Senate race	-.049	-.044	-.518**	-.528**
Gubernatorial race	-.098	-.10	-.404*	-.403*
Competitive election	-.007	-.007	.005	.005
Total spending	----	-.00000022*	----	.000000016
Republican candidate spending	-.00000024	----	.000000054	----
Democratic candidate spending	-.00000018	----	-.00000004	----
Party contact	.929***	.928***	.884 ***	.885***
Contact by someone other than political party				.324
	-.039	-.042	.319	
-2 log likelihood	1172.373	1172.424	1077.740	1077.837
Chi-square	224.591	224.541	146.381	146.284

Note: Cell entries are logit estimates.
*$p < .10$, **$p < .05$, ***$p < .01$ (two-tailed test).

Table C.3   Variable Descriptions

Variable	Description
Senate	Coded 1 if there was a Senate race in the state, 0 otherwise.
Governor	Coded 1 if there was a Governor's race in the state, 0 otherwise.
Competition	The absolute value of the Democratic percentage of the vote minus the Republican percentage of the vote.
Republican incumbent	Coded 1 if a Republican incumbent was running for reelection, 0 otherwise.
Democratic incumbent	Coded 1 if a Democratic incumbent was running for reelection, 0 otherwise.
Democratic spending	Total amount of money spent by the Democratic candidate in 1994.
Republican spending	Total amount of money spent by the Republican candidate in 1994.
Open seat	Coded 1 if no incumbent was running, 0 otherwise.
South	Coded 1 if respondent lived in the South, 0 otherwise.
Education	Coded 1 (less than high school), 2 (high school diploma or equivalency test), 3 (more than 12 years, but no higher degree), 4 (junior or community college degree), 5 (BA degree), 6 (advanced degree).
Income	Coded 1 (less than $2,999) through 24 ($105,000 and over).
Senate race	Coded 1 if the respondent lived in a state with a concurrent senatorial race, 0 otherwise.
Gubernatorial race	Coded 1 if the respondent lived in a state with a concurrent gubernatorial race, 0 otherwise.
Party contact	Coded 1 if the respondent was contacted by a political party, 0 otherwise.
Candidate contact	Coded 1 if the respondent was contacted by a political candidate, 0 otherwise.
Age	Age of respondent in years.
African American	Coded 1 if the respondent was African American, 0 otherwise.
Closing date	Number of days prior to the election that registration was closed.

Appendix D

The Statistical Basis for Chapter Seven

To test the hypotheses presented in chapter 7, we constructed a number of dependent variables aimed at gauging the following. First, the amount of candidate-specific information possessed by individual citizens was measured by their ability to recall, recognize, and ideologically place House candidates. For the purposes of this analysis, we created an index of candidate familiarity based on an individual's ability to recall, recognize, and place House candidates on an ideological scale (Abramowitz and Segal 1992). In analyses not presented in the text, we also tested logit equations on the separate indicators of candidate familiarity. We present the index of candidate familiarity because it provides a nice summary of these analyses.

Second, individual respondents' motivation for acquiring new information was measured by their self-reported level of political interest, concern about the election outcome, and attentiveness to campaign news. We also include measures of respondents' ability to discriminate between the ideology of the candidates and the certainty of these ideological placements. This dimension of cognitive mobilization, we believe, is extremely important if citizens are going to be able to make accurate and valid decisions in congressional elections.

In specifying the statistical models, we assume that these dependent variables are a function of individual characteristics (education, race, gender, age, and partisan strength) and campaign-related factors (candidate spending, party and candidate contact, the presence of a gubernatorial or senatorial campaign, and whether the election involved a Republican or a Democratic incumbent running for reelection). To test these hypotheses, we enhanced survey data from the 1994 and 1996 National Election Studies survey data with contextual data on candidate campaign spending.

There are important differences in the National Election Studies surveys between the midterm election of 1994 and the presidential election of 1996. While the 1994 survey focused largely on the midterm congressional elections, the 1996 survey was, understandably, more focused on the presi-

189

dential election. As a result, there were many more questions in the 1994 survey relating to the congressional races in a respondent's district. For example, in the 1994 survey, respondents were asked about their interest in the congressional races, if they cared about the outcome of the races, and so on. In the 1996 survey, these questions were geared toward interest and concern regarding the presidential election. Since we are looking at the effects of congressional spending, it makes more sense to focus our attention on the cognitive engagement of citizens in the congressional races of 1994. Consequently, we focus primarily, although not exclusively, on the results from the 1994 election.

Nevertheless, while the 1994 National Election Studies survey provides more potential measures of cognitive engagement than does the 1996 National Election Studies survey, we attempted to replicate the results found in 1994 on the 1996 survey wherever possible. One altered question item involves how the survey administrators asked respondents about who contacted them. In the 1994 survey, respondents were asked if they had been contacted by a political party or candidate. In the 1996 survey, respondents were asked if they had been contacted by a political party and, then, in a subsequent question asked if the respondent had "any other" contact. Consequently, in 1994 we have separate measures of direct contact from both a political party and a political candidate, but in 1996 we have only measures of contact by a political party and "any other" contact.

In table D.1, we present the results of separate regression analyses based on partisan classification (Republican versus Democrat) and candidate type (incumbent versus challenger) for 1994. The results in table D.1 confirm the conventional wisdom that candidate familiarity is a function of education, incumbency, the presence of a concurrent statewide election, as well as candidate spending and candidate and party contact. As discussed in past research, the more a candidate spends, the more familiar he or she becomes to respondents. This is hardly a surprising finding given the abundance of research documenting similar findings (see, for example, Jacobson 1997b).

To capture the effects of spending and other campaign-related factors on individual motivations to acquire new information, we regressed the demographic and campaign-related variables presented in table D.2 on an individual's concern about the election outcome, their interest in the election, and their attentiveness to news about the House elections (see below for a more complete description of these variables). As can be seen in table D.2, spending appears to have very little impact on whether individuals care about the outcome of House elections. In fact, the only significant finding indicates that higher Republican spending was associated with a less-concerned electorate. Based on the evidence presented in table D.2,

Table D.1 Regression Analysis of Candidate Familiarity, 1994

Variable	Republican	Democratic	Incumbent	Challenger
Education	.04	.05	.05	.032
	(.02)**	(.02)**	(.02)**	(.018)*
Income	.006	.005	.01	.005
	(.004)	(.005)	(.004)**	(.005)
Age	.007	.016	.015	-.01
	(.008)	(.01)*	(.008)*	(.009)
Age squared	-.0001	-.0001	-.0001	.00007
	(.0001)	(.0001)	(.0001)	(.00009)
Race	.0004	-.09	-.15	.09
	(.09)	(.09)	(.09)*	(.09)
Gender	.05	.12	.07	.09
	(.05)	(.05)**	(.05)	(.05)*
Partisan strength	.07	.09	.06	.09
	(.02)**	(.03)**	(.03)	(.03)**
Dem/Inc spending	.02	.22	.10	.04
	(.03)	(.03)**	(.06)*	(.06)
Rep/Chal spending	.20	.01	-.005	.21
	(.02)**	(.02)	(.02)	(.02)**
Party contact	.22	.20	.15	.29
	(.06)**	(.06)**	(.06)**	(.06)**
Candidate contact	.47	.65	.93	.17
	(.06)**	(.06)**	(.07)**	(.07)**
Dem incumbent	-.19	.44	-.04	-.07
	(.07)**	(.07)**	(.05)	(.06)
Rep incumbent	.44	-.10	----	----
	(.09)**	(.09)		
Senate race	.09	-.12	-.12	.02
	(.06)	(.07)*	(.06)**	(.07)
Governor's race	-.19	-.17	-.36	-.24
	(.06)**	(.06)**	(.07)**	(.07)**
Constant	-2.20	-2.83	-.74	-1.94
	(.40)**	(.42)**	(.69)	(.72)**
r-square	.35	.36	.32	.22
Adjusted *r*-square	.34	.35	.31	.21

$*p < .10; **p < .05.$

there is no reason to believe that greater candidate spending results in a more politically concerned citizenry. Individual citizens may be more familiar with the candidates, but they do not appear to care more (and may in fact care less) about the election outcome. While spending apparently had neither a positive nor a negative effect on concern about House election outcomes in 1994, both party and candidate contact had strong, positive, and significant effects.

In table D.3, we present regression analyses based on an individual's self-reported political interest. As can be seen in table D.3, candidate spending exerts no effect on individual political interest. As with individual concern about the election outcome, however, party and candidate contact exert strong, positive, and significant effects. If higher spending is associated

Table D.2　Regression Analysis of Concern About Outcome, 1994

Variable	Republican/Democratic	Incumbent/Challenger
Education	.11	.09
	(.02)***	(.02)
Income	.009	.011
	(.005)*	(.05)**
Age	.02	.013
	(.01)**	(.01)
Age squared	-.0001	-.00001
	(.0001)	(.0001)
Race	.04	.08
	(.09)	(.10)
Gender	.09	.07
	(.05)*	(.06)
Partisan strength	.18	.19
	(.03)***	(.03)***
Rep/ Chal spending	-.04	-.01
	(.02)*	(.02)
Dem/Inc spending	.02	-.04
	(.03)	(.06)
Party contact	.23	.24
	(.06)***	(.07)***
Candidate contact	.43	.44
	(.07)***	(.08)***
Republican incumbent	.19	----
	(.09)**	
Democratic incumbent	-.003	-.11
	(.08)	(.06)*
Senate race	.03	.02
	(.07)	(.07)
Governor's race	-.09	-.16
	(.06)	(.07)**
Constant	.89	1.76
	(.43)**	(.77)**
r-Square	.22	.21
Adjusted r-Square	.21	.20

$*p < .10; **p < .05; ***p < .01.$

with a less interested and less concerned electorate in House elections, table D.4 presents evidence that higher spending may also result in an electorate that pays less attention to the media reports about the campaign.

According to table D.4, Republican spending appeared to have a slight positive effect on attentiveness to news reports about the 1994 campaign. As a result, higher Republican spending in 1994 may have been associated with greater media attentiveness at the individual level. However, the effect of Republican spending is dwarfed by the effect of Democratic spending associated with less individual attentiveness to the media reports about the campaign. Even presented in the best possible light, it is hard to make a convincing argument that greater spending increased individual attentive-

Table D.3   Regression Analysis of Political Interest, 1994

Variable	Republican/Democrat	Incumbent/Challenger
Education	.07 (.01)***	.06 (.02)***
Income	.008 (.003)**	.01 (.004)**
Age	.02 (.006)**	.009 (.007)
Age squared	-.0001 (.0001)	-.00004 (.00007)
Race	.10 (.07)	.08 (.08)
Gender	.11 (.04)***	.12 (.04)***
Partisan strength	.13 (.02)***	.13 (.02)***
Rep/Chal spending	-.02 (.02)	-.01 (.02)
Dem/Inc spending	-.02 (.02)	-.05 (.05)
Party contact	.19 (.04)***	.18 (.05)***
Candidate contact	.22 (.05)***	.21 (.06)***
Republican incumbent	.15 (.07)**	----
Democratic incumbent	.07 (.06)	-.09 (.05)*
Senate race	-.05 (.05)	-.07 (.05)
Governor's race	-.06 (.05)	-.16 (.06)***
Constant	.10 (.33)	.85 (.58)
r-square	.18	.17
Adjusted r-square	.17	.16

*$p < .10$; **$p < .05$; ***$p < .01$.

Table D.4   Regression Analysis of Media Attentiveness, 1994

Variable	Republican/Democratic	Incumbent/Challenger
Education	.08 (.02)**	.08 (.02)**
Income	.009 (.005)*	.01 (.006)*
Age	.001 (.01)	-.00004 (.01)
Age squared	.00001 (.0009)	.00002 (.0001)
Race	.20 (.09)**	.25 (.11)**
Gender	.05 (.05)	.08 (.06)
Partisan strength	.04 (.03)	.04 (.03)
Rep/Chal spending	.04 (.023)*	-.09 (.07)
Dem/Inc spending	-.10 (.03)**	-.002 (.02)
Party contact	.08 (.06)	.08 (.07)
Candidate contact	-.01 (.07)	.05 (.08)
Republican incumbent	-.06 (.10)	----
Democratic incumbent	.08 (.08)	-.11 (.07)*
Senate race	.08 (.07)	.13 (.07)*
Governor's race	-.20 (.07)**	-.29 (.07)**
Constant	.79 (.46)*	1.37 (.81)*
r-Square	.06	.06
Adjusted r-Square	.05	.05

*$p < .10$; **$p < .05$.

ness to media reports about the 1994 House election campaigns. If anything, it would appear that the net effect of candidate spending decreased individual attentiveness to the media. Party and candidate contact also failed to generate greater individual-level attentiveness to news reports about the campaign. While party and candidate contact may increase interest in and concern about House election outcomes, these contact variables appear to have little or no effect on an individual's willingness to seek out campaign news reports.

The final portion of the analysis for 1994 involves the effect of spending and other campaign-related factors on an individual citizen's ability to make ideological distinctions between candidates. We also examine how spending effects the certainty of such judgments (Alvarez and Franklin 1994). The dependent variable in this part of the analysis is the perceived ideological distance between candidates, defined as the absolute value of Democratic ideological placement minus Republican ideological placement. The results of this analysis are presented in table D.5. As can be seen in table D.5, candidate spending appears to have no significant effect in the equations based on a partisan classification of the candidates. Nor does spending by the incumbent appear to impact the perceived ideological distance of the candidates. Consistent with Charles H. Franklin's (1991) research on Senate elections, spending by the challenger blurs the perceived

Table D.5 Regression Analysis of Ideological Distance, 1994

Variable	Republican/Democratic	Incumbent/Challenger
Education	.15 (.04)**	.12 (.04)**
Income	.02 (.01)**	.02 (.01)**
Age	.01 (.02)	.01 (.02)
Age squared	.000 (.0001)	.00002 (.00002)
Race	-.37 (.19)**	-.35 (.20)*
Gender	.07 (.10)	.10 (.11)
Partisan strength	.17 (.05)**	.16 (.06)**
Rep/Chal spending	-.06 (.04)	-.11 (.05)**
Dem/Inc spending	-.05 (.05)	.11 (.12)
Party contact	.04 (.12)	.05 (.13)
Candidate contact	.94 (.13)**	1.07 (.15)**
Republican incumbent	.14 (.19)	----
Democratic incumbent	.39 (.15)**	.23 (.12)*
Senate race	.07 (.14)	.07 (.13)
Governor's race	.10 (.12)	.11 (.15)
Constant	.36 (.87)	-.12 (1.53)
r-square	.13	.14
Adjusted r-square	.12	.13

*$p < .10$; **$p < .05$.

ideological distance between candidates. Overall, the major political factor driving perceived ideological distances is candidate contact.

If candidate spending fails to highlight perceived ideological differences between candidates, we also failed to find consistent evidence that spending increases ideological certainty. As can be seen in table D.6, the findings regarding the effects of spending on ideological certainty are weak and inconsistent. Democratic spending appears to increase ideological certainty about Democratic candidates, and challenger spending appears to increase ideological certainty about challengers. Incumbent spending, on the other hand, appears to decrease individual certainty about where a challenger stands on a standard ideology scale. Consistent with prior results, this finding suggests that increased spending may confuse rather than enlighten individual voters. Party and candidate contact, however, appear to be a more effective means for increasing an individual's certainty in placing House candidates on an ideological scale (though candidate contact had an insignificant effect on challenger ideological certainty).

The results from the 1996 presidential election show evidence similar to that from the 1994 congressional elections. These results are presented in tables D.7 through D.9. Finally, in table D.10, we present variable descriptions for each variable included in the analysis.

Table D.6 Regression Analysis of Ideological Certainty, 1994

Variable	Democratic	Republican	Incumbent	Challenger
Education	.03 (.02)	.04 (.02)**	.03 (.02)*	-.001 (.02)
Income	.003 (.005)	-.002 (.01)	.01 (.005)*	-.004 (.01)
Age	.0006 (.009)	.01 (.01)	.003 (.09)	.005 (.01)
Age squared	.00003 (.0001)	-.0001 (.0001)	.00002 (.0001)	-.00004 (.0001)
Race	.21 (.09)**	.13 (.11)	.21 (.10)**	.26 (.11)**
Gender	.04 (.05)	.07 (.05)	.05 (.05)	.02 (.06)
Partisan strength	.03 (.03)	.07 (.03)**	.05 (.03)*	.08 (.03)**
Rep/Chal spending	-.02 (.02)	.04 (.03)	-.02 (.02)	.07 (.03)*
Dem/Inc spending	.08 (.03)**	-.02 (.03)	.02 (.02)	-.11 (.07)*
Party contact	.11 (.06)*	.23 (.09)**	.18 (.06)**	.16 (.06)**
Candidate contact	.15 (.09)*	.19 (.06)**	.34 (.09)**	.03 (.11)
Rep incumbent	.03 (.10)	.16 (.09)	----	----
Dem incumbent	.28 (.08)**	-.05 (.08)	-.03 (.06)	.06 (.07)
Senate race	-.06 (.07)	.05 (.07)	-.09 (.06)	.08 (.07)
Governor's race	-.10 (.06)*	-.04 (.06)	-.17 (.06)**	-.26 (.07)**
Constant	.34 (.48)	.41 (.46)	1.02 (.69)	1.98 (.87)**
r-square	.11	.10	.11	.10
Adjusted *r*-square	.09	.08	.09	.06

*$p < .10$; **$p < .05$.

Table D.7   Regression Analysis of Candidate Familiarity, 1996

Variable	Republican	Democratic	Incumbent	Challenger
Education	.086 (.02)**	.082 (.02)**	.081 (.02)**	.113 (.02)
Income	.009 (.004)**	.005 (.01)	.01 (.004) **	-.0006 (.01)
Age	.006 (.01)	.013 (.01)	.003 (.001)**	.021 (.01)**
Age squared	-.00006 (.00008)	-.0001 (.00009)	-.00001 (.00008)	-.00019 (.0001)**
Race	-.437 (.09)**	-.235 (.102)**	-.344 (.093)**	-.455 (.11)**
Gender	.111 (.05)**	.101 (.048)**	.06 (.04)	.136 (.05)**
Partisan strength	.041 (.02)*	.049 (.025)**	.055 (.02)**	.031 (.03)
Dem/Inc spending	.026 (.02)	.121 (.021)**	-.015 (.05)	-.009 (.06)
Rep/Chal spending	.088 (.02)**	-.022 (.026)	.043 (.02)**	.126 (.02)**
Party contact	.166 (.05)**	.082 (.055)	.131 (.05)**	.094 (.06)
Other contact	-.051 (.09)	-.014 (.097)	-.056 (.09)	.022 (.11)
Dem incumbent	-.003 (.08)	.157 (.084) *	----	----
Rep incumbent	.165 (.08)**	.136 (.09)	.019 (.05)	.016 (.06)
Senate race	.003 (.05)	.028 (.052)	-.011 (.05)	-.022(.06)
Governor's race	-.013 (.07)	-.013 (.08)	.034 (.08)	-.047(.09)
Constant	.171 (.38)	.191 (.414)	1.57 (.59)**	-.029 (.71)
r-square	.265	.167	.182	.219
Adjusted *r*-square	.246	.147	.161	.198

*$p < .10$; **$p < .05$.

Table D.8   Regression Analysis of Ideological Distance, 1996

Variable	Republican/Democrat	Incumbent/Challenger
Education	1.02 (.19)**	.50 (.14)**
Income	.02 (.05)	-.01 (.04)
Age	.01 (.11)	.06 (.08)
Age squared	-.0002 (.001)	-.001 (.001)
Race	-2.99 (1.12)**	-2.52 (.83)**
Gender	1.82 (.54)**	-.34 (.40)
Partisan strength	1.76 (.28)**	.60 (.21)**
Rep/Chal spending	.17 (.29)	-.05 (.17)
Dem/Inc spending	.58 (.24)**	.79 (.45) *
Party contact	1.19 (.62) **	1.46 (.46)**
Other contact	1.69 (1.08)	.21 (.79)
Rep incumbent	1.93 (1.00)*	-8.80 (.42)**
Dem incumbent	1.12 (.93)	----
Senate race	.60 (.58)	.48 (.42)
Governor's race	-.05 (.89)	.47 (.69)
Constant	-11.34 (4.59) **	-6.21 (5.2)
r-square	.187	.487
Adjusted *r*-square	.167	.474

*$p < .10$; **$p < .05$; ***$p < .01$.

Table D.9   Regression Analysis of Ideological Certainty, 1996

Variable	Democratic	Republican	Incumbent	Challenger
Education	.04 (.02) *	.05 (.02)**	.05 (.02)**	.04 (.02)*
Income	-.0001 (.001)	.0003 (.005)	.006 (.006)	-.004 (.006)
Age	.01 (.01)	.01 (.01)	.01 (.01)	.01 (.01)
Age squared	-.00002 (.0001)	-.00004 (.0001)	-.0001 (.0001)	-.0001 (.0001)
Race	.01 (.11)	.10 (.12)	.02 (.13)	.09 (.13)
Gender	.12 (.06) **	.22 (.06)**	.22 (.06)**	.10 (.06)*
Partisan strength	.09 (.03)**	.13 (.03)**	.10 (.03)**	.10 (.03)**
Rep/Chal spending	-.04 (.03)	.04 (.03)	-.049 (.03)**	.06 (.03)**
Dem/Inc spending	.08 (.03)**	-.06 (.02)**	.01 (.07)	-.01 (.07)
Party contact	.11 (.07)	.25 (.06)**	.25 (.07)**	.16 (.07)**
Other contact	.09 (.12)	.03 (.11)	-.06 (.12)	.08 (.12)
Rep incumbent	.07 (.11)	.14 (.11)	-.04 (.06)	-.09 (.07)
Dem incumbent	.23 (.10)**	.07 (.10)	----	----
Senate Race	.02 (.06)	.08 (.06)	-.001 (.06)	.07 (.07)
Governor's race	.11 (.09)	.23 (.09)	.30 (.10)**	.25 (.11)**
Constant	.43 (.49)	1.06 (.48)**	1.41 (.79)*	.45 (.81)
r-square	.107	.153	.133	.087
Adjusted r-square	.085	.132	.109	.063

$*p < .10; **p < .05.$

Table D.10   Variable Descriptions

Variable Name	Description
Candidate familiarity	Additive index of separate measures indicating whether respondents could recall, recognize, or place House candidates on ideological scale. Ranges from 0 (unfamiliar with the candidate) to 3 (able to recall, recognize, and place candidate).
Care about election	Indicates how much respondents cared about the outcome of the House election; ranges from not at all to very much.
Political interest	Self-reported interest in the campaign, ranging from not much to very much.
Media attentiveness	Additive index of separate measures indicating whether respondents read about the campaign in the newspaper or in a news magazine and whether respondents watched television news stories about the campaign. Ranges from no exposure to news about the campaign to exposure to newspaper, news magazine, and television stories about the campaign.
Ideological distance	The absolute value of the respondent's ideological placement of the Democratic candidate minus the ideological placement of the Republican candidate.
Ideological certainty	Respondent certainty in placing House candidates on an ideological scale.
Republican incumbent	Coded 1 if a Republican incumbent was running for reelection, 0 otherwise.
Democratic incumbent	Coded 1 if a Democratic incumbent was running for reelection, 0 otherwise.
Democratic spending	Natural log of total spending by the Democratic candidate in 1994.
Republican spending	Natural log of total spending by the Republican candidate in 1994.
Incumbent spending	Natural log of total spending by the incumbent candidate in 1994.
Challenger spending	Natural log of total spending by challenging candidate in 1994.
Education	Coded 1 (less than high school), 2 (high school diploma or equivalency test) 3 (more than 12 years, but no higher degree), 4 (junior or community college degree), 5 (BA degree), 6 (advanced degree).
Income	Coded 1 (less than $2,999) through 24 ($105,000 and over).
Senate race	Coded 1 if the respondent lived in a state with a concurrent senatorial race, 0 otherwise.
Gubernatorial race	Coded 1 if the respondent lived in a state with a concurrent gubernatorial race, 0 otherwise.
Party contact	Coded 1 if the respondent was contacted by a political party, 0 otherwise.
Candidate contact	Coded 1 if the respondent was contacted by a political candidate, 0 otherwise.
Age	Age of respondent in years.
Race	Coded 1 if the respondent was African American, 0 otherwise.
Partisan strength	Coded 0 for independent nonleaners, 1 for independent leaners, 2 for Democrat or Republican, and 3 for strong Democrat or Republican.

References

Abramowitz, Alan I. 1980. A Comparison of Voting for U.S. Senator and Representative. *American Political Science Review* 74:633–40.

———. 1991a. Incumbency, Campaign Spending, and the Decline of Competition in U.S. Elections. *Journal of Politics* 53:34–56.

———. 1991b. "Open-Seat Elections to the U.S. House of Representatives." Paper presented at the annual meeting of the Southern Political Science Association, Tampa.

Abramowitz, Alan I., and Jeffrey A. Segal. 1992. *Senate Elections.* Ann Arbor: University of Michigan Press.

Abramson, Paul R., and John H. Aldrich. 1982. The Decline of Electoral Participation in America. *American Political Science Review* 76:502–21.

Aldrich, John H. 1995. *Why Parties? The Origin and Transformation of Political Parties in America.* Chicago: University of Chicago Press.

Alexander, Herbert E. 1992. *Financing Politics: Money, Elections, and Political Reform.* Washington, D.C.: Congressional Quarterly Press.

Alexander, Herbert E., Eugene R. Goss, and Jeffrey A. Schwartz. 1992. State Experiments with Public Financing. *State Government News* 35:21–25.

Alexander, Herbert E., and Rei Shiratori. 1994. *Comparative Campaign Finance.* Boulder, Colo.: Westview.

Alvarez, R. Michael, and Charles H. Franklin. 1994. Uncertainty and Political Perceptions. *Journal of Politics* 56:671–88.

Ansolabehere, Stephen, Roy Behr, and Shanto Iyengar. 1993. *The Media Game: American Politics in the Television Age.* New York: Macmillan.

Ansolabehere, Stephen, Shanto Iyengar, Adam Simon, and Nicholas Valentino. 1994. Does Attack Advertising Demobilize the Electorate? *American Political Science Review* 88:829–38.

Arkansas Educational Television Commission v. Forbes. 1998. No. 96–779.

Bartels, Larry M. 1986. Issue Voting Under Uncertainty: An Empirical Test. *American Journal of Political Science* 30:709–28.

———. 1996. Uninformed Votes: Informational Effects in Presidential Elections. *American Journal of Political Science* 40:194–230.

Becker, Kerome D., and Ivan L. Preston. 1970. Media Usage and Political Activity. *Journalism Quarterly* 57:122–29.

199

Bennett, Stephen E. 1988. Know-Nothings' Revisited: The Meaning of Political Ignorance Today. *Social Science Quarterly* 69:476–90.

———. 1995. Comparing Americans' Political Information in 1988 and 1992. *Journal of Politics* 57:521–32.

Bennett, Stephen E., and David Resnick. 1990. The Implications of Nonvoting for Democracy in the United States. *American Journal of Political Science* 34:771–803.

Bennett, W. Lance. 1996. *The Governing Crisis: Media, Money, and Marketing in American Elections.* 2d ed. New York: St. Martin's.

Berch, Neil. 1993. Another Look at Closeness and Turnout: The Case of the 1979 and 1980 Canadian National Elections. *Political Research Quarterly* 46:421–32.

Bianco, William T. 1984. Strategic Decisions on Candidacy in U.S. Congressional Districts. *Legislative Studies Quarterly* 9:351–64.

Binkley, Wilfred E. 1964. *American Political Parties: Their Natural History.* 4th ed. New York: Knopf.

Black, Gordon. 1972. A Theory of Political Ambition: Career Choices and the Role of Structural Incentives. *American Political Science Review* 66:144–59.

Bond, Jon R., Cary Covington, and Richard Fleisher. 1985. Explaining Challenger Quality in Congressional Elections. *Journal of Politics* 47:510–29.

Box-Steffensmeier, Janet. 1996. A Dynamic Analysis of the Role of War Chests in Campaign Strategy. *American Journal of Political Science* 40:352–71.

Brians, Craig Leonard, and Martin P. Wattenberg. 1996. Campaign Issue Knowledge and Salience: Comparing Reception from TV Commercials, TV News, and Newspapers. *American Journal of Political Science* 40:172–93.

Broder, David S. 1971. *The Party's Over: The Failure of Politics in America.* New York: Harper and Row.

Brookings Institution. N.d. Working Group on Campaign Finance Reform. <http://www.brook.edu/gs/campaign/round1.htm>.

Brown v. Board of Education, 347 U.S. 484 (1954).

Buckley v. Valeo. 1976. 424 U.S. 1.

Burnham, Walter Dean. 1970. *Critical Elections and the Mainsprings of American Politics.* New York: Norton.

Button, James M. 1989. *Blacks and Social Change: Impact of the Civil Rights Movement in Southern Communities.* Princeton: Princeton University Press.

Caldeira, Gregory A., and Samuel C. Patterson. 1982. Contextual Influences on Participation in U.S. State Legislative Elections. *Legislative Studies Quarterly* 7:359–82.

Caldeira, Gregory A., Samuel C. Patterson, and Gregory A. Markko. 1985. The Mobilization of Voters in Congressional Elections. *Journal of Politics* 47:490–509.

Campaign Finance Overhaul Dies. 1995. In *Congressional Quarterly 1994 Almanac.* Washington, D.C.: Congressional Quarterly Press.

Campbell, Angus. 1960. Surge and Decline: A Study of Electoral Change. *Public Opinion Quarterly* 24:397–418.

Campbell, James E. 1991. The Presidential Surge and Its Midterm Decline in Congressional Elections. *Journal of Politics* 53:477–87.

———. 1993. *The Presidential Pulse of Congressional Elections.* Lexington: University of Kentucky Press.

Chappell, Henry W. 1982. Campaign Contributions and Congressional Voting: A Simultaneous Probit-Tobit Model. *Review of Economics and Statistics* 62:77–83.

Citizens Research Foundation. 1997. New Realities and New Thinking. Report of the Task Force on Campaign Finance Reform. *PS: Political Science and Politics* 30:487–89.

Clubb, Jerome M., William H. Flanigan, and Nancy H. Zinglae. 1980. *Partisan Realignment: Voters, Parties, and Government in American History.* Beverly Hills, Calif.: Sage.

Clymer, Adam. 1997. Mitch McConnell: Fiercest Defender of Campaign Laws. *New York Times,* April 13.

Colorado Republican Federal Campaign Committee v. Federal Election Commission. 1996. 116 S.Ct. 2309.

Corrado, Anthony. 1997a. Party Soft Money. In *Campaign Finance Reform: A Sourcebook,* edited by Anthony Corrado, Thomas E. Mann, Daniel Ortiz, Trevor Potter, and Frank Sorauf. Washington, D.C.: Brookings.

———. 1997b. Financing the 1996 Elections. In *The Elections of 1996: Reports and Interpretations,* edited by Gerald M. Pomper. Chatham, N.J.: Chatham House.

Cotter, Cornelius P., James L. Gibson, John F. Bibby, and Robert J. Huckshorn. 1984. *Party Organizations in American Politics.* New York: Praeger.

Cox, Gary W., and Jonathan N. Katz. 1996. Why Did the Incumbency Advantage in U.S. House Elections Grow? *American Journal of Political Science* 40:478–97.

Cox, Gary W., and Scott Morganstein. 1993. The Increasing Advantage of Incumbency in the U.S. *Legislative Studies Quarterly* 18:495–514.

———. 1995. The Incumbency Advantage in Multimember Districts: Evidence from the U.S. *Legislative Studies Quarterly* 20:329–50.

Cox, Gary W., and Michael C. Munger. 1989. Closeness, Expenditures, and Turnout in the 1982 U.S. House Elections. *American Political Science Review* 83:217–31.

Crotty, William. 1984. *American Parties in Decline.* Boston: Little, Brown.

Dalager, Jon K. 1996. Voters, Issues, and Elections: Are the Candidates' Messages Getting Through? *Journal of Politics* 58:486–515.

Dalton, Russell J. 1984. Cognitive Mobilization and Partisan Dealignment in Advanced Industrial Democracies. *Journal of Politics* 46:264–84.

———. 1996. *Citizen Politics: Public Opinion and Political Parties in Advanced Western Democracies.* 2d ed. Chatham, N.J.: Chatham House.

Delli Carpini, Michael X., and Scott Keeter. 1991. Stability and Change in the U.S. Public's Knowledge of Politics. *Public Opinion Quarterly* 55:583–612.

———. 1996. *What Americans Know About Politics and Why It Matters.* New Haven: Yale University Press.

Denardo, James. 1980. Turnout and the Vote. *American Political Science Review* 74:406–20.

Donnay, Patrick D., and Graham P. Ramsden. 1995. Public Financing of Legislative Elections: Lessons from Minnesota. *Legislative Studies Quarterly* 20:351–64.

Downs, Anthony. 1957. *An Economic Theory of Democracy.* New York: Harper and Row.

Duncan, Philip D., and Christine C. Lawrence. 1995. *Politics in America, 1996: The 104th Congress.* Washington, D.C.: CQ Press.

———. 1997. *Politics in America, 1998: The 105th Congress.* Washington, D.C.: CQ Press.

Dwyre, Diana. 1996. Spinning Straw into Gold: Soft Money and U.S. House Elections. *Legislative Studies Quarterly* 21:409–24.

————. 1997. Pushing the Campaign Finance Envelope: Parties and Interest Groups in the 1996 House and Senate Elections. Paper presented at the annual meeting of the American Political Science Association, Washington, D.C.

Eismeier, Theodore J., and Philip H. Pollock III. 1996. Money in the 1994 Elections and Beyond. In *Midterm: The Elections of 1994 in Context*, edited by Philip A. Klinker. Boulder, Colo.: Westview.

Elving, Ronald. 1996. Shift in Voter Mood Is Key to Incumbents' Fortunes. *Congressional Quarterly Weekly Report* 54:29–49.

Enelow, James, and Melvin J. Hinich. 1981. A New Approach to Voter Uncertainty in the Downsian Spatial Model. *American Journal of Political Science* 25:483–93.

Erikson, Robert S., and Thomas R. Palfrey. 1998. Campaign Spending and Incumbency: An Alternative Simultaneous Equations Approach. *Journal of Politics* 60:355–73.

Evans, Diana M. 1986. PAC Contributions and Roll Call Voting: Conditional Power. In *Interest Group Politics*, edited by Allan J. Cigler and Burdette A. Loomis. 2d ed. Washington, D.C.: Congressional Quarterly Press.

Federal Election Commission. 1995–96. *Summary File.* Washington, D.C.: FEC.

Feldman, Paul, and James Jondrow. 1984. Congressional Elections and Local Federal Spending. *American Journal of Political Science* 28:147–64.

Ferejohn, John A., and James H. Kuklinski, eds. 1990. *Information and Democratic Processes.* Urbana: University of Illinois Press.

Fiorina, Morris P. 1989. *Congress: Keystone of the Washington Establishment.* New Haven: Yale University Press.

————. 1990. Information and Rationality in Elections. In *Information and Democratic Processes*, edited by John A. Ferejohn and James H. Kuklinski. Urbana: University of Illinois Press.

Fiorina, Morris P., David W. Rohde, and Peter Wissel. 1975. Historical Change in House Turnover. In *Congress in Change: Evolution and Reform*, edited by Norman J. Ornstein. New York: Praeger.

Flanigan, William H., and Nancy H. Zingale. 1991. *Political Behavior of the American Electorate.* 7th ed. Washington, D.C.: Congressional Quarterly Press.

Franklin, Charles H. 1991. Eschewing Obfuscation? Campaigns and the Perception of U.S. Senate Incumbents. *American Political Science Review* 85:1193–214.

Fritz, Sara, and Dwight Morris. 1992. *Gold-Plated Politics: Running for Congress in the 1990s.* Washington, D.C.: Congressional Quarterly Press.

Gaddie, R. Keith. 1995a. Is There an Inherent Democratic Party Advantage in U.S. House Elections? Evidence from the Open Seats. *Social Science Quarterly* 76:203–12.

————. 1995b. Negating the Democratic Advantage in Open Seat Elections: A Research Update. *Social Science Quarterly* 76:673–80.

————. 1997. Forgotten Races: Open Seat Congressional Elections. Unpublished manuscript.

Gaddie, R. Keith, and Jonathon Mott. 1997. Realignment or Redux? The 1996 Open Seat Congressional Elections. Paper presented at the annual meeting of the Southwestern Political Science Association, New Orleans.

Gant, Michael M., and William Lyons. 1993. Democratic Theory, Nonvoting, and Public Policy. *American Politics Quarterly* 21:185–204.

Gelman, Andrew, and Gary King. 1994. A Unified Method of Evaluating Electoral Systems and Redistricting Plans. *American Journal of Political Science* 38:514–54.

Gerber, Alan. 1998. Estimating the Effect of Campaign Spending on Senate Election Outcomes Using Instrumental Variables. *American Political Science Review* 92:401–12.

Gilliam, Franklin D., Jr. 1985. Influences on Voter Turnout for U.S. Elections in Non-Presidential Election Years. *Legislative Studies Quarterly* 10:339–51.

Gimpel, James G. 1996. *Legislating the Revolution: The Contract with America in Its First 100 Days.* Boston: Allyn and Bacon.

Goidel, Robert K., and Donald A. Gross. 1994. A Systems Approach to Campaign Finance in United States House Elections. *American Politics Quarterly* 22:125–53.

———. 1996. Reconsidering the "Myths and Realities" of Campaign Finance Reform. *Legislative Studies Quarterly* 21:129–50.

Goidel, Robert K., and Todd G. Shields. 1994. Reconsidering the Political Consequences of Voter Turnout in the United States House Elections. Paper presented at the annual meeting of the Southwestern Social Science Association, San Antonio.

Good Law Yields More Voters. *New York Times,* October 19.

Green, Donald P., and Jonathan S. Krasno. 1988. Salvation for the Spendthrift Incumbent. *American Journal of Political Science* 32:844–907.

———. 1990. Rebuttal to Jacobson's "New Evidence for Old Arguments." *American Journal of Political Science* 34:363–73.

Grenzke, Janet. 1989. Shopping in the Congressional Supermarket: The Currency Is Complex. *American Journal of Political Science* 33:1–24.

Groseclose, Timothy, and Keith Krehbiel. 1994. Golden Parachutes, Rubber Checks, and Strategic Retirements from the 102d House. *American Journal of Political Science* 38:75- 99.

Gross, Donald A., Todd G. Shields, and Robert K. Goidel. 1997. Campaign Finance Reform and the 1994 Congressional Elections. *Policy Studies Journal.*

Gugliotta, Guy, and Ira Chinoy. 1997. Outsiders Made Erie Ballot a National Battle. *Washington Post,* February 10, A1.

Hall, Richard L., and Robert Van Houweling. 1995. Avarice and Ambition in Congress: Representatives' Decisions to Run or Retire from the U.S. House. *American Political Science Review* 89:121–36.

Hamilton, Alexander, John Jay, and James Madison. 1952. *The Federalist: A Commentary on the Constitution of the United States.* New York: Modern Library.

Heard, Alexander. 1960. *The Costs of Democracy.* Chapel Hill. University of North Carolina Press.

Hershey, Majorie Randon. 1997. The Congressional Elections. In *The Election of 1996: Reports and Interpretations,* edited by Gerald M. Pomper. Chatham, N.J.: Chatham House.

Hill, Kim Quaile, and Jan E. Leighley. 1992. The Policy Consequences of Class Bias in State Electorates. *American Journal of Political Science* 36:351–65.

Hill, Kim Quaile, Jan E. Leighley, and Angela Hinton-Andersson. 1995. Lower-Class Mobilization and Policy Linkage in the U.S. *American Journal of Political Science* 39:75–86.

Hinckley, Barbara. 1980. The American Voter in Congressional Elections. *American Political Science Review* 74:641–50.

Hofstadter, Richard. 1956. *The Age of Reform: From Bryan to F.D.R.* New York. Knopf.

Holbrook, Thomas M., and Charles M. Tidmarch. 1991. Sophomore Surge in State Legislative Elections, 1968–1986. *Legislative Studies Quarterly* 16:49–64.

———. 1993. The Effects of Leadership Positions on Votes for Incumbents in State Legislative Elections. *Political Research Quarterly* 46:897–909.

Huckfeldt, Robert, and John Sprague. 1990. Social Order and Political Chaos: The Structural Setting of Political Information. In *Information and Democratic Processes,* edited by John A. Ferejohn and James H. Kuklinski. Urbana: University of Illinois Press.

———. 1992. Political Parties and Electoral Mobilization: Political Structure, Social Structure, and the Party Canvas. *American Political Science Review* 86:70–86.

Jackson, Brooks. 1990. *Broken Promise: Why the Federal Election Commission Failed.* New York: Priority Press.

———. 1997. Financing the 1996 Campaign: The Law of the Jungle. In *Toward the Millennium: The Elections of 1996,* edited by Larry J. Sabato. Boston: Allyn and Bacon.

Jackson, Robert A. 1993. Voter Mobilization in the 1986 Midterm Election. *Journal of Politics* 55:1081–99.

———. 1996a. The Mobilization of the Congressional Electorates. *Legislative Studies Quarterly* 21:425–46.

———. 1996b. *The Influence of Turnout on Congressional Outcomes.* Paper presented at the annual meeting of the Western Political Science Association, San Francisco.

———. 1997. The Mobilization of U.S. State Electorates in the 1988 and 1990 Elections. *Journal of Politics* 59:520–37.

Jacobson, Gary C. 1978. The Effects of Campaign Spending in Congressional Elections. *American Political Science Review* 72:469–91.

———. 1980. *Money and Congressional Elections.* New Haven: Yale University Press.

———. 1985. Money and Votes Reconsidered: Congressional Elections, 1972–1982. *Public Choice* 48:7–62.

———. 1989. Strategic Politicians and the Dynamics of House Elections, 1946–1986. *American Political Science Review* 83:773–93.

———. 1990a. The Effects of Campaign Spending in House Elections: New Evidence for Old Arguments. *American Journal of Political Science* 34:334–62.

———. 1990b. *The Electoral Origins of Divided Government: Competition in U.S. House Elections, 1946–1988.* Boulder, Colo.: Westview.

———. 1992. *The Politics of Congressional Elections.* 3d ed. New York: Harper/Collins.

———. 1996. The 1994 House Elections in Perspective. In *Midterm: The Elections of 1994 in Context,* edited by Philip A. Klinkner. Boulder, Colo.: Westview.

———. 1997a. The 105th Congress: Unprecedented and Unsurprising. In *The Elections of 1996,* edited by Michael Nelson. Washington, D.C.: Congressional Quarterly Press.

———. 1997b. *The Politics of Congressional Elections.* 4th ed. New York: Longman.

Jacobson, Gary C., and Samuel Kernell. 1983. *Strategy and Choice in Congressional Elections.* 2d ed. New Haven: Yale University Press.

Jewell, Malcolm, and William E. Cassie. 1998. Can the Legislative Campaign Finance System Be Reformed? In *Campaign Finance in State Legislative Elections*, edited by Joel A. Thompson and Gary F. Moncrief. Washington D.C.: Congressional Quarterly Press.

Johannes, John R., and John C. McAdams. 1981. The Congressional Incumbency Effect: Is It Casework, Policy Compatibility, or Something Else? *American Journal of Political Science* 25:512–42.

Jones, Ruth S. 1981. State Public Campaign Finance: Implications for Partisan Politics. *American Journal of Political Science* 25:342–61.

Jones, Woodrow, and K. Robert Keiser. 1987. Issue Visibility and the Effects of PAC Money. *Social Science Quarterly* 68:170–76.

Keech, William. 1968. *The Impact of Negro Voting: The Role of the Vote in the Quest for Equality*. Chicago: Rand McNally.

Key, V. O., Jr. 1964. *Politics, Parties, and Pressure Groups*. New York: Crowell.

Kiewiet, D. Roderick, and Langche Zeng. 1993. An Analysis of Congressional Career Decisions, 1947–1986. *American Political Science Review* 87:928–41.

King, Gary. 1991. Constituency Service and Incumbency Advantage. *British Journal of Political Science* 21:119–28.

Krasno, Jonathan S. 1994. *Challengers, Competition, and Reelection: Comparing Senate and House Elections*. New Haven: Yale University Press.

Krasno, Jonathan S., and Donald P. Green. 1988. Preempting Quality Challengers in House Elections. *Journal of Politics* 50:920–36.

———. 1993. Stopping the Buck Here: The Case for Campaign Spending Limits. *Brookings Review* 11:17–21.

Langbein, Laura I., and Mark A. Lotwis. 1990. The Political Efficacy of Lobbying and Money: Gun Control in the U.S. House. *Legislative Studies Quarterly* 14:414–40.

Levitt, Kenneth. 1993. Campaign Finance and the Return of Buckley v. Valeo. *Yale Law Journal* 103:469–73.

Lodge, Milton, Kathleen M. McGraw, and Patrick Stroh. 1989. An Impression-Driven Model of Candidate Evaluation. *American Political Science Review* 87:399–419.

Lodge, Milton, Marco R. Steenbergen, and Shawn Brau. 1995. The Responsive Voter: Campaign Information and the Dynamics of Candidate Evaluation. *American Political Science Review* 89:309–26.

Lowenstein, Daniel. 1990. On Campaign Finance Reform: The Root of All Evil Is Deeply Rooted. *Hofstra Law Review* 18:301–67.

Luskin, Robert C., and Suzanne Globetti. 1996. *Candidate Versus Policy Considerations in the Voting Decision: Information Does Matter*. Paper presented at the annual meeting of the Southern Political Science Association, Atlanta.

Magleby, David B., and Candice J. Nelson. 1990. *The Money Chase: Congressional Campaign Finance Reform*. Washington, D.C.: Brookings.

Maisel, L. Sandy. 1982. *From Obscurity to Oblivion: Running in the Congressional Primary*. Knoxville: University of Tennessee Press.

———. 1994. Competition in Congressional Elections: Why More Qualified Candidates Do Not Seek Office. In *Rethinking Political Reform: Beyond Spending and Term Limits*. <http://www.dlcppi.org/texts/politics/reform.txt>

Malbin, Michael J., and Thomas L. Gais. 1998. *The Day After Reform: Sobering Campaign Finance Lessons from the American States.* Albany: Rockefeller Institute Press.

Mann, Thomas E. 1978. *Unsafe at Any Margin: Interpreting Congressional Elections.* Washington, D.C.: American Enterprise Institute.

Mayer, Kenneth R., and John M. Wood. 1995. The Impact of Public Financing on Electoral Competitiveness: Evidence from Wisconsin, 1964–1990. *Legislative Studies Quarterly* 20:69–88.

Mayhew, David. 1974. Congressional Elections: The Case of the Vanishing Marginals. *Polity* 6:295–317.

McLeod, Jack, Scott Ward, and Karen Tancill. 1965. Alienation and Use of the Mass Media. *Public Opinion Quarterly* 29:584–94.

Miller, Authur H., Edie N. Goldenberg, and Lutz Erbring. 1979. Type-Set Politics: Impact of Newspapers on Public Confidence. *American Political Science Review* 70:67–84.

Morris, Dwight, and Murielle E. Gamache. 1994. *Gold-Plated Politics: The 1992 Congressional Races.* Washington, D.C.: Congressional Quarterly Press.

Nagel, Jack H., and John E. McNulty. 1996. Partisan Effects of Voter Turnout in Senatorial and Gubernatorial Elections. *American Political Science Review* 90:780–93.

Newberry v. U.S. 1921.

Noelle-Neumann, Elisabeth. 1993. *The Spiral of Silence.* 2d ed. Chicago: University of Chicago Press.

Overacker, Louise. 1932. *Money in Elections.* New York: Macmillan.

Page, Benjamin I. 1978. *Choices and Echoes in Presidential Elections.* Chicago: University of Chicago Press.

Page, Benjamin I., and Robert Y. Shapiro. 1992. *The Rational Public: Fifty Years of Trends in Americans' Policy Preferences.* Chicago: University of Chicago Press.

Pateman, Carole. 1970. *Participation and Democratic Theory.* Cambridge: Cambridge University Press.

Patterson, Samuel C., and Gregory A. Caldeira. 1983. Getting Out the Vote: Participation in Gubernatorial Elections. *American Political Science Review* 77:675–89.

Patterson, Thomas E. 1996. Bad News, Period. *PS, Political Science and Politics* 29:17–20.

Patterson, Thomas E., and Robert D. McClure. 1976. *The Unseeing Eye: The Myth of Television Power in National Politics.* New York: Putnam.

Petrocik, John R. 1987. Voter Turnout and Electoral Preference: The Anomalous Reagan Elections. In *Elections in America,* edited by Kay Lehman Scholozman. Boston: Allen and Unwin.

Piven, Frances Fox, and Richard A. Cloward. 1988. *Why Americans Don't Vote.* New York: Pantheon.

Plessy v. Ferguson, 163 U.S. 537 (1896).

Popkin, Samuel L. 1991. *The Reasoning Voter: Communication and Persuasion in Presidential Campaigns.* Chicago: University of Chicago Press.

Potter, Trevor. 1997. Issue Advocacy and Express Advocacy. In *Campaign Finance Reform: A Sourcebook,* edited by Anthony Corrado, Thomas E. Mann, Daniel Ortiz, Trevor Potter, and Frank Sorauf. Washington, D.C.: Brookings.

Powell, G. Bingham. 1986. American Voter Turnout in Comparative Perspective. *American Political Science Review* 80:17–43.

Radcliff, Benjamin. 1994. Turnout and the Democratic Vote. *American Politics Quarterly* 22:259–76.

Ragsdale, Lyn, and Timothy E. Cook. 1987. Representatives' Actions and Challengers Reactions: Limits to Candidate Connections in the House. *American Journal of Political Science* 31:45–81.

Ragsdale, Lyn, and Gerold G. Rusk. 1993. Who Are the Non Voters? Profiles from the 1990 Senate Elections. *American Journal of Political Science* 37:721–46.

Ray, Bruce. 1980. Congressional Losers in the U.S. Federal Spending Process. *Legislative Studies Quarterly* 3:359–72.

Rohde, David W. 1979. Risk-Bearing and Progressive Ambition: The Case of Members of the U.S. House of Representatives. *American Journal of Political Science* 21:1–26.

Romero, David W. 1996. The Case of the Missing Reciprocal Influence: Incumbent Reputation and the Vote. *Journal of Politics* 58:1198–207.

Rosenkranz, E. Joshua. 1998. *Buckley Stops Here: Loosening the Judicial Stranglehold on Campaign Finance Reform.* Washington, D.C.: Twentieth Century Fund.

Rosenkranz, E. Joshua, Andrew L. Shapiro, and Alan B. Morrison. 1998. Should Buckley Be Overturned? /Response. *American Prospect* 37:78–81.

Rosenstone, Steven J., and John Mark Hansen. 1993. *Mobilization, Participation, and Democracy in America.* New York: Macmillan.

Rosenstone, Steven J., Warren E. Miller, Donald R. Kinder, and the National Election Studies. 1995. *American National Election Studies, 1994: Post Election Survey.* Ann Arbor: University of Michigan, Center for Political Studies, and Inter-university Consortium of Political Science Research.

———. 1997. *American National Election Studies, 1996: Post Election Survey.* Ann Arbor: University of Michigan, Center for Political Studies, and Inter-university Consortium of Political Science Research.

Rothenberg, Lawrence S. 1992. *Linking Citizens to Government: Interest Group Politics at Common Cause.* New York: Cambridge University Press.

Royko, Mike. 1971. *Boss: Richard J. Daley of Chicago.* New York: Signet.

Rundquist, Barry, and David Griffith. 1976. An Interrupted Time-Series Test of the Distributive Theory of Military Policy-Making. *Western Political Quarterly* 24:620–26.

Sabato, Larry J., and Glenn R. Simpson. 1996. *Dirty Little Secrets.* New York: Random House.

Sellers, Patrick J. 1997. Fiscal Consistency and Federal District Spending in Congressional Elections. *American Journal of Political Science* 41:1024–41.

Schaffer, Jan. 1997. Introduction to *With the People . . . A Toolbox for Getting Readers and Viewers Involved.* Pew Center for Civic Journalism. <http://www.pewcenter.org>

Schattschneider, E. E. 1942. *Party Government.* New York: Rinehart.

Schlesinger, Joseph. 1966. *Ambition in Politics: Political Careers in the United States.* Chicago: Rand McNally.

———. 1985. The New American Political Party. *American Political Science Review* 79:1152–69.

Schmitt, Eric. 1997. Senate Debates Campaign Party Bill, but Two Sides Remain Divided. *New York Times,* September 27.

Schroedel, Jean Reith. 1987. Campaign Contributions and Legislative Outcomes. *Western Political Quarterly* 40:371–89.

Serra, George, and Albert D. Cover. 1992. The Electoral Consequences of Perquisite Use: The Casework Case. *Legislative Studies Quarterly* 17:233–46.

Serra, George, and David Moon. 1994. Casework, Issue Positions, and Voting in Congressional Elections: A District Analysis. *Journal of Politics* 56:200–213.

Shaffer, Stephen. 1982. Policy Differences Between Voters and Non-Voters in American Elections. *Western Political Quarterly* 35:496–510.

Shepsle, Kenneth A. 1972. The Strategy of Ambiguity: Uncertainty and Electoral Competition. *American Political Science Review* 66:555–68.

Silbey, Joel. 1997. Foundation Stones of Present Discontents: The American Political Nation, 1776–1945. In *Present Discontents,* edited by Byron E. Shafer. Chatham, N.J.: Chatham House.

Smith, Bradley A. 1995. Faulty Assumptions and Undemocratic Consequences of Campaign Finance Reform. *Yale Law Journal* 105:1049–91.

Sniderman, Paul M., Richard A. Brody, and Philip E. Tetlock. 1991. *Reasoning and Choice: Explorations in Political Psychology.* Cambridge: Cambridge University Press.

Sorauf, Frank J. 1988. *Money in American Elections.* Glenview, Ill.: Scott, Foresman.

———. 1992. *Inside Campaign Finance: Myths and Realities.* New Haven: Yale University Press.

———. 1994. Politics, Experience, and the First Amendment: The Case of American Campaign Finance. *Columbia Law Review* 94:1348–67.

Stein, Robert M., and Kenneth N. Bickers. 1994. Congressional Elections and the Pork Barrel. *Journal of Politics* 56:377–400.

———. 1996. The Electoral Dynamics of the Federal Pork Barrel. *American Journal of Political Science* 40:1300–26.

Stern, Philip M. 1988. *The Best Congress Money Can Buy.* New York: Pantheon.

Stone, Peter H. 1998. For Incumbents, a Fistful of Dollars. *National Journal* 30:2680–83.

Teixeira, Ruy A. 1987. *Why Americans Don't Vote: Turnout Decline in the United States, 1960–1984.* New York: Greenwood.

———. 1992. *The Disappearing American Voter.* Washington, D.C.: Brookings.

———. 1996. *Campaign Reform, Political Competition, and Citizen Participation.* <http://www.dlcppi.org/texts/politics/reform.txt>

Thayer, George. 1973. *Who Shakes the Money Tree?* New York: Simon and Schuster.

Thomas, Scott J. 1989. Do Incumbent Campaign Expenditures Matter? *Journal of Politics* 51:965–76.

Thompson, Joel, and Gary Moncrief, eds. 1998. *Campaign Finance in State Legislative Elections.* Washington, D.C.: Congressional Quarterly Press.

Verba, Sydney, Kay Lehman Schlozman, and Henry E. Brady. 1995. *Voice and Equality: Civic Voluntarism in American Politics.* Boston: Harvard University Press.

Wattenberg, Martin P. 1990. *The Decline of American Political Parties, 1952–1988.* Cambridge: Harvard University Press.

Weilhouwer, Peter W., and Brad Lockerbie. 1994. Party Contacting and Political Participation, 1952–1990. *American Journal of Political Science* 38:211–30.

Welch, William P. 1982. Campaign Contributions and Legislative Voting: Milk Money and Dairy Price Supports. *Western Political Quarterly* 35:478–95.

Wilcox, Clyde. 1988. I Owe It All to Me: Candidates' Investments in Their Own Campaigns. *American Politics Quarterly* 16:278.

Wolfinger, Raymond E., and Steven J. Rosenstone. 1980. *Who Votes?* New Haven: Yale University Press.

Wolfinger, Raymond E., Steven J. Rosenstone, and Richard A. McIntosh. 1981. Presidential and Congressional Voters Compared. *American Politics Quarterly* 9:245–55.

Wright, Gerald C., and Michael B. Berkman. 1986. Candidates and Policy in United States Senate Elections. *American Political Science Review* 80:567–88.

Wright, John R. 1985. PACs, Contributions, and Roll Calls: An Organizational Perspective. *American Political Science Review* 79:400–414.

———. 1990. Contributions, Lobbying, and Committee Voting in the U.S. House of Representatives. *American Political Science Review* 84:417–38.

———. 1996. *Interest Groups and Congress: Lobbying, Contributions, and Influence.* Boston: Allyn and Bacon.

Yang, John E. 1995. Gingrich Calls for More, Not Less Campaign Cash. *Washington Post*, November 3.

Yiannakis, Diana Evans. 1981. The Grateful Electorate: Casework and Congressional Elections. *American Journal of Political Science* 25:568–80.

Zaller, John R. 1992. *The Nature and Origins of Mass Opinion.* Cambridge: Cambridge University Press.

Index

ABC News Poll, 7
Abramowitz, Alan, 8, 57–58
Abramson, Paul, 92
Adams, John Quincy, 18
Advertising: commercial, 37–38, 49; political, 26, 37, 64, 93, 128
AFL-CIO, 149, 151, 153, 155, 164
Aldrich, John, 4, 92
Alexander, Herbert, 10, 15, 39, 68, 109, 154
Ansolabehere, Stephen, 89–90, 109, 128, 129
Anti-Federalists, 18
Arkansas Educational Television Commission v. Forbes, 49
Armey, Dick, 66
Arthur, Chester, 20
Australian ballot, 20, 22, 47
Automobile Dealer's Election Action Committee, 54

Barber, Haley, 160
Behr, Roy, 109
Bennett, Lance, 1, 21, 109
Bentsen, Ken, 65
Bentsen, Lloyd, 65–66
BIPAC, 164
Box-Steffensmeier, Janet, 61
Bradley, Bill, 166
Brady, Henry, 89, 91, 104
Brown, George, 95
Brown, Murphy, 123

Brown v. Board of Education, 172
Bryan, William Jennings, 21, 24
Buckley v. Valeo, 2, 27–28, 32, 34, 49–51, 55, 70, 149, 170–172
Bundling, 4, 33, 153
Burger, Warren, 124
Burnham, Walter Dean, 3, 4, 85
Burton, Dan, 66
Bush, George 5, 54, 123

Candidate familiarity, 130–131, 133–134
Candidate ideology: ability to distinguish, 130, 131; certainty, 131, 134–135
Candidate self-investment, 43–44
Center for Responsive Politics, 39, 64
Challenger fund-raising, disadvantages, 31–32, 41–42, 63, 65, 82
Challenger spending, effect on vote percentage, 42, 62–63
Chenoweth, Helen, 151
Civic Journalism, 90
Civil service, 20–21, 35, 47
Clay, Henry, 18
Clinton, Bill, 1, 5, 6, 34, 48, 86, 123, 124, 125, 148, 157, 160, 169, 172, 176
Cloward, Richard, 85, 88
Coca-Cola, 38
Coelho, Tony, 63
Cognitive mobilization, 130–133
Colorado Republican Federal Campaign

Committee v. Federal Election Commission, 2, 28, 49, 55, 152
Common Cause, 39
Concern about election outcome, 136–137
Congress, 168–169: First, 18; 100th 33; 101st 33; 102nd 34; 103rd, 6, 33, 169; 104th, 58, 77; 105th, 58, 77
Congressional Quarterly, 58
Constituency service, 59
Contribution limits, 26–27, 28
Coordinated expenditures, 152
Corrado, Anthony, 144, 145
Corrupt Practices Act of 1925, 22,
Cosby, Bill, 124
Cotter, Cornelius, 4
Credit Mobilier, 19
Cremeans, Fran, 65, 72–73

Dalager, Jon, 129
Delay, Tom, 66
Delli Carpini, Michael, 123, 125, 126
Democratic accountability, 57, 124, 126, 155, 159–160, 164–165, 167
Democratic Congressional Campaign Committee, 148
Democratic Convention, 1968, 26
Democratic fundraising, 24, 25–26, 81–82
Democratic National Committee (DNC), 1; use of issue advocacy, 148
Democratic-Republicans, 17, 18
Disclosure, 27, 29, 143, 146, 153–154, 164
Doheny, Edward, 22
Dole, Bob, 86, 148, 172
Do-little approach, 162–165
Donnay, Patrick, 10
Doolittle, Richard, 162
Downs, Anthony, 128–129
Dwyre, Diana, 146, 148

Eismeier, Theodore 6, 43, 81
Electoral competition, 7, 157, 159, 165, 167; effect of candidate campaign spending, 70–71

Elving, Ronald, 58
Emily's List, 153
Endogenous variables, 176–177
English, Phil, 154
Expenditure limits, 27, 29

Fall, Albert, 22
Federal Election Campaign Act, 2, 12, 26, 46, 143–145, 154; 1974 Amendments, 26–27, 152; 1979 Amendments, 145–146
Federal Election Commission, 31, 144–146, 149, 151, 177; creation, 27; ineffectiveness of, 2, 48, 160
Federalist Party, 17
Federal Trade Commission, 54
Feingold, Russell, 155
Ferejohn, John, 123
Fiorina, Morris, 59
First-time candidates, 45–46
Flannigan, Michael Patrick, 45, 65–66
Foley, Thomas, 97
Fontenot, Gene, 65
Forbes, Ralph, 49
Franklin, Charles, 128, 194
Free advertising, 165, 167
Funding constituency, 31, 45

Gaddie, Keith, 66
Gais, Thomas, 10
Garfield, James, 20
Gelman, Andrew, 178
Gephardt, Richard, 66
Gimpel, James, 6, 43
Gingrich, Newt, 5, 46–47, 48, 128, 138, 160, 169, 170
Glickman, Dan, 45
Goidel, Robert, 8
GOPAC, 46–47
Gore, Al, 160, 172
Goss, Eugene, 68
Grant, Ulysses, 19
Green, Donald, 3, 8
Green, Gene, 94
Gross, Donald, 8

Hamilton, Alexander, 18
Hamilton, Lee, 72, 75, 76, 116

Hanna, Mark, 2, 21
Hansen, John Mark, 90–92, 110, 130
"Harrison Bergeron," 162
Hastert, Dennis, 66
Hatch Act of 1939, 24
Hayes, Rutherford, 20
Heard, Alexander, 25
Hershey, Marjorie Randon, 64
Hieneman, Fred, 151
Hill, Kim Quaile, 88
Hinton-Anderson, Angela, 88
Huckfeldt, Robert, 127
Huffington, Michael, 109

Illegal foreign contributions, 1
Incumbency advantage: fund-raising,
    31–32, 41, 64, 67, 81; sources of,
    57–62
Incumbent spending, effect on vote per-
    centage, 42, 62
Independent expenditures, 32–33, 144,
    149–152; by political parties, 152
Information processing, heuristic mod-
    els, 124–125, 127, 129
In-kind contributions, 47
Interest in campaign, 130
Issue advocacy, 144, 166, 172; by interest
    groups and political action commit-
    tees, 149–152; by political parties,
    148–149
Iyengar, Shanto, 109

Jackson, Andrew, 18, 19
Jackson, Brooks, 48, 81, 144, 148, 151
Jacobson, Gary, 8, 41, 44, 58, 62, 64, 67,
    126, 139, 176
Jefferson, Thomas, 16,17
Jones, Ruth, 10, 68, 81
Jordan, Michael, 38
Jude, Tad, 94

Keeter, Scott, 123, 125, 126
Kennedy, John, 25
Kernell, Samuel, 126
Key, V.O. Jr., 3, 4, 39
King, Gary, 178
Krasno, Jonathan, 3, 8

Labor unions, 154, 162, 172; creation of
    PACs, 24; influence in campaigns, 7,
    24; origins of soft money, 145;
    "Lake Wobegone," 161
Leighley, Jan, 88
Leising, Jean, 72, 75, 76, 77, 79, 116
Lennon, John, 124
Levit, Kenneth, 50, 55
Lockerbie, Brad, 111
Lowenstein, Daniel, 53
Luther, Bill, 94

McCain, John, 155
McCain-Feingold legislation, 166, 167,
    170
McConnell, Mitch 5, 51, 68, 169, 170,
    171
McKinley, William, 2, 21
Madison, James, 17
Maisel, Sandy, 9, 61
Malbin, Michael, 10
Marx, Karl, 124
Matching funds: effect on aggregate
    voter turnout, 98–99; effect on elec-
    toral competition, 74–76, 79; simula-
    tions, 178–179
Mayer, John, 10
Mayhew, David, 57
Media attentiveness, 130
Mineta, Norman, 66
Morris, Dwight, 64

National Conservative Political Action
    Committee, 32, 150
National Realtors Association, 153
National Republican Campaign Com-
    mittee, 148
National Republican Senatorial Com-
    mittee, 148
National Wetlands Research Center, 59
Neathercutt, George, 98
Negative campaigning, 89–90, 128
Negative media coverage, 90
Neumann, Mark, 155
Newberry v. U.S., 23
Newinski, Dennis, 77, 79
Nixon, Richard, 86

Nussle, Jim, 77

Open-seat elections, 40, 65, 66–67
Orton, Bill, 98

Patterson, Thomas, 90
Pepsi, 38
Philip Morris Company, 37
Piven, Frances Fox, 85, 88
Plessy v. Ferguson, 172
Political Action Committees, 2, 9, 24,
    30–31, 33, 41, 43, 143, 161, 164, 166;
    contribution patterns, 63–64, 81–82;
    impact on legislative votes, 52–54
Political corruption, 15–16, 19–21, 23–
    24, 33, 47, 50, 107–108, 160
Political information, 164–165
Political mobilization, 18; effect on cog-
    nitive engagement, 129–139; effect on
    turnout, 85, 104, 109–113, 117; mea-
    surement, 113–114
Political participation, 157, 159; activi-
    ties other than voting, 114, 116; dem-
    ocratic theory, 85
Political parties: contribution patterns,
    63; decline of parties, 3–4, 25, 35,
    60–61, 109, 158; development, 18;
    fund-raising, 144; machines, 18, 107–
    108; state and local, 146
Political patronage, 18–19, 20
Pollock, Philip, 6, 43, 81
Pork barrel legislation, 59–60
Price, David, 151
Proctor & Gamble, 37
Progressive Movement, 3, 22, 108
Public financing, 3, 7–11, 68–69; full
    public financing and electoral com-
    petition, 76–77, 79, 167; full public
    financing and voter information,
    167–168; full public financing and
    voter turnout, 99–100, 103, 167–168;
    in Minnesota, 10; partial public fi-
    nancing and electoral competition,
    77–79; partial public financing and
    voter turnout, 101–103; in presiden-
    tial elections, 27, 29 simulations, 179;

in state elections, 10, 170–171; in
    Wisconsin, 10, 11
Publicity Bill of 1910, 22
Public opinion, 25, 39, 117–118,
    169–170

Quayle, Dan, 123

Ragsdale, Lyn, 89
Ramsden, Graham, 10
Rehnquist, William, 124
Republican fund-raising, 24, 26, 43, 81
Republican National Committee, 158
Retirements, 67, 81; strategic, 59
Revenue Act of 1971, 26, 27
Robber barons, 1, 21
Rohde, David, 59
Roosevelt, Franklin, 22, 24
Roosevelt, Teddy, 22
Rose, Pete, 124
Rosenkranz, Joshua, 50
Rosenstone, Steven, 90–92, 110, 130
Rostenkowski, Dan, 45, 65
Royko, Mike, 107–108
Rusk, Gerold, 89

Sabato, Larry, 2, 15, 33, 47
Schaffer, Jan, 90
Schlesinger, Joseph, 4
Schlozman, Kay Lehman, 89, 91, 104
Schwartz, Jeffrey, 68
Segal, Jeffrey, 57–58
Shapiro, Andrew, 50
Silbey, Joel, 108
Simpson, Glenn, 2, 15, 33, 47
Simpson, O.J., 53
Simulations, use of, 8–9, 11, 68–70, 96
Sinclair, Harry, 22
Smith, Adam, 65, 151
Smith, Bradley, 8
Smith, Donna, 77, 79
Smith-Connally Act, 24
Soft money, 4, 5, 12, 32, 33, 144–149,
    166, 172
Sorauf, Frank, 9, 23, 24, 38, 143, 148
Spending limits, 3, 6, 7–9, 42, 68; effect
    on partisan competition, 71–74, 79,

164, 166; effect on voter turnout, 96–98, 103; simulations, 178
Sprague, John, 127
Standing for office, 16
State campaign finance laws, 10, 23, 34, 46–47, 68, 170–171
Strategic challengers, 61
Strategic elites, 126–127
Strickland, Ted, 65, 72–73

Taft, William, 22
Taft-Hartley Act, 24
Tammany Hall, 19
Tate, Randall, 65, 151
Teapot Dome, 22
Teixeira, Ruy, 87, 92–93
Thayer, George, 17, 19, 20
Thompson, Dixie, 98
Thompson, Fred, 39, 51
Tiahrt, Todd, 45
Ticket splitting, 59–60
Tillman Act of 1907, 22
Type I and Type II error, 53–54

Van Buren, Martin, 4
Vento, Bruce, 77
Verba, Sydney, 89, 91, 104
Vietnam War, 26

Vonnegut, Kurt, 162
Voter information, 7, 38, 123–124, 126, 127, 128, 154, 157, 159, 167
Voter turnout, 7, 165, 167; consequences of low voter turnout, 86–89; education, 91; effect of candidate spending, 70–71, 92–96, 113–114, 115; effect of registration requirements, 91–92, 103; effects of mobilization, 92–93, 96–97, 107–108, 113, 115; in Great Britain, 85;
in midterm elections, 86; in presidential elections, 85–86; property requirements, 17–18;
variation across congressional districts, 94

Wapner, Judge 124
Washington, George, 16, 17, 18, 44
Watergate, 2, 26, 169
Weed, Thurlow, 19
Weilhouwer, Peter, 111
Weimer Republic, 88
Welk, Lawrence, 59
Wellstone, Paul, 148–149
Wilde, Linda, 95
Williams, Dan, 151
Wood, John, 10
Wright, John, 54

About the Authors

Robert K. Goidel is assistant professor of political science at Indiana State University.

Donald A. Gross is associate professor of political science at the University of Kentucky.

Todd G. Shields is assistant professor of political science at the University of Arkansas.